Peter

by

E. F. Benson

Peter
by E. F. Benson
Copyright © 2023

ISBN: 978-93-60464-47-9

Published by

DOUBLE 9 BOOKS

2/13-B, Ansari Road
Daryaganj, New Delhi – 110002
info@double9books.com
www.double9books.com
Tel. 011-40042856

ABOUT THE AUTHOR

Edward Frederic Benson OBE was an English author who lived from July 24, 1867, to February 29, 1940. He wrote novels, biographies, memoirs, histories, and short stories. E. F. Benson was born at Wellington College in Berkshire. He was the fifth child of Edward White Benson, who was teacher and later became chancellor of Lincoln Cathedral, bishop of Truro, and archbishop of Canterbury, and Mary Sidgwick ("Minnie"), who was born. There were three brothers named E. F. Benson: Arthur Christopher Benson wrote the words to "Land of Hope and Glory"; Robert Hugh Benson wrote several stories and works defending Roman Catholicism; and Margaret Benson (Maggie), who wrote books and liked learning about Egypt. I lost two other siblings very young. There were six kids and no grandkids in Benson's family. Benson went to Temple Grove School and then Marlborough College for his education. It was there that he wrote some of his earliest works and the ideas for his book David Blaize came from. He went to King's College, Cambridge, to finish his education. In college, he was a part of the Pitt Club at Cambridge. Later in life, he was made a senior fellow of Magdalene College.

CONTENTS

CHAPTER I

The two who mattered were lounging on the cushioned seat in the low window, of which the lower panes had been pushed quite up in order to admit the utmost possible influx of air. Little came in, for the afternoon was sultry and windless, but every now and then some current moved outside, some trickle of comparative coolness from the grass and trees of the Green Park, sufficient to stir the girl's hair. On this high floor of the house of flats London seemed far remote; the isolation as of an aeroplane, as of a ship at sea, protected them from external intrusion.

Inside the room a party of four were assembled round the tea-table; the hostess, mother of the girl who sat in the window-seat, was wondering, without impatience, as was becoming to so chinned and contented a face, when Mrs. Alston would cease gesticulating with her sandwich and eat it, instead of using it as a conductor's baton to emphasize her points in the discourse to which nobody was listening. The sandwich had already a large semicircular bite out of it, which penetrated well past its centre, and one more application (if she would only make it) to that capacious mouth would render it reasonable to suppose that she had finished her tea. Mrs. Heaton herself had done so; so also had the stout grey-haired man with the varnished face, and as for Mrs. Underwood, she had long ago drunk her cup of hot water and refused any further nourishment. But while Mrs. Alston brandished her crescent of a sandwich, and continued talking as if somebody had contradicted her, it was impossible to suggest a move to the bridge-table that stood ready with new packs and sharpened pencils a couple of yards away. To the boy and girl in the window that quartette of persons seemed of supreme unimportance both by reason of their age and of the earnest futility of their conversation. They talked eagerly about dull things like politics and prices instead of being flippant, in the modern style, about interesting things. Between them and the younger generation there was the great gulf digged by the unrelenting years, and set on fire by the war. It was not flaring and exploding any longer, but lay there in smouldering impassable clinkers.

"High prices and high wages!" asserted Mrs. Alston. "That's what is going to be the ruin of the country. I've said over and over again, 'Why not have an Act of Parliament to halve the price of food and coal and that sort of thing, and another Act, unless you could get it into the same one, to reduce wages by a half also?' High prices, so everybody allows, are the cause of high wages, and if miners and that sort of person could buy their food and their clothes at half the price they pay for them now, there would not be the slightest difficulty in reducing wages by a half, instead of multiplying them by two every time that they threaten to strike. Coal! The root of all the trouble is the price of coal. Reduce the price of coal by half, and instantly the price of transport and gas and electricity will go down in a corresponding manner. Steel, too, and linen; it all depends on coal. The English sovereign has to-day hardly more than half the buying power it used to have. Hardly more than half! Restore it, then, by reducing the price of everything else, including wages. Including wages, mind! Otherwise you will find yourselves in a fine mess!"

She put the rest of her sandwich into her mouth, precisely as Mrs. Heaton had hoped and even foreseen. That made her mouth quite full, and for the moment she was as dumb as the adder. Her hostess, alert for this psychological occasion, gave a short, judicial and fulsome summing-up, addressed to the court in general.

"Well, dearest Mary," she said. "You have made me understand it all now, a thing which I never did before. So well put, was it not, Mr. Steel, and I'm sure quite unanswerable. We must none of us attempt to argue with dearest Mary, because she would show us at once how stupid it was of us, and I, for one, hate to be made a fool of. What a good explanation! Quite brilliant! So now shall we get to our bridge? I expect we're all going to the opera to-night, and so we shall all want to dress early. Dear me, it's after half-past five already! Will nobody have any more tea? Quite sure? Shall we cut, then? Oh, there are Nellie and Peter in the window. Wouldn't you like to cut in, too, dear?"

"No, mother, we shouldn't!" said Nellie.

The four others swooped to the bridge-table, with the swift sure flight of homing pigeons, and hastily cut their cards in order to give no time for repentance on the part of the two others.

"You and I, Mr. Steel," said Mrs. Heaton hastily. "Quite sure you wouldn't like to play, Peter?"

"Quite," said Peter gently. "I should hate it; thanks awfully."

"Well, if you're quite sure you won't—my deal I think, partner. Shall it be pennies?"

Mr. Steel had a whimsical idea.

"Oughtn't we to halve our points, too, Mary?" he said. "Like wages and coal?"

For a moment he was sorry he had been so rashly humorous, for Mrs. Alston opened her mouth and drew in her breath as if to speak on a public platform to the largest imaginable audience. Then, luckily, she found something so remarkable in her hand that her fury for political elucidation was quenched, and she devoted the muscles of her athletic mind to considering what she would do if the dealer was so rash as to call no trumps. Thereafter the great deeps, dimly peopled with enemies ready to pounce out of the subaqueous shadows and double you, completely submerged the four of them. They lit cigarettes as in a dream, and smoked them in alternate hells and heavens.

Nellie looked at them once or twice, as an anæsthetist might look at his patient to see whether he was quite unconscious. The third glance was convincing.

"It must be rather sweet to be middle-aged, Peter," she said. "For the next two hours they'll think about nothing but aces and trumps!"

"Sign of youth," said Peter.

"Why?"

"Because they're absorbed, like children. When you were little, you could only think about one thing at a time. It might be dentist or it might be hoops. But you and I can't think about anything for more than five minutes together, or care about anything for more than two. I suppose that when you're old you recapture that sort of youthfulness."

He paused a moment.

"Go on: tell me about it all," he said.

Nellie did not reply at once, but began plaiting her fingers together with the little finger on the top. They were slender and small like her face, which narrowed very rapidly from the ears downwards to a pointed chin. Loose yellow hair, the colour of honey, grew low over her forehead, and just below it, her eyebrows, noticeably darker than her hair, made high arches, giving her face an expression of irony and surprise. Her forehead ran straight into the line of her nose, and a short upper lip held her mouth in imperfect control, for it hinted and wondered, and was amused and contemptuous as its mood took it. Now it half-smiled; now it was half serious, but always it only hinted.

Peter apparently grew impatient of her silence and her finger plaiting.

"You're making them look like bananas on a street-barrow," he observed.

Nellie smoothed them out and gave an appreciative sigh.

"Oh, I bought two to-day," she said, "and ate them in the street. I had to throw the skins away, and then I was afraid that somebody would slip on them and break his leg."

"So you picked them up again," suggested Peter.

"No, I didn't. I was only sorry for anybody who might slip on them. I couldn't tell who it was going to be, and probably I shouldn't know him——"

"Get on," he said.

"Oh, about Philip. Well, there it was. He asked me, you see, and—of course, he's rather old, but he's tremendously attractive. And it's so safe and pleasant, and I like being adored. After all, you and I have talked it over often enough, and you knew just as well as I did that I was going to accept him if he wanted me."

Nellie suddenly felt that she was justifying what she had done, and she did not mean to do that. What she had done justified itself by its own inherent good sense. She changed her tone, and began counting on those slim fingers which just now had introduced the extraneous subject of bananas.

"Peter, darling," she said. "If his grandfather and an uncle and two children of the uncle die, there is no doubt whatever that I shall be a peeress. Won't that be fun? I feel that Uncle Robert and the two children may easily die; they're the sort of people who do die, but I doubt whether grandpapa ever will. He's like the man with the white beard; do I mean the Ancient Mariner or the Ancient of Days, who comes in Ezekiel?"

Peter Mainwaring rocked backwards in the window-seat with a sudden little explosion of laughter that made all the bridge players look up as if their heads were tied to the same tweaked string. Then they submerged again.

"Not Ezekiel, anyhow," he said. "It's either Daniel or Coleridge. I expect Coleridge."

"Yes, I mean Coleridge," she said. "The man who stops the wedding guest; wedding guest was what suggested it. Grandpapa always wanted Philip to marry one of those cousins of his, who look like tables with drawers in them. Long legs and bumps on their faces like the handles of the drawers. But Philip wouldn't."

Peter ran his fingers along the line of his jaw as if to be sure that he had shaved that morning. His face for a man of twenty-two was ridiculously smooth and hairless; it did not much matter whether he had shaved or not.

"Naturally Philip wouldn't," he said, "but that's got nothing to do with it. I don't want to know why Philip didn't do something, but why you did. I want to see your point, to do you justice. At present I feel upset about it. You know quite well that there's only one person you ought to marry."

"You?" asked Nellie, feeling that the question was quite unnecessary.

"How clever of you to guess. You are clever sometimes. Oh, I know we've talked it over enough and seen how impossible it was, but when it comes to your marrying someone else— —"

He lit a match and blew it out again.

"I know," he said. "You've got threepence a year, and I've got twopence, so that in the good old times we should have been able to buy one pound of sugar every Christmas. Even then we should have had nothing to eat with it. But what you haven't sufficiently reckoned with is the fact that by the time I am a hundred and fifty years old, I shall get a pension of a hundred and fifty pounds from the Foreign Office. But it's rather a long time to wait."

Nellie's eyes suddenly grew fixed and rapt.

"Oh, Peter, one moment!" she whispered. "Look quickly at mamma's face. When that holy expression comes on it, it always means that she is intending to declare no trumps. So when I'm playing against her, if it's my turn first I always declare one no trumps, and then she has to declare two. Wait one second, Peter."

"No trumps," said Mrs. Heaton.

"There, I told you so!" said Nellie. "Yes; it is rather long to wait, though I don't mean to say that a hundred and fifty isn't a very pleasant age, dear. The people in Genesis usually lived five hundred years before they married, and begat sons and daughters. Anyhow, I shall be a widow before you're a hundred and fifty, and then we shall be engaged for three hundred and fifty years more, and then we shall totter to the altar. I can't help talking drivel; it's all too serious to take seriously. By the way, I shall be richer than you eventually, for when mamma dies I shall have two thousand a year, but that won't be for two thousand years. We have been born too soon, Peter!"

Peter thought this not worth answering, but lifting one of his knees, nursed it between his clasped hands in silence. For her loose honey-coloured hair, he had a crisp coal-blackness; he was tall for her small slim stature, and his lips were set to definite purposes, whereas hers were malleable to adapt themselves to any emotion that might waywardly blow on her. But both, in compensation for differences that were complementary, were triumphantly alike in the complete soullessness of their magnificent youth; without violation of any internal principle they might, either of them, shoot up singing with the lark, or pad and prowl with the ruthless hunger of the tiger, or burrow with the mole. They were Satyr and Hamadryad, some ancient and eternally young embodiment of life, with whim to take the place of conscience, and the irresponsible desire of wild things to do duty for duty, and impulse to take the place of reason. Each, too, had developed to an almost alarming degree that modern passion for introspection, which is an end in itself, and like a barren tree, yields no fruit in the ways of action or renunciation.

Peter hugged his knee, and his eye grew hazy and unfocused in meditation.

"Am I in love with you, do you think?" he asked at length.

She laughed, quite disregarding the ears of the bridge players. With Peter she was more herself than with anyone else, or even than when alone.

"Oh, that's so like you," she said, "and so wonderfully like me. Certainly you're not in love with me; you're not in love with anybody. You never have been; you never will be. You're fonder of me than of anybody else, but that's a very different thing."

"But how do you know I'm not in love with you?" he asked. "I may be. You're not so unattractive. Why shouldn't I be in love with you?"

"It's obvious you aren't. To begin with, you don't feel the smallest jealousy of Philip. Besides, though you so kindly say that I'm not so unattractive, you're the one person who really sees and notes and mentions my imperfections. You wouldn't be so critical of me if you were in love. And then, as I said, you're not jealous of Philip."

"Good Lord, how could I be jealous of Philip?" asked he. "I should have to want to be Philip before I could be jealous of him, and I wouldn't be Philip, even as things stand, for anything in the world. Besides, you don't really think him so tremendously attractive though you said so just now. You said that out of pure conventionality, not out of conviction."

Some momentary perplexity, like a cloud on a sunny windy day of spring bowled its shadow over her face, and creased a soft perpendicular furrow between her eyebrows.

"Peter, I think I want to become conventional," she said, "and, if you wish, I will confess I was practising for it when I said that. Oh, my dear, we're all human, cast in a mould and put in a cage, if you don't mind mixed metaphors. I'm going to marry in the ordinary way, just because girls do marry. Mamma married, so did my two grandmammas, and four great-grandmammas, and eight great-great-grandmammas. In fact the further you go back, the commoner marriage seems to have been. Some awful human hereditary spell has been cast on me."

Peter leaned forward, bright-eyed and faun-like. "Break it!" he said. "Exorcise it! Spells don't exist except for those who allow themselves to be bound by them. The fact is we all weave our own spells."

"But if I did refuse now, what then?" said she. "If you don't obey conventions, you must have conviction to take their place, and I haven't got any. Besides, if I don't marry I shall become an old maid, unless I die young. Oh, we are all in a trap, we girls. There are three awful alternatives to choose from, and I dislike them all. I don't want to die young, but if I live to be sixty I've got to be a grandmother or a stringy old maid."

"You've got to be stringy, anyhow, at sixty," said Peter.

"Not at all. Grandmothers are usually plump and comfortable: it is great aunts who are stringy. And grandmothers remain young, I notice, whereas elderly maiden ladies are only sprightly. I think that it's because they cling to youth, and there's nothing so ageing as to cling to anything. If you want to retain anything, the best plan is to drop it, and then it clings to you instead."

"That's rather ingenious," said Peter. "You may go on about it for a minute."

"I was going to. It's perfectly true. All the people who don't eat potatoes and sweets for fear of getting fat become elephants, like mamma, who lives on cracknel biscuits."

"Does she?" said Peter with deep interest. "How wonderful of her."

"And all the people who take immense care of themselves die at the age of forty, because they are clinging to life, while those who break every ordinance of health never die at all. And all the people who lay themselves out to be brilliant are crashing bores——"

"Oh yes; proved," said Peter. "Let's go on to something else. What's to happen to me when you marry?"

"Nothing," said Nellie. "Why should it? You'll go on being quite different from anybody else. That's a career in itself. You aren't human, anyhow, however many great-grandmammas you may have had. You're a wild thing, partly domesticated, and when you're tired of us all, you go waving your tail, and walking in the wet woods, and telling nobody. Kipling, you know. Then you come back rather sleepy and pleased, and allow us to put a blue riband round your neck and tickle you under the chin, and then you lie down on a cushion in front of the fire and purr. You don't purr at us, though, you purr at yourself."

"Lor!" said Peter. "All that about me!"

Nellie pushed back her hair from her forehead, and again plaited her fingers together. But this time it was no deliberative, meditative process, but a swift unconscious action.

"Yes, my dear, and there's more, too," she said. "It's my swan-song, remember, for soon I am going to become ordinary and conventional. I used to go in the wet woods, too, you know, though we never met each other there. But that has been the bond between us, up till now we have been completely independent. You're going to remain so, but not I. Oh, Peter, there was a bond! My dear, do you think that I'm rather mad? I have serious doubts about it myself."

"You always were rather mad," said he. "But go on; sing your swan-song."

"Then don't look as if you had taken a guinea stall to hear me," she said. "Where had I got to? Oh, yes. There was a bond; you know it yourself. I've never been conscious of anybody else as I've been conscious of you, nor have you ever been conscious of anyone else as you've been conscious of me. You've never been in the least in love with me, nor have I with you. But we're the same kind of person, and one doesn't often see the same kind of person as oneself. Do you understand at all, or am I simply reading out of my own book?"

He was silent a moment.

"Nellie, would you marry me if I were rich?" he asked.

She made a gesture of impatience.

"How on earth can I tell?" she said. "If you were rich you would be quite a different person."

"No, I shouldn't— —"

"Oh, Peter, how stupid you are," she said. "And how frightfully Victorian. That is so shallow. Wealth is just as much part of a man or a woman as brains or beauty. I don't say that a girl loves a man for his brains, or his money, or his beauty, but they all make a part of him. Wealth isn't an accident; it's an attribute. A poor man—I'm not talking about you and me, but only speaking in the abstract—may be the same in character and charm as a rich man, but what a gulf money makes between them! Let one man be poor, and another, his absolute double in every way, be rich. They cease to be doubles at once."

"But if you happened to love the costermonger——" began Peter.

"We can leave that out, because neither of us has the slightest idea what love means."

"How about the bond you spoke of, then?" asked he. "Hasn't that got anything to do with it?"

She considered this, and then laid her hand on his arm.

"If I could choose now, this minute," she said, "in what relationship we should stand to each other, I would choose you as my brother. I haven't got one; I should like to have one tremendously. And yet, if I might have it all just the way I liked, I think I should have you for my sister. I don't so much want you to take care of me as I want to take care of you. I want——"

"Oh, come now," said Peter.

"It's true, though."

They had turned themselves about in the window-seat, so as to secure for this surprising conversation a greater privacy from the party at the bridge-table, and were leaning out of the window. A hundred feet below Piccadilly roared and rattled, but here the clatter of it was shorn of its sharp edges; it was as if a stir of bees was swarming in some hive down there. Seen like this from above, passengers and vehicles alike were but crawling dots and blots; everything, from the swiftest motor down to the laziest loiterer, seemed to be drowsily and soundlessly sauntering. Often had Peter and Nellie leaned out here looking on the traffic at the base of the cliff, capturing for themselves a certain sense of isolation. Even leaning out they could see nothing of the precipitous cliff side of the house, for a couple of feet below the window a stone cornice jutted out some ten or twelve inches, and beyond the edge of that the nearest visible objects below were the tops of motor buses and the hats of the foot passengers along the pavements. So still was the air that now, when Peter flicked the ash off his cigarette, it floated down, still cohering, till it dwindled into invisibility. He followed its fall with that detached intentness which the surface mind gives to the ticking of a clock or the oscillation of some flower-head, when the whole psychic attention is focused elsewhere; and it seemed that Nellie, as far as her surface mind went, was trotting in harness with him, for though he had not hinted at what occupied his eyes, scarcely knowing it himself, she was equally intent.

"I've lost sight of it, Peter," she said, breaking the silence of a whole minute.

"Of what?" he asked.

"Of your cigarette end. You were watching it too. Don't pretend that you weren't."

"Well, if I was, what then?" he asked.

"Nothing particular. I only felt you were watching it—just the bond."

He shifted himself again. Hitherto, as they leaned out, his left shoulder touched hers. Now he broke the contact.

"I think that's about the extent of the bond," he said. "And your marrying Philip shows precisely what sort of value you put on it. You've made it clearer than you know, for you've defined your feelings for me as being a desire to have a brother, or rather a sister to take care of. I don't think that's worth much. You defined it further by saying that you couldn't tell whether you would marry me or not if I were rich, because if I were, I should be a quite different person. If the quality of the bond would be affected by that, it must be of remarkably poor quality, and you're quite right to break it. When you began talking about the bond I thought you might be going to say something interesting, something I didn't know, something that, when you stated it, I should recognize to be true. If that's all your swan has got to sing it might as well have been a goose."

Nellie's eyebrows elevated themselves up under the loose yellow of her hair.

"Peter dear, are you quarrelling with me?" she asked.

"Yes. No. No, I'm not quarrelling. But the whole thing is such a bore. Where's my tail, and where are the wet woods?"

She leaned her chin on her hands, that lay along the window sill.

"I wish you were in love with me," she said.

"I'm extremely glad that I'm not," said he. "Otherwise I suppose I should want to be Philip, or, as the madrigal says, some other 'favoured swain.' But for you to talk about a bond between us is the absolute limit. You want everything your own way, and expect everybody else to immolate himself, thankfully and ecstatically, on your beastly altar."

"So do you," murmured Nellie. "We all do."

"I? How do you make that out?" demanded Peter.

"Because you object to my marrying Philip when you haven't the smallest desire to have me yourself. If you knew that I should say 'Yes,' supposing you asked me to jilt Philip and marry you, you wouldn't ask me to. You want me to marry nobody and not to marry me yourself. That's not good enough, you know."

Peter's mouth lengthened itself into a smile, and broadened into a laugh.

"It's a putrid business," he said. "Why shouldn't I take a neat header from the window and have done with it? I'm twenty-two, and already I think the whole affair is rot. And if it doesn't amuse me now, when is it going to amuse me? It was even more amusing during the war, when one came back for a fortnight's leave before going out to that hell again. One did grab at pleasure then, because in all probability one would be blown to bits very soon afterwards. But now that one is not going to be blown to bits very soon afterwards the whole seasoning has gone out of it. No, not quite. I want to be admired. What is love? Good Lord, what is love? As I haven't the slightest idea, the best thing I can do is to grab at pleasures."

"Or the worst," suggested Nellie, rather sententiously.

"Now get off the high horse," said Peter. "Or, rather, don't attempt to get on it. You can't, any more than I. Let's be comfortable. Marry your silly Philip, and I'll—I'll—— Shall I take to drink? No, that wouldn't do, for people would say I was trying to drown my despair at your marriage. I haven't got feelings of that sort, and I should hate anybody to think that I had. I loathe being pitied, anyhow, and to be pitied for something you don't suffer from would be intolerable. And though you will remain just the same to me after you're married, and I shall certainly remain the same, our relations will be altered."

Nellie let her eyes flit over him, never quite alighting. They skimmed over his crisp hair, over the handsome, smooth, soulless profile, over his shoulders, over the knee he was nursing, over the hiatus where white skin showed between his rucked-up trouser and a drooping sock. At this moment she, with the knowledge of the definite step that she had taken in life by engaging herself to Philip Beaumont, felt far older and more experienced than he. She, anyhow, could look ahead and see a placid, prosperous life in front of her, whereas Peter, a year older than she, was still as experimental as a boy. All the same, if he wanted anything, he had remarkable assiduity in the pursuit of it until he caught it, but nothing beyond the desire of the moment was to him worth bothering about. Her own prudence, her own commitment of herself she knew to be a development of to-day and yesterday, and now it seemed suddenly to have aged and consolidated her. But she had no answer for that voice crying in the wilderness "What is love?" Or was there some sort of signpost by the wayside enveloped in mist? She passed over that point.

"If it really all seems to you so putrid," she said, "I can't imagine why you don't, as you say, take a header into the street. But you've no intention of doing anything of the sort. You would firmly resist any attempt of mine to tip you out. You like life quite passably as it is, you know, and also you do expect something more from it. In fact, I never saw anyone so thoroughly unlikely to give up living or to run any risk that could reasonably be avoided. You say it's a putrid business, but really you find it a pleasant one."

Peter sighed.

"Oh, yes, it will have to do," he said. "Don't tip me out, Nellie. But don't, on the other hand, think that I cling so desperately to life."

"Not desperately, but instinctively. It would be silly of anybody to throw up a hand that may contain some glorious ace without looking very carefully through it. Everyone goes on playing and clutching at the new deals until he is sure that there isn't an ace in the pack for him. Indeed, it's when you've found the ace that you don't value the rest of the hand so much."

"I don't follow. Explain," said Peter.

"Well, this kind of thing. For instance, if you found the ace, that is to say, if you fell tremendously in love, you might not care about the rest of the hand. If the adorable was in my bedroom, two windows off, and if she was locked in there, and if the house was on fire——"

"Any more 'ifs'?" asked Peter.

"Not one. But supposing all these things, you would instantly get out on to that cornice, at peril of your life, and shuffle your way along it. You would *have* to be with her. You wouldn't give two thoughts as to what might happen to you."

Peter thought this over.

"I should be a consummate ass, then," he remarked. "A fellow with a grain of sense would go down the passage and bash the door in."

"But let's pretend that for some reason you couldn't. If the only way of reaching the room was along the cornice you would go."

Peter looked at the ledge.

"And if I got there in safety, what then?" he asked. "I couldn't carry her back along the ledge."

"But that wouldn't prevent your going," said she. "Whatever the risk to yourself was, and however useless your going was, you would go."

Peter was silent a moment, frowning.

"I feel as if all this has happened before," he said. "Do you know that feeling? Did we ever sit here before and talk about just this?"

"Not that I remember. No, I'm sure we never have. Isn't it odd, that sensation? Does it seem to you like remembrance of a previous occasion, or a presentiment of a future one?"

"Or a slightly faulty action of the two lobes of the brain?" said Peter. "What were we talking about? Aces?"

"Yes. That's what I mean about throwing the rest of your hand away for the sake of an ace."

Peter looked at his watch.

"I must go," he said. "I've got to get home to dress, and rush back to the Ritz to dine early before the opera."

"Oh, not just yet," said she. "But I wish you wouldn't live in South Kensington. Why do you?"

Peter had a direct glance and a direct answer for this.

"Because it's cheaper living with my father and mother than being on my own," he said. "Also— —"

"Well?" she asked.

"I was going to say because they like having me with them," said he. "But I don't think that's true, so I didn't say it. I mean, if I had plenty of money I should take a flat of my own, quite regardless of whether they liked to have me with them."

Nellie gave a little sigh, with a click of impatience at the end of it.

"There's an odd kind of honesty about you," she said. "You state that sort of thing quite baldly, whereas I should conceal it. If I had been you I should have said that I lived at home because my mother liked having me with her. It wouldn't have been true, but I should have said it. Very likely by saying it often I should have got to believe it."

"Nobody else would have," remarked Peter.

"You're rather a brute, my dear," said she. "Go away to South Kensington."

"I'm going. But about aces for one second more. Have you found your ace, Nellie? Don't bother to answer."

"That is spoken like a rather spiteful woman," was Nellie's perfectly justifiable rejoinder.

"Maybe. I'm your spiteful sister," said Peter.

He walked gracefully and gently over to the card-table.

"Good-bye, Mrs. Heaton," he said. "Nellie and I have had a lovely talk. I hope you've won every rubber."

"And three aces, thirty," said Mrs. Heaton. "Good-bye, dear Peter. I suppose you'll be at the Opera to-night. *Parsifal*. My deal? So it is."

CHAPTER II

Peter descended from these heights into the hot dusty well of the streets, and soon was on his way home to dress and return to the Ritz, where an early dinner preceded the opera and any other diversions that might present themselves. On this sweltering June evening the top of a bus was a cooler progression than a taxi, besides advancing the sacred cause of economy, which he had just confessed was more real to him than that of filial piety, and at Hyde Park Corner he could catch a conveyance that would deposit him not fifty yards from his father's house. Coolness and economy were sufficiently strong of themselves to make him board it with alacrity, and the detachment of a front seat just suited the meditative mood which his talk with Nellie had induced.

Peter knew himself and her pretty well, and with the admirable contributions she had made to their discussion there was little to puzzle out, but much to appraise and estimate. The notion that the news of her engagement had been a blow of any sharp or stunning quality could be at once dismissed, for never had he known so well, as when she, earlier in the day, had communicated the news of her engagement to him over the telephone (that was like her), how whole-heartedly he was not in love with her, and how unintelligibly alien to him, as she had pointed out, was that emotion. During the last year which had witnessed a very decent flowering of intimacy between him and her, there had never been, on either side, the least attempt at love-making; their relations had been wholly free from sentiment, and not once had either of them tripped or stuttered over the foreign use of love-language. But in ways wholly unsentimental they had certainly arrived at some extremely close relation of intimacy; there had emphatically been a bond between them, which to his mind her engagement, if it did not actually loosen it, would shift, so to speak, on to a new place; the harness must be worn elsewhere. If it was to be maintained, he, at any rate, must accustom himself to its new adjustment. She had defined that comradeship this afternoon in a way that was rather surprising, for the ideal relation of him to her, apparently, was that of a brother, or, with greater precision, that of a sister. That had not struck him before, but even when first presented, it did not in the least puzzle him. Indeed, it satisfactorily accounted for that elimination of sex which had always marked their intimacy. She had not sought the male element in him, nor he in her the female. So far he was in complete agreement with the casual conclusion they had jointly arrived at, but at that point Peter detected the presence of something that seemed to show a lurking fallacy somewhere. For he had no doubt that if he had been rich, he would before now have proposed to her, and in spite of her provision that, since riches were an attribute of a man and not an external accident, they turned him into a different person, and that thus she could not tell whether she would have accepted him or not, he did not, for himself, believe that she would have hesitated in doing so. Finally, as material to meditate upon, came her firm statement that though Peter did not want or intend to marry her, he objected to anybody else doing so. With the extreme frankness with which he habitually judged any criticism on himself, he instantly admitted that there was a great deal to be said for Nellie's assertion. When it was stated brutally like that, he recognized the justice of her outline. She might have made a caricature of him, but her sketch contained salient features, the identity of which, as he contemplated this scribble of her inspired pencil, he could not disclaim. Without doubt she had caught a likeness; more tersely she had "got him." Even as he acknowledged that, he felt a resentment that she had so unerringly comprehended him, and shown him to himself. He enjoyed, rather than otherwise, his own dissection of himself, without bias or malice, but he felt less sure that when Nellie was the dissector he welcomed so deft an exposure.

The retrospect had been sufficiently absorbing to make him unaware that, somewhere in Knightsbridge, the top of the bus had become a strenuous goal for travellers. Every seat was occupied, and beside him a young man had planted himself in the vacant place and was talking to a girl who had plumped herself into a seat two tiers behind his. Peter instantly jumped up.

"Let me change places with your young lady," he said, "and then you'll be together and talk more conveniently."

The change was made with a tribute of simpering gratitude on the part of the "young lady," and Peter, with laurels of popularity round his straw hat, took the single place. He knew perfectly well that he had disturbed himself from no motive of kindliness; he did not in the least want to please either the man or the girl. His motive had been only to appear pleasant, to obtain cheaply and fraudulently the certificate of being a "kind gentleman." For himself, he did not care two straws if the pair of sundered lovers bawled at each other from sundered seats....

And then as he took his new place it struck him that the quality which had prompted the transference of himself from one seat on the top of a bus to another, was precisely the same as had led him to resent Nellie's dissection of him. In the one case his vanity was gratified, in the other his vanity was hurt.

"That's it," he said to himself, and mentally he prinked, like a girl, in the glass that had so unerringly shown him to himself. Yet it did not show him an aspect of himself that was in any way surprising, either for pleasure or distaste, for he knew well how prolific a spring of native vanity was in him. He would always take an infinity of trouble in order to appear admirable, or, on the other hand, to conceal what was not so admirable. He would always inconvenience himself in order to appear kind, exert himself to appear amusing, bore himself, while preserving the brightness of an attentive and interested eye, in order to confirm his reputation for being sympathetic. But though vanity was the root of such efforts, there was, at any rate, no trace of it in his acknowledgment of it. He never deluded himself into thinking that he suffered fools gladly, because he liked them, or desired to secure for them a pleasant half-hour in which they could tediously inflict themselves on him; he suffered them with the show of gladness in order to be thought kind and agreeable in the abstract, and in the concrete to pick up the gleanings of welcome and entertainment which, for such as him, lie so thick on the fields of human intercourse, when the great machines have gone by. He had no reason to complain of these gleanings; there was no one among the youth of London who was more consistently in request, or who more merited his mild harvestings. In a rather fatigued and casual generation, tired with the strain of the last five years, and now suddenly brought to book after the irresponsibility of wartime, when for all young men each leave snatched from the scythe of the French front might easily be their last, there was a certain license given, Peter had always been a shining exception to such slack social conduct of life. He did not, as he had told Nellie, expect much from it, but as long as you were "on tap," it was undeniably foolish not to present yourself presentably. Your quality was certainly enhanced by a little foam, a little effervescence. "That nice Mr. Peter, always so polite and pleasant," was his reward; and at this moment Nellie's divination of his true attitude towards her engagement was his punishment.

The bus hummed and droned along the Brompton Road; there was still a solid stretch before it halted just opposite the side street which was his goal, and there was time to consider her further criticism that he went off, waving his tail, into the wet woods and saying nothing to anybody. What had she meant exactly by that? He had, at any rate, his own consciousness that she had hit on something extremely real and vitally characteristic of him. Surely she meant his aloofness from any intimate surrender of himself, the self-sufficiency that neither gave nor sought strong affection. He had acknowledged the vanity as of a be-ribanded cat, and now he added to that his desire for material comfort, a quiet, determined selfishness, and the reservation to himself of solitary expeditions in the wet woods with a waving tail. Probably she meant no more than that, and though Peter quite acknowledged the justice of these definitions, he again felt a certain resentment against her clear-sightedness. She had a touch of these defects and qualities herself; it was that which made the bond between them.

Peter let himself into his father's house in the grilling, dusty street nearly opposite the Oratory with the anticipation of finding a speedy opportunity for a domestic exhibition of vanity, for he felt sure that something ludicrous or tiresome and uncomfortable would await him; something he would certainly tolerate with bland serenity and agreeableness. The house, the front of which had been baking in the sun all the afternoon, was intolerably hot and stuffy; the door at the head of the kitchen stairs had, as generally happened, been left open, and the nature of the dinner which would presently ascend could be confidently predicted. Beyond, at the back of the hall, the door into his father's studio was also open, and a languid, odorous tide of oil-paint and Virginian tobacco made a peculiarly deadly combination with kitchen-smells, and indicated that Mr. Mainwaring had been occupied with his audacious labours. Just now he was engaged on the perpetration of a series of cartoons (suitable or not for mural decoration). The practical difficulty, if these ever attained completion, would be the discovery of the wall that should be large enough to hold them; indeed, the great wall of China seemed the only destination which, though remote, was sufficiently spacious. The subject of them was the European war from a psychic no less than from a sanguinary point of view, for the series (of which the sketches were complete) started with a prodigious cartoon which depicted Satan whispering odious counsels into the ear of the Emperor William II, who wore a smile of bland imperial ambition at the very attractive prospects presented by the Father of Lies. In the background an army corps of the hosts of Hell stretched from side to side of the picture like some leering, malevolent flower-bed. Thereafter the series was to traverse the annals of all kinds of frightfulness: Zeppelins dropped bombs on Sunday-schools, submarine crews, agape with laughter, shot down the survivors from torpedoed liners. All these existed only in sketches; the first, however, as Peter knew, was rapidly approaching completion on the monstrous scale, and took up the whole end of the studio. Neither Peter nor his mother had as yet been permitted a glimpse of it; the full blast of its withering force, so Mr. Mainwaring had planned, was, on completion, to smite and stun them.

He had heard Peter's entrance into the house, for an outburst of jubilant yodelling came to the young man's ears as he put down his hat.

"Tirra lirra, tirra lirra," sang out the boisterous voice. "Is that my Peter? Ha-de-ah-de-ho!"

Peter's eyebrows went up, his mouth slackened to a long sigh, and his slim shoulders shrugged. But his voice—all of him that at present could convey his mood to his father—was brisk and cordial.

"Hallo, father," he said. "Do you want me?"

"Yes, my dear; come in a moment. I have something to show you."

Peter closed the door of the kitchen stairs and went into the studio. His father was standing high on a stepladder in front of his canvas, dashing the last opulent brushful of sombre colour on to the thundercloud which, portending war, formed so effective a background of Prussian blue to the Emperor's head. He painted with swoops and dashes; such things as "finish" were out of place in designs for the wall of China.... Even as Peter entered he skipped down from the steps of the ladder and laid aside his palette and brushes.

"*Finito, e ben finito!*" he cried. "Congratulate me, my Peter! I made the last stroke as you entered, an added horror—is it not so?—in that cloud. Ha! You have not seen it yet; sit down and drink it in for five minutes. Does it make you hot and miserable to look at? Yes, you'll see more of that cloud and of what it holds for distracted Europe before I come to the end of my cartoons. Bombs and torpedoes are in that cloud, my Peter; devastation and destruction and damnation!"

He struck a splendid attitude in front of the tremendous canvas, and with a sweep of his hand caused his thick crop of long, grey hair to stand out in billows round his head. Physically, as regards height and fineness of feature, Peter certainly owed a good deal to his father, for John Mainwaring's head—with its waves of hair, its high colour, its rich exuberance—was like some fine manuscript now enriched with gilt and florid illuminations, of which Peter was, so to speak, the neat, delicate text unadorned by these flamboyant additions. Peter's vanity, doubtless, came from the same paternal strain, for never was there anyone more superbly conscious of his own supreme merits than his father. Highly ornamental, he knew that his mission was not only to adorn the palace of art with his work, but to enlighten the dimness of the world with his blazing presence. Like most men who are possessed of extraordinary belief in themselves, of high colour and exuberant spirits, he was liable to accesses of profound gloom, when, with magnificent gestures, he would strike his forehead and wail over his own wasted life and the futility of human endeavour. These attacks, which were very artistic and studied performances, chiefly assailed him when the Royal Academy had intimated that some stupendous canvas of his awaited removal before varnishing day. Then, with bewildering rapidity, his spirits would mount to unheard-of altitudes again, and, brush in hand, he would exclaim that he asked no more of the world than to allow him to pursue his art unrecognized and unhonoured, like Millet or Corot. His temperament, in fact, was that of some boisterous spring day which, opening with bright sunshine, turns to snow in the middle of the afternoon, and draws to a close in lambent serenity; and whether exalted, depressed, or normal, he was simply, though slangily, the prince of "bounders."

He clapped his hand on Peter's shoulder.

"I need not point out to you the merits, or, indeed, the defects of my composition," he said, "for my Peter inherits something of his father's perceptions. Look at it then once more and tell me if my picture recalls to you the method, even, perhaps, the inspiration of any master not, like me, unknown to fame. Who, my boy, if we allow ourselves for a moment to believe in psychic possession, who, I ask you—or, rather, to cast my sentence differently—to whom do I owe the realization of terror, of menace, of spiritual horror, which, ever so faintly, smoulders in my canvas?"

He folded his arms, awaiting a reply, and Peter cudgelled his brains in order to make his answer as agreeable as possible. The name of Blake occurred to him, but he remembered that of late his father had been apt to decry this artist for poverty of design and failure to render emotional vastness. Then, with great good luck, his eye fell on some photographic reproductions from the ceiling of the Sistine Chapel that decorated the wall of the studio, and he felt he had guessed right.

"No one but Michael Angelo," he said. "That's all the influence I can see, father."

Mr. Mainwaring rested his chin on his hand and was gazing at his work with frowning, seer-like scrutiny. It was difficult to realize that it was he who had yodelled so jubilantly just now.

"Curious that you should have said that, Peter," he said in a deep, dreamy voice. "For days past, as I worked, it has seemed to me that M.A.— Master of Art, as well as Michael Angelo, note you—that M.A. was standing by me. At times, indeed, it seemed that not I, but another, controlled my brush. I do not say he approved, no, no; that he was pleased with me; but he was there, my boy. So, if there is any merit in my work, I beseech you to attribute it not to me but to him. It was as if I was in a trance...."

He closed his eyes for a moment and bowed his head, and then, as if at the last "Amen" of some solemn service, he came out of the dim cathedral into sunlight.

"Your mother!" he said. "We must not forget her in this great moment. Is she in? Tirra lirra! Ha-de-ah-de-ho! My own!"

He pranced to the door, ringing the bell, as he passed, and repeated his yodelling cries. From upstairs a quiet, thin voice gave some flat echo of his salutation; from below a hot parlourmaid opened the door of the kitchen stairs and set free a fresh gale of roastings.

"Three glasses," he said to the latter. "Three glasses, please, and the decanter of port. *Maria mia!* Come down, my dear, and, if you love me, keep shut your lustrous eyes and take my hand, and I will guide you to the place I reserve for you. So! Eyes shut and no cheating!"

Mrs. Mainwaring, small in stature, with a porcelain neatness about her as of a Dresden shepherdess, suffered herself to be led into the studio, preserving the scrupulous honesty of closed eyelids. By her side her rococo husband looked more than ever like some preposterous dancing-master, and if it was correct to attribute to him Peter's inherited vanity, it was equally right to derive from the young man's mother that finish and precision which characterized his movements and his manners. Easily, too, though with a shade more subtlety, a psychologist might have conjectured where Peter's habit of walking in the wet woods and telling nobody was derived from, for it was not hard to guess that Mrs. Mainwaring's tranquil self-possession, her smiling, serene indulgence of her husband's whim, was the result of a quality firm and deeply rooted. Self-repression had, perhaps, become a habit, for her conduct seemed quite effortless; but in that tight, thin-lipped mouth, gently smiling, there was something inscrutably independent. She was like that, secret and self-contained, because she chose to be like that; her serenity, her collectedness, were the mask she chose to wear. Thus, probably, Peter's inheritance from her was of more durable stuff than the vanity he owed to his father, for how, if his mother had not been somehow adamantine, could she have lived for nearly a quarter of a century with this flamboyant partner, and yet have neither imbibed one bubble of his effervescence nor lost any grain of her own restraint? Indeed, she must have been like some piece of quartz for ever dashed along by the turbulence of his impetuous flood, and yet all the effect that this buffeting and bruising had produced on her had been but to polish and harden her. She went precisely where the current dashed her, but remained solid and small and impenetrable.

Such was her relation to the bounding extravagance of her husband; he swept her along, quite unresisting, but never parting from her self-contained integrity, and all his whirlings and waterfalls had never stripped one atom off her nor roughened her surface. To him she appeared transparently clear, though, as a matter of fact, not only had he never seen into her, but, actually, he had never seen her at all. He bounced her about, demanding now homage, when the exuberance of creation was his, now sympathy when the rejection of a picture by the Royal Academy made him a despairing pessimist; but she never varied with his feverish temperature, and on the surface, at any rate, remained of an unchangeable coolness. His trumpets never intoxicated her small, pink ear; his despair of himself and the world in general never came within measurable distance of sullying her serenity, any more than a thunderstorm disturbs the effulgence of a half-moon that neither waxes nor wanes. She still continued calmly shining behind his clouds, as was obvious when those clouds had discharged their violence. John Mainwaring never dreamed of considering what, possibly, might lie below that finished surface; it was enough for him that she should always be ready to pay a scentless homage to his achievements, or sit quietly like a fixed star above the clouds of despair that occasionally darkened his day. She was "*Maria mia*, my beloved," when he was pleased with himself, and, when otherwise, it was enough that she should repeat at intervals: "Fancy their rejecting your picture. I am sure there are hundreds in the exhibition not half so good."

To Peter she was an enigma to which he never now attempted or desired to find the key. She seemed to him quite impervious to external influences behind that high wall of her reserve. Nothing, so far as he knew, roused emotion in her; nothing excited, nothing depressed her. Sometimes, when a boy, he had gone to her with a trouble to confide, and she would say: "How tiresome for you, dear," and perhaps suggest some sensible course of action. But neither his troubles nor her own (if she had any) seemed to touch her emotions; while, on the other hand, if there was something agreeable to communicate, if his father sold a picture, or Peter had the announcement of promotion in the Foreign Office, her sympathy and pleasure (if she felt any) were just as iced as her condolence had been. The event—to Peter's apprehension—that most had power to move her was the fact that somebody had left open the door at the top of the kitchen stairs. When that was "quite shut," and when all household cares had their sunset after dinner, her habitual mode of self-employment was to read a page or two of a novel (returning it to the library next day) and then to take some sort of railway guide and scan the advertisements of hotels situated in agreeable places on the south coast or among the Derbyshire Highlands. Often and often had Peter returned from dinner to find his mother thus employed. His father, when in the throes of creation, went early to bed in order to be fresh and spry for the light of the morning hours; but she slept badly, and slept best if she went late to bed. There she would be then when Peter latch-keyed himself into the house on his return from dining out, or even, occasionally, when he returned far later from a dance, with the Bradshaw in her hand open among the advertisements of hotels. She would put a paper-knife in the leaves to keep her place while she exchanged a few words with him; then, when he went to bed, she would resume her reading. Quite naturally and warrantably he had always considered this a "sad narcotic exercise" on her part, producing, it was to be hoped, the drowsiness which she was wooing. A more promising device for dulling the activity of the brain, than reading about unknown hotels at unvisited places, could hardly be desired, and so reasonable a process provoked no curiosity on his part.

But the door at the top of the kitchen stairs was the most active of her interests, and took precedence in her mind of any mood of her husband's. So when to-day he led her with a prancing processional movement to a throne of Spanish brocade at a suitable focusing distance from the finished cartoon, she, with nostrils open though with shut eyes, gave the door to the kitchen stairs the first claim on her attention.

"That door has been left open again," she said. "How careless Burrows is! Please shut it, my dear. I will keep my eyes tightly shut."

It struck Peter at this moment that both he and his mother treated his father as if he had been a child. They both played his games, treating them with due seriousness, lest they should damp the excited pleasure of the young. She was playing now without collusion, for, led in as she had been, with closed eyes, she had no idea that Peter was present. Then, faintly up the kitchen stairs came the jingle of the glasses, and Burrows entered with the tray that had been ordered, once more leaving that fatal door agape. By some exercise of domestic intuition Mrs. Mainwaring divined the sort of thing going on round her, and with eyes still honourably closed said:

"Be sure you close the door at the top of the stairs, Burrows, when you go down again."

John Mainwaring, with a wealth of gesticulation in order to enjoin silence on Peter, and with much stealthiness of action, completed his festive preparations. Demanding from his wife steadiness of hand and no questions, he thrust between her fingers a brimming glass of port, took one himself, and filled a third for Peter. In obedience to his pantomime Peter stood on one side of his enthroned mother and elevated his glass.

"Open your dear blue eyes, *Maria mia!*" exclaimed John Mainwaring, "and before you say a single word drink to your husband's offering to Art!"

Mrs. Mainwaring opened her eyes, and found as she had already guessed from previous experience, her brimming glass.

"I couldn't possibly drink all that, my dear," she said, "but I will sip it with pleasure before I say anything. There! Dear me, what a fine great picture! All success to it! So that's what has kept you so busy all these days when I wasn't allowed to come into your studio. Oh, there's Peter! Are you going to dine at home, dear? I thought you said you were going out."

"I've only come home to dress," said he.

"I see. Now let me look at your father's picture. Why, there's the German Emperor! And what a quantity of other people. Dear me! And who is that whispering to the Emperor? What a horrid expression he has!"

The artist drank his glass of port at a gulp, and at another the rest of hers.

"Horrid? I should think it was. If you had said devilish you would have been even more on the bullseye. Now you shall be our Molière's housemaid. Speak, voice of the British public! Tell me and Peter what you see before you."

Mrs. Mainwaring, with the aid of her glasses, and the slight hint already given, was perfectly certain that it must be Satan who was whispering to the Emperor, and that all those dreadful faces behind must have something to do with him. Then there was that huge dark cloud in the background.

"The Emperor and Satan," she said with a sort of placid excitement, like an adult trying to guess a child's riddle. "Now wait a minute, my dear. Yes, I'm sure that dreadful thundercloud behind is the war, and if the Emperor wouldn't listen to Satan it would go away. But he's looking pleased and proud; he is listening. I suspect that Satan is telling him that he will win the war and be Emperor of the earth, as you've always said he would have been if the Germans had won. Well, I do think it's clever of you to have made me think of all that. Such a few weeks, too, to paint such a big picture! How well you kept your secret! You only told me that you were very busy, and that I mustn't come into your studio. I never thought that when you allowed me in again I should see anything so large and remarkable. Most striking! Isn't it, Peter?"

"Splendid!" said Peter. Then he wondered if he had put enough conviction into his voice to satisfy the *gourmandise* of his father.

"Quite splendid!" he said, rather louder.

Then it was Mrs. Mainwaring's turn in this game.

"And it's only the first of a series," said she. "You must send it to some exhibition at once, John, in order to make room for the rest. So large, is it not? It fills up all the end of the studio. Such an important picture. Dear me, how wicked the Emperor looks! And what will the next picture be?"

"War. Picture of war. Allegorical. Shells bursting into shapes of devilish malignity."

He leaned on the back of the throne, regarding the picture intently.

"It will kill me, painting the rest of them," he said with a fell intensity. "I've got to go through the hell of it all myself before I can paint them."

The calm of Mrs. Mainwaring's voice was untouched by this gloomy prospect.

"No, dear, it won't kill you," she said consolingly. "That's your artistic temperament. You will have a good holiday afterwards. You must be sure to do that. I see; the other pictures will all come out of that dreadful thundercloud. Such a poetical idea! And I hope you'll have a picture of Peace for the last one. Everything quite serene again, and the thundercloud vanished, and no Emperor at all, unless you paint a very little figure of him in the background to show how small he has become. Just him in the background, somewhere in Holland."

John Mainwaring left his domestic position, leaning on the throne, and strode up and down the studio.

"Ah, that intolerable happy ending!" he said. "That's the convention that spoils all art. Art's a stern, bitter business; you mustn't expect to find a bit of sugar at the bottom of your cup. Art, as the Greeks said, is meant to move pity and terror."

Mrs. Mainwaring stepped from her throne.

"Well, I shall think of a peaceful picture for myself, then," she said, "and when I have looked at all yours I shall imagine my own. After all, the war is over, and it's had a happy ending for us, since the Germans have been beaten and Peter has come back from it all safe and sound. That's my ending."

He projected his fine grey hair again with a dexterous sweep of the hand.

"Well, well," he said, as if he was an adult playing with a child, whereas certainly the relation was the other way about. "I will do my best for you, Maria. But I make no promise, mind. Remember that."

As Peter started off again for the various entertainments of the evening he tried to imagine himself in serious sympathy with either of his parents, and ruinously failed. Beginning with his father, he surveyed with the critical clear-sightedness of his terribly sensible nature those hysterical daubings of paint, those mysteries as to what his father was engaged on, those prancing port wine ceremonies when his labour was finished, that crystal confidence, never clouded, in the worth of his fatuous achievements. Long ago it had soaked into his soul that his father was a magnificent buffoon, who, decking himself in the habiliments of Hamlet, had no idea that instead of being engaged in heroic drama, he was a figure in a farce so outrageous that you could not really laugh at him; you could only marvel. Had his pictures, every one of them, been masterpieces, his own enthusiasm over them would have verged on the grotesque. As it was they were preposterous and childish performances, inspiring the observer with pity and terror for the perpetrator rather than, in the sense of Aristotle, whom his father so often quoted, for the works themselves. How was it possible to feel sympathy with one whose impenetrable egoism burned radiantly unconsumed like that? Yet, while he rejected that possibility, Peter found himself somehow envying the temperament that transmuted life for its owner into an endless orgy and carouse. Even the deepest despairs into which reaction plunged his father were psychical feasts to him, served up with the same sauce of transcendental egoism as were his raptures. That was like some pungent essential oil of so ammoniacal an aroma that it pervaded its whole accessible atmosphere. No neutral quality on the part of others, no individual indifference was permitted to exist, or, if it existed, it was either wholly unnoticed or, if noticed, sublimely pitied. Peter's father, so it struck the young man, galloped through life "like a ramping and a roaring lion," the king of the beasts.

It was no manner of good to attempt to sympathize with so predatory an animal, and from the thought of his father Peter switched off to the thought of his mother, who was the habitual prey. There he was confronted with the mild enigma, of which he had not the faintest comprehension, and for the hundredth time, guessing out of a dubious, incurious twilight, he wondered if there was, could be, anything to comprehend. He tried to sum up his knowledge of her. She ordered dinner, she wore day and night some family inheritance of her own of splendid pearls, she read advertisements in railway guides of hotels on Cornish Rivieras and Derbyshire Switzerlands. That she should order dinner and wear her own pearls was an accidental happening, because she was mistress of a house and had some pearls, but beyond that she receded, as far as Peter was concerned, into a dreamland without logic. Indeed, as he devoted his mind to her now, the most illogical thing about her was that for twenty-three years she had contrived to live with his father, and had preserved a certain personality of her own. It seemed frankly impossible that anyone who had lived so long with that maniacal egoist should not have been in any way affected by him. But there she was. His father had neither crushed her nor vitalized her, and whatever her real personality might be, Peter felt sure that the ramping and the roaring lion had not invaded an atom of it. If his father sustained himself on the flamboyance of his own existence, she, none the less, was self-sufficient, demanding neither sympathy nor comprehension from others. The chasm that yawned between himself and his father was a mere rabbit-scrape compared to the abyss on the other side of which there sat his mother, delicate and immovable, covered with hoar frost and decked with her pearls, and reading her railway guide.

Peter owed that deep-seated vanity of his to his father; to his mother he owed that aloofness which was no less characteristic of him. But to himself he seemed to have nothing to do with either of them; they both appeared to him to be distant and ancient phenomena, and he waved a mild salutation to them as acknowledgment of the debt of his own existence. Between them they had projected him, but his own individuality swamped that as completely as his father's egoism drowned all other flavours. Was it always like that nowadays? Were all the last generation so far sundered from the adolescent present as he from his father and mother?... Was there a new plan of life, a new outlook, a new everything?

CHAPTER III

Peter's dinner at the Ritz was no dinner-party, and there were but three young men, of whom he was one, and their hostess who assembled in the Yawning-place. People always yawned there; they were either waiting for somebody to come, or they were waiting for somebody to go away....

His hostess to-night was the perennial Mrs. Trentham, with whom a party of herself and three young men was a favourite form of entertainment. She always professed a coquettish contrition at not having been able to get some girls to meet her young men—which, indeed, she had been quite wonderfully unable to do, since it never occurred to her to take the preliminary step of asking them, and no nice girl would come to dine with Mrs. Trentham without being asked. So the girls, not being asked, stayed away, and Mrs. Trentham apologized.

She was considerably older than the rest of her youthful assemblage; but she looked almost as young as any of them, and might charitably have been supposed to be a sister, or a wife, or something. She had only one real passion in her excited life, and that was to dine as publicly as possible with several young men, sending her husband, to his great contentment, to amuse himself comfortably at his club. There he talked politics and played Bridge, and the very number of these public entertainments on the part of his wife, and the diversity of the youths who partook of them, were guarantee against any breath of scandal sullying herself or anybody else. With perfect justice, nobody believed anything against her; yet this delightful immunity from gossip rather annoyed her. But, in order to give colour to compromise, she would have been obliged to descend to duets in quiet corners, which would have been no fun at all. The loss of publicity, the loss, too, of the pleasing phenomenon that batch after batch of young men, in groups of two or three, so constantly accompanied her to one of the most strategic tables at the Ritz, would not have been compensated for by the added chance of scandalous talkings. After all, London was not so violently likely to care what she did, especially since she did not care either, and it was far more agreeable to continue doing what she liked rather than gain an entirely spurious loss of reputation by less enjoyable methods. She had a pleasant, prurient mind, and her morals were beyond reproach. She called attention to her age, when she was with the young, in a somewhat excessive manner, and often alluded to her beautiful hair, which had been grey before she was thirty. "Such an old woman as me," was an ungrammatical phrase which she often affected, and this was a preventive measure against anybody else thinking of such a thing. Her favourite subject of conversation was love.

Mrs. Trentham was not really quite so silly as she sounded, though her immense sprightliness often seemed to plunge her into the nethermost depths of fatuousness. During the war she had taken to dressing in the uniform of a nurse, which she discovered suited her, though, for fear of witnessing distressing sights, she kept well away from hospitals; since then, having realized the decorative value of black and white, she had adopted a garb which seemed to indicate that she was a widow, though not quite recently bereaved. An occasional bright note of colour in her hair or round her charming waist seemed to have forgotten about her widowhood and was extremely becoming.... So garbed, so minded, she awaited Peter, who was the last of her conspicuous party of young men. He was certainly late for her appointed hour, but she did not dislike that as the Yawning-place was full, and, instead of scolding him, she had her usual apologetic greetings volubly ready.

"My dear, you will be furious with me, I know," she said, "but I simply couldn't get hold of any girls, so you and Charlie and Tommy will just have to put up with an old woman until we go to the opera, and then you will breathe loud sighs of relief, and I shall see you no more. Why are you so late, Peter? Whom have you been flirting with?"

"My father and my mother," said Peter. "He has just finished the largest picture in the world."

"How sweet of him! Ah, they have brought some cocktails at last."

She waited till the servant was well out of hearing.

"But how stupid the waiter is," she said. "I am sure I told him to bring three not four. Shall I taste it? Shall I like it, do you think?"

It seemed not too optimistic to hope that she would, for, otherwise, she would long ago have ceased not only tasting the fourth cocktail which she was sure she had not ordered, but consuming it so completely that the strip of lemon-peel overbalanced against the tip of her pretty nose.

"My dear, how strong!" she exclaimed. "I feel perfectly tipsy, and one of you must give me your arm, as if you were a nephew or something if I stagger or reel. Let us go in to dinner at once. I promised Ella we would get to Mrs. Wardour's box by the beginning of the opera."

"Who is Mrs. Wardour?" asked Charlie Harman.

"Oh, quite new," said Mrs. Trentham. "Hardly anyone has seen her yet. Rich, fabulously rich. Her husband was one of the hugest profiteers—not eggs at fourpence, but steamers at a quarter of a million. He bought up everything that floats and sold it to the Government, and most of it got sunk. He died a couple of years ago. Too sad."

"More about her, please," said Peter.

"I haven't seen her yet, my dear, but Ella Thirlmere is being her godmother—sponsor, you know—and she asked me to take people to her box and her dinners and her dances. Her name's Lucy: it would be. I shall begin by calling her Lucy almost immediately. There's no time nowadays to get to know people. You have to pretend to know them intimately almost the moment you set eyes on them."

"And pretend not to know them afterwards, if necessary," said Peter.

May Trentham gave a hasty glance round the room and, becoming aware that quite a sufficient number of people were looking at her and her party, slapped the back of Peter's hand with the tips of her fingers, and gave a scream of laughter to show what a tremendously amusing time she was having.

"You naughty boy!" she said. "Is he not cynical about Lucy? I shan't talk to you any more. Tommy, my dear, tell me what you've been doing. You look flushed. I believe you're in love."

"No. I've been playing squash," said Tommy.

"What is squash? I believe it's one of your horrid new words and means flirting. Who is she?"

"She is Charlie. At least, I was playing squash with Charlie," said Tommy, with laborious precision. "He didn't like it."

Charlie fingered two little tails of blond hair that grew directly below his nostrils and formed his moustache. Otherwise his face was completely feminine—plain and pink and plump. He gesticulated a good deal with his hands, flapping and dabbing with them.

"Odious game," he said, showing a great many teeth between his red lips. "You go on hitting a ball against a putrid wall until you're too tired to hit it any more, and then Tommy says 'One love.' When you've done that fifteen times, he says 'Game,' and then you begin another one. I hoped I should never hear of it again."

"You shan't, my dear; but don't be such a cross-patch. I know you're annoyed with me for not getting you some pretty girl to talk to. You must talk to Peter. He's in disgrace with me. Oh, Peter, is it true about Nellie Heaton's engagement?"

"Perfectly," said Peter.

"Then why aren't you broken-hearted? I don't believe any of you young men have got hearts nowadays."

"That accounts for their not being broken," said Peter.

It was time to laugh loudly again in order to remind the rest of the diners what a brilliant time she was having, and May Trentham did this.

"There he goes again!" she said. "Is he not shocking? My dear, have you had a dreadful scene with her?"

"No. I only had tea with her."

"Oh, don't pretend you weren't desperately in love with her. But never mind. I will find some other girl for you, who will adore you so violently that you will lose your heart to her, though you say you haven't got one. She shall be rich and lovely, and we shall all be frantically jealous of her. And you shall both call me Aunt May, because I have brought you together."

"Thank you, Aunt May," said Peter. "Go on about her, please."

"No, I've talked to you long enough. Tommy is feeling left out. When the opera is over, by the way, I want you all to come on to Ella Thirlmere's dance. I promised to bring you all. Mrs. Wardour is sure to be coming, and she will certainly have plenty of motor-cars to take us. Oh, there is that marvellous Spanish boxer, is it not, dining alone with Ella. How gentle and kind he looks! Darling Ella! I wonder if she will have six rounds with him in the middle of her dance. I would certainly back her: look at her chest. But how daring of her to dine with him here! They say he marries again after each of his fights and settles all the money he has won on his new wife. But, after all, I suppose it's just as daring of me to dine with three such attractive young men as for her to dine with just one Solomon like that!"

Tommy puzzled over this for a moment. He was very good-looking, but there was no other reason for him.

"Solomon?" he asked.

"Yes, my dear; think of his wives. I was talking to Anthony Braille to-day, who makes all those wonderful tables about population, and what encourages and hinders it. He said the only chance for England was to close all the music-hall bars and introduce polygamy. Every Englishman, after this dreadful war—you know I was a nurse during the war—must have fifty children a year for two years—or did he say two children a year for fifty years?—in order to bring up the population again to its proper level. It was all most interesting—if he only didn't stutter so much!"

"He seems to have stuttered out the main facts," said Peter.

"Oh, I couldn't tell a young man half the things he said to me. We ought all to be Patagonians and polygamists. The birth-rate among Patagonians is colossal. They behead all women of the age of thirty-five who aren't married, and all bachelors at the age of forty. It has something to do with eugenics."

The intoxication of a restaurant now crowded with people had gained complete ascendancy over Peter's hostess. She never felt quiet and contented unless she was surrounded by a host of friends, acquaintances, and people she knew by sight, and had to shout at the top of her voice in order to be heard above the roar of other conversations and the blare of a band. It was equally necessary for the establishment of this tranquil frame of mind that several young men, and, if possible, no women, should be with her, and that she should constantly be convulsed by shrieks of laughter, and should have both her elbows on the table. A finer *nuance* in success was that she must appear wholly absorbed in the brilliance of her own table, and quite unconscious of the hubbub round her, though presently, when she got up, she would seem to awake to the fact that she was in a crowded restaurant, and would blow kisses all over the room, and have dozens of little smiles and words for all those whose position between her and the door she had unerringly noted. Just a sentence or two for each, reminding her "my dears" of a meeting to-morrow, or a meeting yesterday with a phrase of flattery and a bit of whispered scandal and the conclusion: "I must fly; those boys will be so cross with me if I keep them waiting. Meet you at dearest Ella's? Yes? Lovely!"... All this was faithfully performed on her part, and her face, with its pretty little features all bunched together in the middle of it, like the markings in a pansy, had expanded and contracted again sufficient times before she reached the door of the restaurant to enable a weary conclave to express itself as it waited for her.

"*Parsifal*, too," said Charlie. "Thank God we've missed the first act. Aged stunt—flower-maidens and grails. Can't we get away, Peter? Come home with me. Say we're busy at the F.O. German complications. Bolshevists on the Rhine."

Tommy stood first on one leg scratching a slim calf with the other instep, and then on the other leg scratching in a corresponding manner.

"You simply can't," he said. "How am I to deal with her and Lucy? And *Parsifal*?"

"Polygamy and Patagonians," said Peter, with a vague remembrance of the preposterous conversation that had garlanded their dinner. "Flirt, Tommy. Can you flirt? Hold hands. Sigh. Beam. Can't you manage it?"

"No," said Tommy.

"Then Tommy and I will go away," said Charlie. "After all, she doesn't want us, except as a stage crowd. She wants you most, Peter. I say, I like your studs. Who?"

"Nobody. I liked them, too, so I got them. But we've all got to go on. After all, we've had dinner."

"All the more reason for not going on," said Charlie.

"That's no good. It doesn't pay. Besides, she's awfully decent——"

"Don't be priggish, Peter. I say, is Nellie really going to marry Philip Beaumont? Do you mind?"

This atrocious conversation was interrupted by the sprightly tripping advent of their hostess, who put her fingers in her ears, which she knew were "shell-like," as she passed through the direct blast of the band, and consoled them for her want of appreciation of their professional functions by distributing more of her little smiles.

"Now I know you are all going to scold me," she said, "because I've kept you waiting. But there were so many dears who insisted on my having a word with them. They nearly tore my frock off. Let's all cram into one taxi, and I will sit bodkin. And after Ella's dance we'll all go on to Margie Clifford's. She specially told me to bring all of you, and scold you well first for not having talked to her on your way out. I don't know what everybody will think when I appear at the Ritz and the Opera, and two dances with the same young men. I shall have to tell my darling Bob that the *Morning Post* hasn't come, or he'll storm at me. What a lovely white lie."

There flashed through Peter's consciousness at that moment an insane wonder as to what would *happen* if he said calmly and clearly and genuinely, "My good woman, who cares? As for the compromising young men who accompany you, they are all dying to get away, and only the debt of the excellent dinner you gave us, of which I reminded them, prevents us from doing so." There was the truth of the matter, and it was all rather mean and miserable. Her guests were spending the evening with her and ministering to her hopeless delight in daring situations simply because she had, on her side, administered the nosebag. They consented, with a grudging sense of honourable engagement, to plough their way in her wake merely because she had fed them. If she had asked them severally or collectively to drop in after dinner, in the way of a friend, for conversation and soda water, none of them would have dreamed of gratifying her. And now, when they had fed deliciously at her expense, they would all have preferred to go back to Charlie's rooms in Jermyn Street, or to Tommy's flat (Peter's house was handicapped by the presence of parents), rather than trail along to *Parsifal*, and to a dance, and yet another dance. The dances, perhaps, might be amusing, for there would be girls there, and some sitting about on stairs, and some sliding about on slippery floors, and an irresponsible atmosphere, and certainly some more champagne. You had to get through the night somehow, and nowadays you could smoke while you were dancing, and you needn't dance much. The nuisance—rather a serious one—was that Mrs. Trentham would be there all the time, screaming and dabbing at them to show how amusing and brilliant they all were, keeping them firmly planted round her while she told them that they must go away and dance and make themselves agreeable to others rather than hang round an old woman like her, and continually whistling them back if they attempted to do anything of the sort. She would take up a position where she could most advantageously be seen and heard, and get them all plastered about her, swiftly talking to each in turn, so that he could not possibly go away as long as she so volubly told him to. She had that artless art to perfection; no one had such a gift for making young men adhesive as she, while all the time she was scolding them for wasting their time on an old woman. There was no semblance of sentiment in these proceedings; the entire objective of the manœuvres was to demonstrate to the world that these boys insisted on crowding round her and not leaving her. That was her notion of a successful evening, and since they had signed their bond by eating her dinner, she managed to exact the full pound of flesh.

The curtain went down on the first act of *Parsifal* precisely as Mrs. Trentham led her shrill way into one of the two boxes that bore the name of Mrs. Wardour. She tripped in, all feather fan and stockings, like some elegant exotic hen, proudly conscious of the brood of most presentable chicks, though not of her rearing, which followed her. The house at that moment started into light again, and black against the oblong of brightness were the backs of two female heads, both of which turned round at the click of the opened door. One of them had a great tiara on, sitting firmly on a desert of pale sandy hair.

May Trentham advanced with both hands held out.

"My dear, how late we are," she said. "You must scold these boys, for they kept me in such shrieks of laughter at dinner that I had no idea of the time. Dearest Ella has so often talked to me about you; always asking:

'Haven't I met Mrs. Wardour yet? Was it possible I had not met her great friend Lucy Wardour?' Charmed!"

In the hard light of the theatre, Mrs. Wardour's face appeared to her to be quite flat; the shadows on it looked like dark smudges applied to the surface with a brush, rather than markings derived from projections and depressions. This apparition of a diamond-crowned oval of meaningless flesh was slightly embarrassing, and she turned to the second occupant of the box. There, in the younger face, she saw what Lucy might, perhaps, once have been like, before the years had flattened her out. Obviously this was a daughter, though Ella Thirlmere had altogether omitted to mention such a thing. Then, with her rather short-sighted eyes growing accustomed to the staring light, Mrs. Trentham observed that her first impression of her hostess's face was an illusion, though founded on fact; just as when the figure of a man resolves itself into a hat and coat hanging on the wall. There was nothing, in fact, abnormal about Mrs. Wardour's countenance: it was just blankish. She had large cheeks of uniform surface, a nose of small elevation, no eyebrows, and eyes set in very shallow sockets. Then another shadow came on to her face; but this time, without delay, May Trentham saw that it was her mouth opening. When she had opened it, she spoke, but she did not conduct both processes simultaneously.

"Well, I'm pleased to see you," she said; "but there are so many friends of Lady Thirlmere—Ella, I should say; she told me always to say Ella—there are so many of Ella's friends visiting me to-night that I don't quite seem to know your name."

May Trentham felt that her brain was giving way. Here was a perfectly empty box, except for Mrs. Wardour and her daughter, and yet here was Mrs. Wardour assuring her that so many friends of Ella were here.... Where were the friends? Were they invisible? Was the box in reality crowded with unseen presences?...

"I'm Mrs. Trentham," she said, clinging firmly to that sure and certain fact. "May Trentham. Ella told me you would expect me."

Mrs. Wardour appeared to be making an effort of recollection. This, in a few moments, seemed successful.

"That's correct," she said. "I remember; and this is my daughter Silvia."

For a moment her face slipped off its sheath of meaninglessness, and something homely and kindly and simple gleamed in it.

"I've got two boxes to-night, Mrs. Trentham," she said. "This and the next, as Lady Thirlmere—Ella—so kindly sent along such a quantity of her friends. That's what it is; and so Silvia and I (didn't we, Silvia?) we left the other box, seeing that it was so full, and came in here, for, naturally, I wanted to put my guests where they could see the play, and Silvia and I, we wanted to see, too. Mrs. Trentham was it? And I'm sure I'm very glad to see you and your young friends. I should like them all to be introduced to me and Silvia."

Charlie had hung up his hat and coat during this amazing conversation, and now came forward.

"How-de-do?" he said.

"I haven't caught the name yet," said Mrs. Wardour. The sheath had gone back over her face again.

"This is Lord Charles Harmer," said Mrs. Trentham.

"Indeed. The son of the Marquis of Nairn?" asked Mrs. Wardour.

Charlie opened his mouth very wide.

"Brother!" he exclaimed, as if he were saying "Murder!" on the Lyceum stage.

Tommy and Peter were less important; the latter, when the introductions were over, found himself sitting between Silvia and her mother. On the further side of Mrs. Wardour was May Trentham between the other two young men and already absorbed in identifying the occupants of boxes opposite and blowing kisses.

"There! There's just room for all of us," said Mrs. Wardour, "without squeezing each other. We were too squeezed in the other box, weren't we Silvia? There's six in the other box, and now we're six here. Let me think; there's Lord Poole and there's Lady Poole. There's Mrs. Heaton, and there's Miss Heaton, and there's Mr. Philip Beaumont. That's five. Miss Heaton is engaged to Mr. Beaumont; isn't that it, Silvia? I want to get it clear."

"Yes, that's right," said Peter.

"Indeed! Do you know Miss Heaton?" asked Mrs. Wardour.

"Yes, very well," said he.

"That's what's so pleasant," said she. "Just to sit here and know everybody. That's what we want, Silvia, isn't it? Just to sit and know everybody. But that only makes five. Who's the other one? His name began with F, and he was very fat."

"Perhaps that was his name," said Peter. He was beginning to enjoy himself; the whole thing was such complete nonsense. What kept up the high level of it was that Mrs. Wardour replied with seriousness:

"No; if his name had been Fat, I should have remembered it," she said. "It wasn't Mr. Fat, nor Lord Fat. He seemed to know everybody, too. He just sat there and knew everybody."

From Peter's other side, where Silvia sat, there came some little tremor of a laugh, hardly audible, and turning, he saw that her face dimpled with amusement. It was singularly sexless; the curve of her jaw, the lines of her mouth were more like a boy's than a girl's; boyish, too, was her sideways cross-legged attitude. If she was laughing at her mother's remark, her amusement was clearly of the most genial kindliness.

Mrs. Wardour continued in a perfectly even voice that almost intoned the words, so void was it of inflection.

"It's a pity your party has missed so much of the opera," she said. "There's been a lot of pretty music; some of it reminded me of being in church and hymns. It'll seem quite strange going to a dance afterwards. A lot of knights singing hymns. *Parsifal*, you know. Some say it's the best opera Wagner ever wrote."

This time Silvia certainly laughed, and again her laugh had not the smallest hint of satirical enjoyment; she was just amused. Peter found himself, though he had scarcely yet glanced at her, somehow understanding her. He recognized in her amusement all that he himself failed to feel with regard to his father's cartoons and his mother's readings in Bradshaw. He knew intuitively that Silvia had got hold of the right way to regard absurdities; to see comedy without contempt. Whether she knew it or not (it was quite certain that she did not), she had given him a glimpse, a hint, an enlightenment, not only of what she was, but of what he was not. Looking at her now directly for the first time, his handsome face caught some reflection of her boyish brightness.

"And what do you think of *Parsifal*?" he asked.

She raised her eyebrows.

"How can I tell?" she asked. "I never saw an opera before."

"I envy you," said Peter.

"Why? For not having seen one, or because I am at last seeing one?" she asked.

Peter, as usual, found himself wanting to make a good impression. If he had been in a lift with a crossing-sweeper he would certainly have tried to make the crossing-sweeper like him, and have exerted his wits to hit upon something which the crossing-sweeper would think to be admirable, even though on arriving at the next floor he would never see him again.

He quickly decided now that the girl would not admire mere drivel.... She happened to want to know what he envied her for.

"For both," he said. "For getting a new impression. That includes both. You mustn't have seen an opera before, and you must be seeing one now."

She looked at him with perfectly unshadowed frankness.

"I believe you meant the first," she said. "I believe when you said you envied me, that you meant I was lucky in not having spent a quantity of boring evenings."

"In any case, I don't mean that now," said Peter.

"Ah, then you did. Why do you mean it no longer?"

Peter found himself criticizing her. A conversation between the acts of an opera was not meant to degenerate into a catechism. You talked in order to mask the ticking of the minutes. But as he was in for a catechism, it was better to be an agreeable candidate.

"Why?" he asked. "Because I expect that you never spend boring evenings. Probably you are not a person who is bored."

Clearly, as he suspected, she was not going to commit herself to any statement without consideration, even when so violently trivial a subject was under discussion. Her eyebrows, much darker than the shade of her hair, like Nellie's, pulled themselves a little downwards and inwards, so that they nearly met.

"Oh, I could easily be bored," she said. "A lot of bored people would infect me and make me bored."

She leaned a little forward towards him, again with that boyish appeal.

"Please don't be bored," she said. "Be interested and amused. Make yourself into a sort of disinfectant to protect me."

"Is there an epidemic?" he asked.

"Yes; the place is reeking with it. My mother, for instance, detests music. Isn't it darling of her?"

"How very odd of her, then— —" he began.

He stopped because, in some emphatic, intangible way, the girl retreated from the platform of intimacy on to which she had stepped. She moved her chair an inch or two away from him, hitching it back with her foot, but that was only a symbol of her change of attitude. What to Peter made the significance of that small steering was a certain quenching of light in her face, as if, over it, she had put up some mask of herself that might easily have been mistaken for her, if the beholder had not, for a glimpse or two, seen her unmasked. She shifted from the personal ground on which, for a minute, they had met, and became Miss Silvia Wardour, generalizing in small talk, in the usual imbecile and social manner. She also became much more feminine....

"I wonder how many people in the house, who have come to hear Wagner, really dislike it," she said. "Probably we all of us like some species of noise, and dislike another species of noise. If you like the Beethoven noise, you probably dislike the Wagner noise. Only nobody will say so. They come to look at each other."

She had carried back the conversation on to the personal platform again, as if she was sorry to have slipped off it so suddenly. But she carried it on to another part of the platform. Quite clearly she did not intend to discuss her mother's presence at the opera.

"Tell me," she said. "What sort of noise do you really like? This or somebody else's?"

Peter wondered for the moment whether she was to prove to be the earnest sort of girl, who, whatever you said, insisted on discussing your random statements, until you contradicted yourself (which usually happened quite soon), and then, vouchsafing a gleam of daylight, found an explanation for them in order that you might be encouraged to entangle yourself further. The earnest girl, the inquisitorial girl; he did not like that type.... They gave you pencils and pieces of paper after dinner and made you write acrostics; they took letters out of a box and gave you eight of them, from which you had to make a word; they divided the guests up into equal numbers, told them that this was "Clumps," and that two people were going to leave the room and guess whatever had been thought of. These were their lighter, intellectual motions, and you feverishly played "Clumps" in order to avoid intolerable abstract discussions. Yet Silvia had not the sleuth-hound expression that usually accompanied these hunters after intellect.

"What a searching question," he said. "But, really, I'm omnivorous about noises. I like the noise I'm listening to. I like it particularly."

There was not in her face the smallest consciousness that he might conceivably be alluding to the fact that she was talking to him. She let her eyes sweep across the crowded theatre.

"That noise?" she asked. "All those people talking? I love it, too. Oh, wouldn't it be interesting to be somebody else for a minute, and know what he meant, what he felt like when he said anything?"

Clearly she had used the masculine gender quite unconsciously. Peter's answer, on the other hand, was deliberate.

"Yes, I should love to know what she feels like, even over the most trivial speech," he said.

Silvia dropped on to this with a precision that only showed how complete her own unconsciousness had been.

"She?" she asked.

"Certainly 'she,'" he said. "I know well enough the kind of thing which men feel like."

She leaned forward again.

"Oh, tell me about that," she said.

Certainly they were together on the personal platform again. Peter was quite at home there; his passion for making a good impression on new acquaintances, his rather uncanny skill in extracting intimacy from them, gave him a confident gait on these boards. He felt that this queer, attractive girl did not in the least wish to be talked to in the ordinary, nonsensical manner. In the gabble of the ballroom, and in the more intimate duologue on the stairs outside it, girls, the generality of them, liked to be told that men thought exclusively about them, and spent their waking and sleeping moments in the contemplation of their divinity and pricelessness. Nellie, of course, was an exception, for between them there certainly was some peculiar bond of understanding; but the majority of girls, so ran his indolent and incurious creed, just wanted to be told that they were too priceless for anything, and some wanted to be kissed. It was all nonsense; they knew that as well as he did; but such was the inherited instinct, or, if you wished to be precise, the inherited instinct acting on the new conditions. But he knew that Silvia was not like that; there was some eager, friendly quality about her. She was not quite the normal girl of the ballroom; nor again, was she the earnest girl, who wanted to explore your brains and prove that you hadn't got any. She seemed merely interested in the topic, not because it would lead to a demonstration of her cleverness.

"Men?" he said. "What do men feel? They are as vain as peacocks, and they think entirely about themselves. They think of you as an inferior sex designed to amuse them."

"Ah, the darlings!" said Silvia, quite unexpectedly.

The great pervading brilliance of the lights went out. A row of veiled illuminations only remained in front of the red confectionery of the curtain, against which the conductor's head was silhouetted. Silvia, after her surprising exclamation, drew her chair more into the corner in order to enable Peter to pull his up to the front of the box.

"Klingsor's Castle," said Mrs. Wardour, with a final desperate glance at her programme. "Who is Klingsor, Silvia?"

Peter wondered whether he could whisper, "Who is Silvia?"; but decided against it.

"A magician, darling," said Silvia, with the same underlying bubble of amusement.

CHAPTER IV

There was a mad brutality of discordant noise, and the risen curtain disclosed an astrologer. He roared and yelled, and soon a dishevelled female, in an advanced stage of corruption, shrieked back at him. Silvia found herself disliking the Wagner noise, and her attention came closer home; came, in fact, to the quarter-view of Peter's face, as he sat low in his chair in order to give her a clear view of Klingsor. She was not sure that she liked Peter any better than the hurly-burly that was going on, and though she knew she had been liking him during the interval between the acts, she now seriously set herself to the task of disliking him, and the easiest method of achieving that result was to class him as just one of the crowd which had come that night to occupy, by request, her mother's two boxes. She perfectly understood the situation: Lady Thirlmere, the woman with the pearls and the blue-black hair, had told a lot of her friends that they could go to see *Parsifal* for nothing, and reap a quantity of subsequent benefits at the price of knowing Mrs. Wardour, of frequenting her house, and of permitting her to eddy round in the general whirlpool. For some reason, inscrutable to Silvia, her mother wanted that; she and her mother, in fact, were like a pill, which Lady Thirlmere had guaranteed that the world should swallow. The pill was nobly gilded, and there was any amount of jam to assist the swallowing of it.

Without doubt Peter was one of the open mouths.

Klingsor and Kundry continued to rave at each other, and so far from listening, Silvia used that external noise to drive her own thought into seclusion; much as a dull sermon, a tedious lecture, makes for introspection in the audience. And hardly had she classed Peter among the open mouths than she wondered if she had been quite fair in doing so, for the talk they had had was not of the same timbre as the conventional quackings which for the last week had made her mother's house like a farmyard, with her, like Mrs. Bond of the nursery rhyme, calling "Dilly, dilly ... you shall be stuffed," and stuffed they were. Silvia could no more enter with sympathy into her mother's aims than she could enter with sympathy into stamp-collecting; but out of love for the stamp-collector—the dear, weary, steadfast stamp-collector—she was eager to feel the highest possible interest in the collection and collect for her with all her might. But she knew that she despised the spirit of the stamps, which, in return for food and drink and opera-boxes, were so willing to be collected. Next week there was to be a dance "for her," in that immense mansion which had been re-christened Wardour House, and pages of the stamp-book would on that occasion be filled with adhesive specimens. "Everybody," so she understood Ella Thirlmere to say, would come, and no doubt it would be tremendous fun....

There were certainly some stamps here now. Lord Charles was one, though why had he been willing to be collected? He sat with his head propped between two long hands, and a queer sort of nose, just protruding, indicated by its downward angle that he was profoundly meditating. Next him was her mother, whose pearls clinked rhythmically to her breathing, and nearest to herself she could see the half-averted profile of the young man whom she was encouraging herself to dislike. He appeared to be looking at the stage; certainly he was paying no attention to her, and she got back to what she actually thought of him, instead of forcing herself into a defensive attitude against him. Somehow they seemed (not that it mattered) to have been talking to each other from odd standpoints. When, ridiculously interested for the moment, she had asked him what men "felt," he had not given a masculine answer. He had spoken to her as if he had been a girl; he had said that men were as vain as peacocks, and thought of women as an inferior sex, designed for their amusement. Very likely that was quite true; but now in this isolation of darkness and loud noises, which cut her off from him and everyone else in the box, it seemed to her to have required a woman to state that. That was a woman's view of a man; a man, though he shared it, could scarcely have said it. Instead, he would have told her that women were the angelic sex, meant to be adored....

Some violent concussion had occurred on the stage; there was no longer a gloomy black man with a photographic lens, but some insane sort of flower-bed; and remembering her programme, she recollected that this was the enchanted garden. The enchantment seemed to lie in a quantity of prodigious calico or cardboard flowers. Presently they burst. If they had not burst they must have burst, for mature females, singing loudly, were hatched out of the centre of each. The change had awakened Charlie, and he opened his mouth very wide.

"My dear, what unspeakable wenches!" he said loudly to Mrs. Trentham.

"Silvia, look at the flower-maidens," said her mother. "They all came out of the flowers. Was not that wonderful? Look at the one from the blue convolvulus! Isn't she sweet?"

Silvia choked a laugh with an audible effort, swallowing it whole.

"Yes, darling," she said. "Aren't they pretty?"

Peter turned to her quickly.

"Oh, that's just how I talk to my father!" he said, and instantly looked back at the stage again.

She reconsidered her verdict of him as merely belonging to the open mouths which Lady Thirlmere showered on her mother. They, at any rate, did not behave in that unwarranted way. Her neighbour was ill-bred, odious, familiar, and having thrown an impertinence like that over his shoulder, he did not even wait for her rejoinder. What it would have been she did not quite know. But ... was it impertinent of him after all? Was it, perhaps, rather a pleasant indication of intimacy? For intimacy, in the ordinary sense, there had not been time or opportunity; but had he, perhaps, just spoken quite naturally, assuming a corresponding naturalness on her part?

If so, she had failed him....

Silvia was annoyed with herself for such a suggestion. How could she have "failed" a young man whom she had seen for the first time half an hour ago, who was only one specimen out of that flock of rooks which had alighted there in this new field, where worms were to be had for the mere picking of them up....

There was a long interval at the end of this second act, and a reseating of the occupants of the two boxes. Lord Poole, whom Mrs. Wardour's godmother had chosen as a genial acquaintance, came in with his great towering frame and his immense red face and his unlimited capacity for enjoying himself.

"Lucky dog, Parsifal," he remarked to Silvia, "to have had all those girls to choose from. He should have taken the one that came out of that great white lily. My word, she did surprise me when she came out of that lily. I wish I knew where I could get some of those lilies. Hallo, Peter! Get out of that chair like a good boy, and let me sit between Miss Silvia and her mother. Haven't had a word with either of them yet. Go and make love to my wife for ten minutes; you'll find her next door, and come back and tell me how you've been getting on."

When this great licensed victualler of London appeared on the scene and made some such suggestion, it was usual to go and do as he told you. But now Peter glanced at the girl as if to ask whether she wished him to make way or not. She gave him no sign, however, no hint that he was to stop where he was, and so the best thing, as his cool, quick brain told him, was to answer Lord Poole genially according to his folly.

"You condone it, then," he said.

"Lord, yes, I condone anything," he said. "We all condone everything nowadays. Saves a lot of trouble in the courts."

The frankness of these odious sentiments made it quite impossible not to treat them as a farce. No one in his senses took Lord Poole seriously; he was so jolly and so preposterous, and so successfully sought safety in numbers. He instantly spread himself over Peter's chair and firmly put one arm round Silvia's waist and the other round her mother's.

"Nice young fellow that," he observed as Peter went out of the box. "What a pair he and Miss Silvia make, hey? He's black and she's fair, and he's a clever fellow and won't have a penny, and I wish I was his age. Do you know his father? He's a rum 'un."

These remarkable statements were addressed in a loud, hoarse whisper to Mrs. Wardour, and were, of course, perfectly audible to Silvia. Then he turned to the girl.

"I've been asking your mother to elope with me," he said, "so I hope you didn't overhear. Now I'm going to talk to you and she mustn't listen. You're perfectly delicious, my dear, you and your golden hair, and that little foot that's kicking me. Let it go on kicking; I like it. Wonder how Peter's getting on with my missus. Peep round the corner, Miss Silvia, and see if she looks like going off with him. There are several topping girls in that box, but she's the pick of them, bless her heart. What! Here's your mother getting up and leaving me. More friends coming in! I never saw such a lot of friends. Why, it's Ella! I'm in luck to-night. And there's May Trentham only one chair away. Look at her profile against the light. Did you ever see anything so perfect? Looks rather like the head on a postage-stamp, but don't say I said so."

Lord Poole was now satisfactorily engaged in his usual evening occupation of getting as many girls and pretty women round him as possible, while Mrs. Trentham was performing a similar office with regard to every young man who came into the box. Her pansy face was growing sillier than ever as she kept telling them all to go and talk to somebody else. The object of these two middle-aged magnets was precisely similar: one wanted to attract to itself all the men, the other all the women; but there was an infinite divergence in their methods. May Trentham, pretending to be young, kept asserting how old she was; Lord Poole, pretending to be old, could not conceal the fact of how young, he was. He, again, was not thinking one atom about himself, but was entirely absorbed in his collection of sirens; she was thinking exclusively about herself, and was only anxious that every one in the house should turn green with envy at her galaxy of adorers.... Then Ella Thirlmere and a friend or two joined the group, and he returned blatantly, fatuously, delightfully to the opera.

"Well, now, I do feel like Parsifal," he said. "Here I am in the middle of such flower-maidens, any of whom could give a couple of furlongs in a mile to those on the stage and come romping home in a canter. Look at Ella now: there's a picture for you! Why, my gracious, here's Winifred, too! Come and tell us all about it, Winifred; how many hearts, not reckoning mine, have you broken to-ight? Look at that hair of hers! Did anybody ever see hair like that? I never did, and I've seen a lot in my time. May Trentham, too! Do you wonder that all the young men go swarming round her? I'm sure I don't, and I'd join the swarm myself if I wasn't so blissfully situated just where I am. Haven't enjoyed an evening so much for years. Wish this interval would last till Doomsday, and then we'd all go up to heaven together! St. Peter would let me in without a question when he saw whom I'd brought along with me."

Among the people who had drifted in at the end of the act was Philip Beaumont, whom Mrs. Trentham had instantly rendered adhesive by her voluble commands to go back to Nellie Heaton at once. Nellie, however, had very designedly sent him here, for she had become aware by a glimpse, a sound (an instinct, perhaps even more) that Peter was in the box next door, and her dispatch of her lover there would certainly signify to Peter that she wished him to take the chair now vacant by her and resume the talk in the window that had taken place that afternoon. Somehow that talk had made for itself an anchorage uncomfortable to her consciousness; it had been like a fishbone in her throat. She had taken gulps of her *fiancé*, so to speak, in order to dislodge it; but she had not succeeded in swallowing it. She had tried to divert her attention from it; had pounced with fixed claws on the opera in front of her; had jotted down in her memory, with the fell example of Lady Poole as an object-lesson, a quantity of ways of behaviour and of the presentation of yourself to others which were undesirable when you were fifty or seventy or whatever Lady Poole happened to be. You must be quiet and calm when you had tottered up to those hoary altitudes; you must leave your hair to turn any colour it chose.... You mustn't wriggle and snort, for whereas wriggling in the young might exhibit (quite advantageously) a graceful litheness, it suggested in the old that a galvanic battery had been unexpectedly applied to the knees and the elbows and the middle part of the person. But there was something remote about these gleanings of knowledge; they might prove to be nutritious (and possibly palatable) if preserved and remembered for thirty or forty years; at the present moment they were not of sufficiently arresting a quality to divert her mind from this fishbone of her interview with Peter.... There had been a harshness, a crudity in it; there had been, to her mind, a certain hostility in it; there had been also a certain hunger in it, an emptiness that ached. He had clearly pronounced that their relationship—the bond, in fact, of which she had spoken—must be changed by her engagement, and, though she would have combated that with wit and good sense, some internal fibre of her throbbed, vibrated to the truth of it. She wanted to convince Peter (and even more to convince herself) that the old bond, the old relationship, still flowered and had lost no petal of its fragrance.

She had not to wait long for his entry; Philip had barely left the box before Peter appeared in the doorway, and she applauded his quickness in answering the signal she had waved to him in the ejection of the other. He was silhouetted there for a moment as he spoke to someone in the corridor outside, cool and crisp and complete. Peter was always like that; nature had applied to him some extra polish, some exquisite finish, which detached him from all others in the moist or dusty crowd. Adorable though that was, the thought came to the girl that, above all else, she wanted to disturb and disarrange that. Peter excited and dishevelled. Peter enthusiastic. Peter undetached and clinging was perhaps the real Peter.... A clamorous, turbulent Peter....

He looked round as he entered; he clearly saw her, and as clearly disregarded the obvious movement of her hand to the vacant seat which Philip had just quitted. Though that rejection—that "cut" you might call it, considering their friendship—was in no way premeditated, it was, when he saw Nellie beckoning as with proprietorship, or so it struck him, quite deliberate. He had given no thought to it before, and apparently gave no further thought now, for he instantly placed himself next Lady Poole, beside whom there was another empty seat. There was a great green feather nodding a welcome from her violent hair; it matched her green shoes and the large slabs of false emerald with which her dress was hazardously held together. She was quite as absurd as her husband, and had a witty poison under her tongue, which she sprayed profusely over most subjects of discussion. But her poison hurt nobody, since nobody ever believed a word she said. She was, in fact, as harmless as a serpent, and certainly not as wise as a dove.

The serpent aspect showed its innocuous fangs.

"Monster," she said to Peter. "Sit down and tell me at once what's going on next door. Whom's my Christopher flirting with?"

"Everybody," said Peter. "He sent me away to flirt with you. Let's begin. Shall I begin? Tell me why you and he should always remain young when all the rest of us are as old as the hills."

The wisdom of the mature dove peeped out for a moment, but was driven back by a hiss of the serpent, as a loud squeal of laughter sounded from the next box.

"That's May Trentham," said Lady Poole unerringly. "My dear, what a woman! Why do all you young men crowd round her like moths round a night-light. Whom has she got?"

"The rest of the males," said Peter. "Male and female, you know— —"

"Stuff and nonsense. There are people who are things! Look at our hostess, whom Christopher is probably embracing at this moment. I assure you she hasn't got a face; she's got a slab. What are we coming to? Then there's her daughter. She's a boy; a nice, handsome, healthy boy, doing well. I wish my son was like her. Do you know him? He's like a pincushion."

Peter was not actively listening to these extraordinary remarks; he was taking in and assimilating just what he had done in not occupying the place indicated to him by Nellie. He came to the conclusion that he had not done so precisely because she intended him to. She was meaning to get on perfectly well without him, and had better begin at once.

"Why pincushion?" he asked.

"Because I put pins into him whenever I see him, which isn't often, and he just sits there and keeps my pins. He doesn't mind; he doesn't bleed. He's nothing at all, poor wretch. I beg him to steal or bear false witness or break any commandment that comes handy so long as he does something. He eats chocolate and trims hats. I shall have no pins left soon.

"Never mind Eddy! But what a horrible opera; must have been written by an organist in collaboration with a choirboy. I wonder if Christopher is in the next box at all. I expect he's gone behind to scrape acquaintance with some flower-maiden—probably that voluptuous crone who came out of a large white lily, though how she got into it originally is more than I can say, because she was bigger than anything I ever saw. If only Eddy would do that sort of thing: so much more suitable. Anæmic; that's what you all are. The women aren't quite so bad as the men. I know personally five grandmothers who have married again in the last fortnight. But the grandmothers who continue optimistically marrying will die in time, and what's going to happen to England then? What's the use of saying 'emigration,' when there won't be anybody to emigrate?"

"I didn't say 'emigration,'" said Peter, with his head whirling. This sort of speech was characteristic of Lady Poole. She dashed pictures on to a screen like a magic lantern, and took them off again before you had seen them, leaving darkness and the smell of oil.

"May Trentham, too," said this amazing lady. "I hear you've been dining with her. She would like every boy in the kingdom to remain celibate for her antiquated sake. I will say for Christopher that he doesn't want that. He would like every woman to do just the opposite.... Good gracious, here's another act and I thought it was all over and that we were only waiting for our motors. Come and see me to-morrow. Any time, I'm always at home. Where is one to go in these days? Profiteers and Bolshevists and Jews! That's England; mark my words!"

Peter groped his way out of the box in the sudden eclipse of the lights, sidling by others who were tip-toeing back again, without any response to Nellie's signal. He knew quite well that there was an unoccupied seat next her, and that it would have been the most natural thing in the world for him to have appropriated it; but he chose to consider that it was more suitable yet that Philip should find his way back to it. She had given him the right to be there, and Peter, with a tinge of insincerity, told himself that he was behaving with extreme correctness in not occupying it; the insincerity lying in the fact that his root-reason for going back to the other box being that he was determined that Nellie should not have everything quite her own way.

Then again—another reason for behaving so properly—she had said herself that afternoon that she meant to fit herself to the conventional mould, and here was he helping to secure a perfect fit. No doubt she was right; she was right also in divining that the nature of the bond between them must now necessarily be changed. It had never been a passionate one; their individual independence, no less than the material obstacles in the way of declared and complete surrender to each other, had always stood between them; but there seemed, now that the bond was slackened, to have been potential passion woven into it. Perhaps the slight collision with Philip in the doorway, and the knowledge that he was groping his way back to the chair by Nellie again, accentuated that perception. For a moment Peter paused; he had yet just time to slide past Philip and occupy the chair; but there seemed to glimmer in the seat of it some label "Reserved," and he checked his impulse. No doubt he would resume natural relations with Nellie again to-morrow, or probably even to-night in the dance—or two dances, was it?—where they would be sure to meet, and a certain subtle antagonism which had begun to smoke and smoulder within him would be quenched. He left it, for the present, at that.

For three or four hours more that night, after the conclusion of the opera, Sivia found herself in touch with one or other of the guests who had so agreeably and with so little ceremony decorated the fronts of her mother's boxes. They seemed just as much at home in Lady Thirlmere's house, taking genial possession of it, dancing to her band, drinking her champagne in the same clubable manner. Lord Poole was greatly in evidence, surrounding himself with the gay moths that positively stuck in the spiced honey of his outrageous compliments and could scarcely disentangle their feet therefrom. He squeezed their hands, he put his arm round their waists, he made the most amazing speeches right and left as to their irresistibility. He was like some mirror into which every woman looked and saw there a fascinating reflection of herself, that presented an image of herself more delicious than, even when trying on a new hat, she had ever supposed herself to be. "What's to happen to us poor men," he asked Silvia, "if you're all of you going on being so tip-top? We shan't do a stroke more work; we shall spend all our time in looking at you, and then who's to pay your bills? I've lost my heart twenty times already to-night, and that's enough for an old chap like me, so I shall take myself off to bed. Where's my wife, I wonder? Can your bright eyes pick out any extra dense crowd of young men? If you can, I shall plunge straight into them, like taking a dive after a pearl-oyster, and I'll find her right in the very middle of them."

There seemed to be an unusual congregation at the end of the drawing-room, which opened on to the dancing floor, and Lord Poole accordingly took his dive. Silvia could see, as the waves of black coats and white shirts split up round him, that it was Mrs. Trentham who was the pearl-oyster just there; but the dive must have been satisfactory, for Lord Poole disappeared fathoms deep.

Silvia began to revise her judgment on the nonchalant greed of the mouths that flocked to be fed. Everyone was so gay and pleasant, so intent on laughter and amusement; everyone knew everyone else. She had done no more than set eyes on a young man who had come in with Mrs. Trentham to her mother's box, but Tommy confidently claimed her as an old friend, and she stalked and slid about the floor with him. At the conclusion of that a girl whom she remembered with even mistier vagueness disentangled herself from another young man (the one who had slept so quietly and cried out so audibly at the appearance of the flower-maiden) and ejected Tommy from the seat next Silvia. She was entrancingly pretty in some wild, dewy manner, and had all the assurance that the knowledge of a delightful appearance gives its possessor.

"I haven't had a word with you all the evening," she said, "and I want to tell you how delicious it was of your mother to let me come to her box. I saw you round the edge of the curtain talking to Peter. He raves about you; so, as I wanted to rave too, I—well, here I am. Don't send me away."

Silvia was utterly unaccustomed to exercise any critical faculty where friendliness seemed to be offered. There were no outlying forts to her heart, no challenging sentries; if a girl seemed to like her, that was passport enough. Who this was she could not for the moment remember, though doubtless her name was among those which her mother had repeated as being occupant next door. Then the name, Nellie Heaton, found a lodging in her mind and seemed secure. She was not sure that she liked the information that Peter was "raving" about her; but it was surely friendliness, the desire to be pleasant, that had prompted the retailing of it to her.

"You must be Miss Heaton," she said. "Am I right? There were so many new faces to-night, you know...."

She looked at Nellie with that direct gaze that sought only to appreciate. There was certainly a great deal to appreciate: the girl was dazzlingly pretty.

Nellie laughed.

"Yes; I suppose I am Miss Heaton for the present," she said.

A little more of her mother's commentaries came into Silvia's mind. Had there not been a man in the next box—name missing for the moment— to whom Miss Heaton was engaged? Perhaps her phrase, "for the present," alluded to that.

"Ah, I'm beginning to remember," she said. "I remember that you are soon to be married. I hope you'll be tremendously happy."

"That's dear of you," said Nellie. "But when I said I was Miss Heaton for the present, I didn't quite mean that."

Silvia, with all her friendliness, shrank ever so slightly from this. There was a certain reserve about her which did not quite allow the indicated response. But the welcome of her manner was not abated.

"Do be kind and sort out all these nice people for me," she said. "I have grasped Lord Poole, and isn't it Mr. Mainwaring who is Peter? He sat next me for an act. All the Christian names are a little puzzling at first. Then there's Tommy; I haven't the slightest idea what his surname is, though I shall know him again, because I danced with him just now. And there's Lord Charles, who went to sleep—I shall know him again——"

"And won't you know Peter again?" asked Nellie. "That's one for Peter."

"Oh, but I shall," said Silvia. "He's——"

The two were sitting close to the door into the ballroom, and at that moment Peter passed in front of them talking to a girl. He just glanced at them, took them both in, and melted into the crowd.

"Yes; that's Mr. Mainwaring," said Silvia confidently. "I—I liked him. Don't you like him?"

Nellie made a little sideways, bird-like movement of her head. Out of her changed relations with Peter she felt that something like antagonism had minutely sprouted. She wanted ... yes, she would give an answer that would seem wholly appreciative of Peter, and that would yet contain something that Silvia possibly (just possibly) would not like.

"Dear Peter!" she said. "Of course, we're all devoted to Peter. It's the fashion to be devoted to Peter."

CHAPTER V

During the next month the foam and froth which spouted from the weir of London, into which Mrs. Wardour, of her own design and desire, had been so expensively plunged, began to be less tumultuous as she floated away from the occasion of her first bewildering dive. Lady Thirlmere, that admirable godmother, had chucked her into it, holding her breath and shutting her eyes, and now Mrs. Wardour was getting her head above water and beginning to paddle on her own account. The sponsor had provided the richness of total immersion, and Lucy Wardour was certainly swimming. As she came up to the surface, she found herself surrounded by iridescent bubbles; she was bobbing along in a mill-race of desirable acquaintances. She had made no friends—there was no time for leisurely processes of this sort; but when she had decided that she wanted to spend her months and her money in the pursuit of some such indefinite goal as now loomed promisingly in front of her, she had not expected to make friends. She had not "gone for" friends; she had gone for something that attracted the attention of the accomplished gentlemen who wrote those small and exquisite paragraphs in the daily papers. Inscrutably enough, that happened to be her ambition; what she wanted was to see (though she knew it already) that "Mrs. Wardour was among those who brought a party to the first night of *The Bugaboo*."... "Mrs. Wardour gave a dinner at Wardour House last night, followed by a small dance." ... "Mrs. Wardour was in the Park, chatting to her friends, and wearing a green toque and her famous pearls."... Among her secretary's duties was that of pasting these juicy morsels, supplied by a press-agency, into a red morocco scrapbook. In fact, she was streaking her way across the bespangled firmament of London, like a comet, with a blank face and an anxious eye. But those who thought that the anxious eye received no impressions just because they were not instantly recorded on the blank face, made the mistake of this season.

May Trentham had undeniably been guilty of this error. From that first night, when she had brought her young men to the opera, she had thought that Mrs. Wardour was not sufficiently alive to her value, and as Mrs. Wardour did not appear to be learning any better, she had certainly permitted herself to indulge in little rudenesses, little patronizations, little contempts, which Mrs. Wardour did not appear to notice. Certainly she made no direct allusion to them, and her rather meaningless countenance showed no sign of having perceived them....

This afternoon she was occupied with her secretary in making out a list of a favoured few, not more than eighty all told, who were to be bidden to an entertainment at which the Russian ballet was to figure. She ran her short, blunt forefinger down the alphabetical pages of her "visiting-list," and dictated names to the gaunt Miss Winterton, who took them down in an angry scribble of shorthand. The last few pages were approaching.

"Then there's Mrs. Trentham," she said to Silvia. "I think we'll leave out Mrs. Trentham."

Silvia put in a mild plea.

"She rather enjoys things, mother," she said.

There was a pause, in which Mrs. Wardour slowly and deliberately recalled certain moments which nobody would have thought she had noticed.

"Well, she isn't going to enjoy my things," she said.

They were seated in Mrs. Wardour's private sitting-room in the great house in Piccadilly. It was hung with French brocade; an immense Aubusson carpet covered the floor, and a Reisener table and bureau, with half a dozen very splendid chairs, echoed the same epoch. Mrs. Wardour had found this a little too stiff for domestic ease, and a decidedly more homely note was struck by a few wicker chairs, upholstered in cretonne, and a tea-table of the same imperishable material, with flaps which let down on hinges and formed convenient shelves for cakes and teacups. On the top of the bureau was a large photograph of the late Mr. Wardour in watch-chain and broadcloth. There were but a few more names, and Mrs. Wardour closed the book.

"Then you'll send invitations to the names I've given you, Miss Winterton," she said, "on R.S.V.P. cards. There's no one else you'd like to ask, Silvia?"

Silvia knew quite well what she was intending to say, and wondered why she hesitated.

"Will you ask Mr. Peter Mainwaring?" she said.

"Mr. Mainwaring? I don't seem to recollect— —"

"Darling, of course you can't recollect everybody," said the girl; "but I should like him to be asked."

"Certainly then. What's his initials and address?"

Silvia supplied this information, and Miss Winterton gathered up her papers and left them. She had the air of some dethroned queen, for whom disastrous circumstances had made it necessary to perform menial offices. Mrs. Wardour breathed a sigh of obvious relief when she had gone.

"She terrifies me, Silvia," she said, when the door had closed. "She and that new butler. To think that one of them is called Summerton and the other Winterton. Well, I'm sure!"

Silvia blew out a little bubble of laughter.

"Stand up to them, dear," she said.

"Yes, it's all very well to talk; but how am I to stand up to them when my knees tremble? I wouldn't have it known, but that's the fact. Well, we are going to have a grand party next week."

Mrs. Wardour relaxed herself in the wicker chair.

"It's been a job and a half," she said, "and I wish your father was alive to see what a good job and a half I've made of it. He always had a hankering for high life himself, but he was too busy to catch hold of it. 'When I give the word, Lucy,' he's often said to me, 'we'll start in and show them all how to do it.' Often he's said that to me. And I always had a taste for it, too; and sure enough it came natural to me from the first. We're pretty well sitting down and knowing everybody now."

Hard work it certainly had been; for the last two months Mrs. Wardour had worked as hard at securing the goal she had so steadfastly set before her as her husband had ever done in providing the paraphernalia for the enterprise; but now she might fairly claim that she was beginning to sit and know everybody. She had brought to her task an unremitting industry, and—when the tide was once flowing in her favour, so that it was possible to consider not so much whom she would ask but whom she would leave out—a steely ruthlessness. That ruthlessness, indeed, had been a weapon throughout the campaign; if a desirable guest was unable to come on Monday, Tuesday, or Wednesday, Mrs. Wardour had adamantinely proceeded with Thursday, Friday, and Saturday; she had even taken her place at the telephone and demanded in her flat, firm voice that her quarry should consult his engagement-book and let her know which was the first disengaged night. Ruthless, also, she had now become, as in the case of Mrs. Trentham, when the question was one of exclusion, and the party for the Russian ballet had been selected on the sternest principles. Thinking over that now, her mind reverted to Silvia's final invitation.

"And who is your Mr. Mainwaring?" she asked.

Silvia again had to stifle some embarrassment that, since it did not exist on the surface at all, must have had some more secret origin.

"Oh, I've met him a score of times," she said. "He's one of the people who is always there. He sat between us once at the opera, I think I remember. One evening when Lord Poole made love to you, dear. But, somehow, he's never been to your house yet."

"That's more than most can say," remarked Mrs. Wardour, so nearly smacking her lips that an impartial umpire might have said that "it counted." This set Silvia laughing.

"And what have I said now?" asked Mrs. Wardour.

It was not so much what her mother was saying as what she was being that so continually kept Silvia in a state of simmering hilarity. Contemplate it as she might, she had never been able to comprehend the impulse, or rather the steady, unwavering devotion, that had kept Mrs. Wardour at such high pressure all these weeks. She did not enjoy the process of these eternal entertainments; the gaiety of others did not make her gay; music made no appeal to her; she was long past the age of dancing (though so many of her contemporaries were not), and yet she would sit benignly content through the short hours of the summer night, with her great tiara on her head, and feeling the heat acutely, for the mere pleasure of being there. That she *was* there was now undeniable, and, happily, having got there, she suffered no disillusionment. The mere *chasse*, the acquisition, was certainly not the mainspring of her activities. She had engaged in the *chasse* not for the sake of getting but of having....

The second terror of her busy life entered.

"Miss Heaton wants to know if you are at home, miss?" said the formidable Summerton.

It was a relief to Silvia's mother that she had not got to "stand up" to Summerton, and, indeed, there was no crisis at all, for close behind him was Nellie.

"My dear, I was so afraid you might say that you weren't at home," she said, "that I thought it only my duty to save you telling lies. Am I interrupting? How are you, Mrs. Wardour? Send me away if I am intruding, or say that you have just gone out if you don't want me to stop, and I will promise to believe you."

Silvia had risen with a flush of pleasure on her face at the entrance of her friend. From all the new acquaintances of London, Nellie had made a shining emergence; through all the mists and bewilderments of the new life she shone with a steady beam, like the luminous finger from a lighthouse, clear and steadfast above the complicated currents.

"But this is lovely," said Silvia. "Sit down. Tea? Something? Anything?"

She stood looking at her with frank, surrendered gaze; a little dazzled, as she always was, with such easy unconscious splendour. She regarded Nellie, if she could have put her appreciation into words, as she might have regarded some golden casket, set with gems, which seemed to have been laid in her hands. She had, as yet, no idea what was inside it; she had not attempted to raise the lid. It was enough at present to be allowed to hold it in shy, adoring fingers.

"No, nothing," said Nellie; "not even to sit down. I came, in fact, to make you stand up."

"I'm doing that," said Silvia.

"That's not enough.... My dear, what a delicious frock! But my horrible Philip has been obliged to go out of town, and I'm at a loose end till dinner, and thought it would be wonderfully pleasant to sit on the grass somewhere. Isn't that original? At the moment when that rural idea occurred to me, I passed your gilded portals and thought it would be even more wonderful if you came and sat there too. I don't mean ordinary, dirty grass, but clean grass. Richmond Park, or something. Top of a bus, of course. Old hats."

There could have been no more attractive notion to Silvia. She felt that it was just that she had long been wanting; namely, to be with Nellie on the grass in an old hat. She could still ecstatically be dazzled, could follow the beam of the lighthouse with steady rapture; but a fresh aspect of her, away from ball-rooms and crowds, just that old-hat aspect, she felt at once to be what most she desired. She might, it is true, be just as dazzling thus, she might, indeed, be more dazzling when other lesser brightnesses were withdrawn from her vicinity; but however she turned out, she could not fail to show a new enchantment.

"Of course I'll come," she said. "Let me go and get an old hat. You don't want me, mother, do you?"

"No, dear. But if you'll ring the bell, I'll order the car for you. Far more comfortable and far quicker than the top of a bus."

Nellie had been taking in the appurtenances of this room, to which she had not previously penetrated, with those quick, bird-like glances which were away again, scarcely alighting, before you knew they had perched at all. Mrs. Wardour's hospitable suggestion seemed to contrast with her own project in just the manner in which those creaking cretonne chairs contrasted with the brocade on the walls and the Aubusson on the floor.

"Ah, how kind," she said; "but, dear Mrs. Wardour, the point of our expedition is not to be comfortable and quick, but uncomfortable and slow. I yearn for that, and for being rustic and common. Otherwise, I should ask you to lend me one of those glorious chairs and let me sit and look at Buckingham Palace."

"Yes, you can see it out of the window," said Mrs. Wardour. "But the top of a bus—let me see, Miss Heaton, isn't it—is the top of a bus quite the thing for girls like Silvia and you?"

"But absolutely," said Nellie. "It wouldn't be a bit the thing to drive in your lovely Rolls-Royce. And we shall have tea somewhere quite unspeakable, with dirty napkins."

Mrs. Wardour shook her head.

"Now a nice tea-basket and the car," she insinuated. "Ready in ten minutes, I beg you, Miss Heaton."

Why the notion of Richmond Park and a bus and a tea-shop had blown in upon Nellie she had no clear idea; but as she and Silvia swayed and bounced westwards, it easily yielded an unconscious analysis. Her morning had been taken up with dress and trousseau for the imminent wedding, her mother had joined her at the dressmaker's flushed with triumph over some grabbing business called settlements, and over the afternoon there had hung, rather sultrily, the prospect of long hours with Philip, who was coming to lunch. Her mother, as usual, had a bridge party of harpies, and no doubt she and Philip, just as she and Peter had done not many weeks ago, would sit in the window and pass for being absorbed in each other. It was owing, no doubt, to the hymeneal morning, and the prospect of a similar afternoon, that, on the outpouring through the telephone of Philip's calm, but sincere, regrets that business claimed him in the country, reaction had opened its sluice-gates and overwhelmed her with the desire for hours physically and morally remote from rich fabrics and opulent comfort, and from the ambient atmosphere of things connected with just one theme. She was perfectly well satisfied with the general prospect, matrimonially considered; but she wanted just now, as celibacy was so soon to vanish, a foreground of it and simplicity and freedom to her picture. Originally, when the telephone had first told her of Philip's defection, she had scarcely made the needful pause of ringing off before getting into communication with Peter to know whether he could slip the official collar for an afternoon. Certainly that was "ringing off" Philip with some completeness, and with whom better than with the other could she take a last excursion into the country that would so soon be severed from her by the sea, placid she hoped, of matrimony? But the official collar could not, so Peter's very distinct voice told, be shifted. He, Peter's voice, at any rate, said he was sorry; but he added no superlatives of regret, and before she had removed her ear she heard the click of the replaced instrument at the other end. He rang off, so it seemed to her, with a certain finality, not lingering to gossip. That had been rather characteristic of him lately; though she had constantly met him, he had always appeared in that light, impenetrable armour of his aloofness, never raising his visor, nor showing a joint in his harness where she could get at him. Ever since the interview on the window-seat six weeks ago he had been withdrawn like that.

Failing to get Peter, her next inclination had been to sip her celibacy alone, for though Peter, better than anybody, symbolized the things that were passing away (the wet woods and the roving and the independence), she would, in his absence, get nearest to them alone. So she had already started on her suburban pilgrimage, strolling down the glare and wilderness of Piccadilly to get on to a Richmond bus at the corner of Hyde Park, when, finding herself dazzled by the sun on the newly-gilded gates of Wardour House, the notion of Silvia's companionship suggested itself, and she paused weighing its advantages. Silvia would certainly give her an eager, appreciative comradeship (so much was instantly clear), and on the heels of that a tangle of other interesting little curiosities, with tentacles protruding, plumped themselves into the same scale. She did not trouble to unravel them now; they would straighten themselves out as the afternoon went on.

Richmond Park proved very empty of loiterers; occasionally a motor-bicycle, with a wake of dust hanging in the air behind it, streaked down the yellow road; but, by the Pen Ponds, no more than the distant throb of such passenger was audible. Summer was in full leaf among the oaks and beeches, retaining still the varnished freshness of spring, and populous in the shade of the leafy trees were herds of fallow-deer, which lay sleepy and yet alert, with twitching ears and whisking tail against the incorrigible menace of flies, until an abatement of the heat restored appetite for the young tussocky grass. The hawthorn was nearly over; smouldering coronets of faded flame, or grey ash of dazzling blossom represented the glories of May; but round the ponds the humps of the rhododendron banks were still on fire.

Such talk as had flourished between the two girls had not yet penetrated beyond the barrier where triviality ceases, and past dances, with keen criticism on their merits, and dances to come, and the adequacy of various partners (among whom Peter's name flitted by like blowing thistledown) had been flashed on and off the public plate. There had been a little longer exposure for the projected party at which the Russian ballet were to supply the entertainment, and Nellie had been informed, with horrified eagerness on the part of Silvia, that, of course, she had been bidden: the invitation had only been inscribed that afternoon. Her acceptance of it was equally "of course," and with the luck that attended friends, the date of it was a clear two days before her marriage. Trivial though it had all been, she felt that the Hamadryad (herself) had been doing spade-work in the shade. The ground was cleared and levelled; every topic that she might now wish to work up into a more elaborate tapestry had been put in on tentative threads, much as characters in a decently-written drama, flit, at any rate, across the stage in the first act. The two, delightfully grouped, hatless, and secure from interruption, had come to anchor in the circular shade of an old thorn-bush not far from the edge of reeds that fringed the pond. The red petals of the spent blossom dropped down from time to time; the hum and murmur of June woods was a carpet on which more intimate conversation could lightly spread itself.

Nellie drew up and clasped her knees.

"Fancy my impertinence in dragging you out to Richmond Park when I know that you had a hundred things that you wanted to do," she said. "Tell me, what would you have done if I hadn't appeared like some bird of prey and clawed you? Now don't say that you would have had tea with your mother and gone for a drive in the Park. If you do, I simply shan't believe you."

Yes, she was more dazzling, so Silvia found, when there was no one to contrast her with. The sheer, silly, conventional tittle-tattle took a sparkling quality quite alien to it when it came from her mouth. Her personality was like coloured lights playing on a fountain and turning the drops to gems.

"I must be silent, then," she said.

"Oh, don't be silent! When people are silent it means they are only being polite. If they were less polite they would say that they were excruciatingly bored. Then, after a suitable silence, they say, 'How charming it is here!' Don't say 'how charming it is here.' That will be the last straw, Silvia. Dear me, I said 'Silvia' by accident. It—what they call—slipped out."

"Oh, do say it on purpose, then," said Silvia.

"Very well; me too, you understand. What a funny business is Christian names! The Christian name is never really ripe till it drops. I wonder if you know what an unutterable boon you and your mother have been to that smoky place over there. And to crown it all, you are giving the most delightful party with the most gorgeous punctuality, as far as I am concerned. Do say you settled it for that night because you knew I couldn't come on any subsequent night."

Silvia gave a little moan like a dove in a tree.

"I can't say that," she said.

Nellie sighed, wholly appreciatively.

"That's so refreshing of you," she said. "You're one of the real people, I expect; the people who mean what they say. I usually mean what I don't say."

Silvia turned round and lay facing her friend.

"Don't say it, then, Nellie," she said. "I mean—do say the things you mean. How complicated it sounds, and how simple it is. Shall we stop talking about me, do you think? I've got another subject."

"I know it," said Nellie. "What about Peter? I adore Peter, by the way; don't say anything horrid."

A certain sense of shock came to Silvia. Peter had not, ever so remotely, been the subject to which she alluded. But when Nellie suggested him, he was flashed on the screen with disconcerting vividness.

"But I didn't mean him at all," she said. "I wasn't thinking about— about Mr. Mainwaring."

"He wouldn't like that," said Nellie.

Silvia sat up. She had a perfectly clear conscience to endorse an immediate repudiation. What caused that suspicious, that questionable little leap of blood to her cheeks, was, indeed, not that she had been thinking of Peter, but that Nellie supposed she had.

"Oh, but this is quite silly!" she exclaimed. "Indeed, he wasn't in my mind at all. Why should he be? I scarcely know him."

Nellie knew that she had ceased for that moment to dazzle Silvia, to whom the suggestion that Peter had been in her mind was clearly unwelcome and unexpected. It might be true or it might not (so ran Nellie's swift argument) that Silvia was not thinking of Peter at all; but that she should be ruffled—ever so delightfully—at the notion that she had been, constituted a symptom, did it not?... But it was enough to note that, and pass on at once to the easy task of dazzling Silvia again.

"You are too delicious," she said. "Yes, I'm going to stick to my subject for a minute longer, which is you, since yours isn't Peter. You've got the most lovely lack of self-consciousness, do you know? Of course you don't, or you wouldn't have it. But when I talk to other girls, we each think about ourselves. It's like talking to a boy—not Peter, mind—to talk to you."

Silvia made some gesture of deprecation.

"No, I will go on," said Nellie. "Look at the glass I hold up to you, please. It isn't only the lovely parties that you and your mother have given us that have polished up the rusty old season: it's your quality—what shall I call it—wind and sun, sexlessness. You just move along like a spring day, with all your banners streaming, in the most entrancing glee. You're absolutely *insouciante*, if you understand French."

Silvia had lost sight of Peter by now; he was round the corner, and how near that corner was, was immaterial. She wanted to put herself round the corner, too, and seized on this as a possible diversion.

"Oh, yes, I do," she said. "I only came back this spring from three years in France."

"There you are again! There's another of your completenesses. You're spread evenly, richly, like butter (when we're all eating margarine) over the whole slice of life. I wish I could bite you! I believe that with a little trouble I could, and, if so, I should hate you, not for what you've got but for what I haven't."

At this moment Nellie became aware that her day in the wet woods had changed the character with which, prospectively, she had endowed it. She had meant, first with Peter as her companion, and next by herself, to enjoy the last hours of her celibacy. With Silvia, on the other hand, she was now not enjoying her own, but envying her companion's. What she envied her most for was her decorated simplicity. Silvia wore her decorations externally; she didn't attempt to swallow them and, by digestion, make them build up a complicated identity. Worst of all—from the envious point of view—she didn't know how splendidly embellished she was.... It was as if you said to a gallant soldier, "Have you got the V.C.?" sarcastically almost, and then he looked down—not up—at his decorations, and found that the little piece of riband was there.

Silvia moved a shade away from her companion. The break in the thorn tree, with the consequent oval of hot sunlight, quite accounted for that.

"But what haven't you got?" she asked. "You live, as naturally as drawing breath, the life that's so new to me, and so puzzling and so delightful; and below and beyond all that, you're on the point of being married. He chose you, out of all the world, and you found all the time that you had chosen him. What is there left for you, just you now and here, to want? You're adorable— —"

Silvia wrestled and threw the bugbear of shyness which so often sat on her shoulders and strangled her neck. There it writhed on the grass, not in the least dead, but, for the moment, knocked out.

"Oh, sometimes I wish I was a boy," she said. "I'm more in that key than in ours. Sometimes I think— —"

Nellie projected herself into that gap of sunlight from which, possibly, Silvia shrank. She had no definite scheme of exploration for the moment, but it seemed to her that something in the tangle of motives with which she had invited Silvia to share her afternoon was faintly stirring as if with unravelment. Those loops and knots might get more inextricably muddled, it is true; but, conceivably, the whole thing might "come out" like a conjuring trick.

"Ah, what is it that you think?" she asked. "Don't stop so tantalizingly. As if thinking wasn't everything! Whatever one *does* is only a clumsy translation of what one has thought. Think aloud!"

Nellie looked more than ever at that moment like some exquisite wild presence of the woodlands, Dryad or Bacchante, delicate and subtle in face and limb and brain, and merely proto-plasmic in soul, a creature made for the bedazzlement and the undoing of man. Certainly she had woven her spells over Silvia again; the momentary check in the incantation, when she had attributed "Peter-thought" to her, had passed as swiftly as the shadow of one of those light clouds which drifted over the grass.

But at that moment, when she so bewilderingly shone out again, there formed itself in Silvia's mind, as she tried to follow this injunction to think aloud, not the image of her at all, but of Peter. For if Nellie was divinely akin to the blossoming thickets and the shadows that were beginning to lengthen over the grass, making cool islands on which the deer were grazing now, he, too, would be no less harmoniously bestowed by this reflecting lake-side. It was not that either of them suggested rurality; no one, indeed, was more emphatically of the street and the ballroom and the complication of the city than they. But by some secret pedigree of soul they were of the house and lineage of the things that glowed and enjoyed and were lovely, and gave as little thought to yesterday as they took for to-morrow. All this, not catalogued in detail, but fused into a single luminous impression, passed through Silvia's consciousness like the wink of summer lightning....

"As if it wasn't difficult enough to think at all," she said, "and as for thinking aloud, thinking articulately—if I'm to sum it up, ever so clumsily, it's merely that I adore, with all the incense I've got, the thought of your happiness. It does matter so much to me, and ... and isn't it noble fun to find someone who matters? Very few people really matter; I suppose little, silly, finite hearts like ours can't take in many. But those who do matter must come right in, if they don't mind. They mustn't risk themselves by hanging about on the doorstep; they might catch cold. Aren't I talking nonsense? It's your fault for taking me into the country, for assuredly it has gone to my head. Where there's a stifle of roofs and a choke of streets nobody matters and everyone is quite delightful. What a stupid word that is, and how expressive of a stupid thing."

Silvia very deliberately shot off into the backwater of nonsense, so to speak, out of the main stream, for the sun was on the water, in this dazzle of Nellie's personality, and she could not see towards what weir the hurrying river might be taking her. Very likely there was no weir; the glistening tide, running swift, would very likely spread out into some broad expanse of Peace-pools; but it was the brightness that prevented scrutiny.

By some flash of woodland instinct, by some uncanny perception, Nellie divined the cause of this retirement into the backwater of triviality. With a ruthlessness that rivalled Mrs. Wardour's pursuit of desirable guests, she caught the rope of Silvia's boat, so to speak, before she could tie it to the security of some overhanging branch, and shot it out into the main stream again.

"Yes, my dear," she said, "you talk nonsense delightfully. Ah, I didn't mean stupidly; I didn't mean in the sense you had just labelled it with. I meant delightfully, charmingly. But just for a change after that delightful (now I mean stupid) London, we're talking sense. You interested me indescribably just now. You said you were more in a boy's key than a girl's. What did you mean exactly?"

Silvia watched the receding shore to which she had hoped to tie up....
After all, what did it matter if there was a weir, not a Peace-pool down there
in that dazzle of benignant sunshine? But there was another difficulty in the
way of expression.

"I can't really explain," she said. "There are things so simple that no
explanation is possible. If I said, 'It is a hot day,' and you told me to explain,
I couldn't. I could only say, 'If you don't feel it, if you don't know what that
means, I can't help you.' It's the same with all elemental things."

Nellie regarded her with eyes that were framed in some steely sort of
interest; eyes that were eager to know not from the kindly tenderness of
friends but from some surgical curiosity.

"I think I know what you mean by a 'boy's key,'" she said. "Let me see
if I can explain you to yourself, Silvia, since you won't—ah, can't—explain
yourself to me. If you were in love, for instance, you would passionately
want to give love, to pour yourself out, instead of, like most girls, provoking
love and permitting it and ever so eagerly receiving it. You wouldn't want
a man's homage so much as you would want to be allowed to love him.
You would want, and how queer and delicious of you—you lovely upside-
down, inside-out creature."

This abrupt termination of the presentment of Silvia in love, as
imagined by her friend, was due to something quite unexpected. There
came on Silvia's face, as her own privacy was thus invaded, a dumb, but
none the less violent signal of protest. She shrank and withdrew herself, as
if a burglarious bullseye had been shot through the window of her room,
where she lay lost in cool, soft maidenliness. The contact was even more
direct than that; it was as if some pitiless incision had been made in her
very flesh. But with this pause in the application of the knife, this shuttering
of the bullseye—for any further beam would have disclosed the deliberate
attempt to rifle the jewel-chest—there came the complete withdrawal of her
protesting signal.... It had been the bullseye of a friend that looked in, the
scissors of a dear amateur manicurist....

She was sitting there hatless in the shade, and with her hand she pushed
her hair back.

"Oh, you're a witch, Nellie," she said. "Two hundred years ago you
would have been burned, and I should have helped to pile the faggots. I
expect that you're magically right. I can't tell, you know, because I assure
you, literally and soberly, that I never have been in love. Literally never.

Soberly never. But, somehow, what you suggested (how did you divine it, you witch?) touched something, made something vibrate and sing. I didn't know anything about it; I didn't know it was there. Then you put your finger on it, and I knew ... I knew I *had* it."

"And then you just hated me for a moment," said Nellie.

Silvia did not quite accept this.

"You made me wince," she said in correction. "And, oh, yes, I'll confess: just for a moment you seemed to me hostile and hurting. You aren't; you're heavenly and healing. You taught me, bless you. But I think you're a witch all the same. It wasn't telepathy; you told me something about myself that I didn't know, and couldn't have known, and can't know now, for that matter. Oh, you lucky creature. You've fallen in love. You know it all. Did you do it in the manner you attribute to me? Did you savagely give, not wanting anything but to give, give.... How did you put it just now? To be allowed to love, to pour yourself out, to pay homage instead of exacting it? The boy's key! My dear it seems ages and ages since that phrase came up. I've had a whole drama since then, you know."

Nellie, in point of fact, had had her drama, too. But it was as yet undetermined. She had not got at the root facts for which she was burrowing. Silvia's volley of questions, anyhow, were easy of response. They were, barring, a certain inversion, very Victorian questions, dating from the days when men blindly adored and women swooned at the declaration of the passion which they had done their level best to excite. But that inversion made to her, and for particular reasons, a wildly interesting speculation. Silvia, when she loved (so much was certain), would love in the "boy's key," the eager, evocative key. She acknowledged herself, in contemplation of the event, as blindly adoring, as being "allowed" to love. Whether that was entirely a prognostication, or whether it was already partially, potentially fulfilled was another question, and the application of that concerned Nellie, and her own purposes, alone. Soon, deftly now, with the lesson of Silvia's revolt against surprises, she would get a further result from her dissection. At present there was the impatient, intimate volley of questions to answer.

"Oh, my dear, I understand so well the 'boy's key,'" she said. "A triumphal, victorious surrender, with all the bells ringing—isn't that it? A march out with white flags insolently flying. I should love to be like that, if I *was* like that. But that isn't my key. I just surrendered, rather terrified, you know. But I couldn't be terrified of Philip for long: he's such a dear."

This could not be considered more than an approximate account, a vague sketch, very faintly resembling the scene it portrayed—a quiet, feminine disclosure. But Nellie did not want to discuss that; she wanted to get back to her tangled skeins again.

"I should like to see you in love, Silvia," she said. "Promise to tell me when it happens. At least, you needn't; it will be wonderfully obvious, you in your 'boy's key.' Whom can we find for you who will just fall in with that, and be the complement of it, making, it complete and round and perfect? Hasn't ever so little a bit of him, just the top of his head, come over the horizon yet?"

Silvia did not withdraw or raise any signal of protest this time. She made no signal at all; none, at any rate, that could be perceived by the girl who sat watching her very narrowly. And once more Nellie fumbled, so to speak, at the shutter of her bullseye, which would flash on the light.

She looked at the watch on her wrist.

"My dear, how late it is!" she said. "We must go at once. I promised to go to Mr. Mainwaring's studio. Peter's father, you know. Peter will be vexed if I don't come."

Then came the signal. Silvia jumped up with wholly unnecessary alacrity. But more nimbly yet did the high colour mount to her face.

CHAPTER VI

One evening, a week or so before the date fixed for the wedding, Philip Beaumont and Nellie had dined and gone together to the first night of some new play. It was saliently characteristic of him—a peak, so to say, prominently uprising from the smooth level of his cultivated plains—that when arrangements for such diversions and businesses were in his hands they always went without a hitch. Nellie had expressed a desire to see this play, without giving long notice to him of her wish, and it followed, as a matter of course, that he managed to get gangway seats in the stalls at the most advantageous distance from the stage.

Things happened like that with him: his own unruffled smoothness, which seemed immune from any of the attacks of asperities of one kind or another, to which human nature is subject, seemed to create a similar well-ordered decorum in his activities. Tonight, for instance, the dinner which preceded the theatre was punctual and swiftly served, so that neither hurry nor undue lingering followed it: his motor slid up to the kerb-stone precisely as they quitted the restaurant, and it might be taken for granted that at the conclusion of the piece it would be bubbling up opposite the portals of the theatre precisely as they emerged. Once in their seats there had been but a few minutes to wait before the lights were lowered for the first act; these afforded a convenient time to grasp the real and the histrionic names of the actors and see where the acts were laid.

In those few minutes Nellie's glance had swept over stalls and boxes, noting the position of various friends. Silvia was in a box with her mother, and loud screams of laughter from another box opposite, perhaps temporarily turned into a parrot-house, made it almost certain that Mrs. Trentham was having her usual splendid time surrounded by a bevy of young men. A glance verified that, and the same glance showed her that Peter, who, she knew, was to be present, was not among them. Then someone entered the box where Silvia and her mother sat, and she knew where Peter was. Immediately a loud flamboyant voice just behind her informed her that Peter's entry had been noticed by someone else.

"Glance, *Maria mia*," it said, "at that box next the stage on the right, where is the lady with the wealth of Golconda (I allude to diamonds) on her head. You and I have no reason to be ashamed of that tall handsome boy. Ah, behold just in front of us the adorable Miss Heaton, Miss Heaton, the box by the stage, the lady in diamonds: her name. A word, a whisper ...!"

The quenching of lights gave suitable cover for the emotions evoked by this particular brand of theatrical slosh. There were whimsicalities, there was slyness, there was maidenliness and womanliness, there was the sense of looking through a keyhole; but all these qualities were soaked and dyed with slosh. Mr. Mainwaring, to Nellie's sense, seemed to make himself spokesman for the house: he thrilled to every slyness, however subtle, and he advertised, on behalf of the rest of the audience, his appreciation. His resonant laugh proclaimed the gorgeousness of the less abstruse humours, as when the heroine, being asked to give her lover a kiss, wore a face of horror and said, "Eh, on the Sawbath!" His giggling and his slapping of his great big thigh gave the cue for more recondite deliciousnesses; he exclaimed *"Bravá! Bravá!"* at the end of a long speech; he blew his nose loudly at the blare of the Highland Vox Humana, and bestowed one splendid sob on his handkerchief when the author really let himself go and opened all the sluices of sentimentality. Mr. Mainwaring had to recover with gulps and hiccups from that, but he pulled himself together like a man, and ran his fingers through his hair to make it stand out from his interesting head.

Though these convulsions were resonant only just behind her, Nellie gave them no more attention than she would to raindrops on the window: and the doings of the stage occupied her as little, and as little the presence next her of the perfect organizer.

... A certain antagonism had grown up, had seeded itself and was rapidly propagating. A vigorous seedling was the fact of Peter's being where he was. It was no business of hers, so she told herself, with whom Peter went to the play, and she tried to divert her mind by ironical comment. Peter, poor and parasitic, would always dance a graceful attendance on anyone who would give him dinner and a seat in the box. Peter was like that, and for his grace and politeness there was due reward. He had a trick of sympathetic listening, of intelligent interrogation that made his companion feel herself interesting. You could put him next the most crashing bore, and he would wreathe himself in smiles until the crashing bore felt herself to be the wittiest of sirens. And then suddenly the stupidity of her comments and their irrelevance failed to divert Nellie altogether.

There was the antagonism, hugely grown by now. Peter, so she made out, was as conscious of it as she, and had certainly during the last week or two contributed to its growth. He had answered Nellie's formalities with similar politeness: he had watered where she had sown, and she wondered whether he contemplated with the dismay of which she was conscious, the lively crop of their combined husbandry.

It was the fashion, as she had once said to Silvia, to be devoted to Peter, and Silvia seemed to have "picked up" the fashion with the same ease as she had exhibited all along her social pilgrimage. She welcomed all that came up with a frolic, boy-like enjoyment, but there was, as Nellie perfectly well knew, a real Silvia, a serious Silvia, somebody with a heart and the shy treasures of it, a personality curiously ungirl-like, something eager and hungry and wholesome. She knew in advance what her way of love would be, and her feet, firm and unstumbling—Silvia would never stumble—were on the high road. Of all the saunterers that she might meet there, would she not, by the mere instinct of divination, choose the complement to her own unusual personality? The complement certainly was someone feminine but not effeminate, indeterminate in desire, somebody, in fact, extraordinarily like Nellie herself. In the way of a girl, Silvia had already quite succumbed to a charm that Nellie had not troubled to exercise: she had recognized and surrendered to it with that victorious white-flag abandonment. With what ringing of bells would she not march out to the mildest call for capitulation when a boy of that type blew his lazy horn?

Long before the act was over Nellie had known that she would present herself in the interval at Mrs. Wardour's box. She would, in anticipation, have much to say to Silvia: there would be plans for the next day, or regrets over the dreadful occupations that made plans impossible. There would be some flat steady compliment about diamonds and parties for Mrs. Wardour, and—there would be nothing at all for Peter. She wanted, as far as she was aware, just to take him in in the new situation which was surely forming, as clouds form on a chilly windless day. She wanted to get used to it, she wanted—or did she not want?—to put the weed-killer of familiarity on the crop of antagonism which was certainly prospering in a manner wholly unlocked for. And then, much quieted and reassured, she would return to Philip, and feel for his hand when the lights went down again. He had a good hand, cool and secure and efficient: there was the sense of safety about it, of correctness: it was all that a hand should be. Then, still secure, and vastly more content than she was now, he would take her back to her mother's flat, and perhaps drop in for a half-hour. She would say, quite correctly, "Come upstairs and talk to mother and me for a few minutes." She would work the lift herself, and he would be surprised at her mastery of it. Then, when they were vomited forth at the fifth floor, she would remember that her mother had gone to a bridge-party and would certainly not be home before twelve. That would give them their half-hour alone.

Nellie was not prepared for the companionship in her expedition with which Mr. Mainwaring decorated her. Standing in the middle of the gangway, he made her a sonorous and embellished little speech when, rather rashly, she revealed her destination at the end of this interminable first act.

"Peter's friends, my Peter's friends, are mine," he magnificently observed, "and I feel it my duty to pay my respects to them. Oblige me, Miss Heaton, by accepting my escort to the box that glitters with the combined distinction of diamonds and Peter's presence. My wife—will you not, *Maria mia*?—will prefer to remain precisely where she is. Chocolates, my beloved? A cup of coffee? I will leave my purse with you. Refresh yourself!"

Mrs. Mainwaring declined refreshment, except in so far as it was ministered to by some advertisements of Brighton hotels which appeared on the back of the programme. There was one there which she had not previously heard of and which seemed very reasonable.

Her husband offered the sleeve of a velveteen-clad arm to Nellie, and they proceeded upstairs with pomp and the slight odour of turpentine, which was all that was left of a dab of paint which had dropped from his brush on to the skirt of his coat as a profound inspiration seized him after he had dressed for dinner. Philip gave a slightly iced negative to Nellie's inquiry whether he was to join this pilgrimage.

Mr. Mainwaring did all the usual things. He clapped his hand on Peter's shoulder when the introductions had been made, and hoped, with a stately bow, that his boy had been behaving himself. He waved his hand when Mrs. Wardour pronounced the first act "very interesting," and recognized a fellow artist. Before ten minutes were over Mrs. Wardour was committed to look in next afternoon and see "his few poor efforts." Then he became more confidential and whispery.

"A marvellous, an incomparable type!" he said, looking at Silvia, and back again at her mother. "Who has had the felicity, the difficult felicity, of painting that glorious head? No one? I am astonished. I would be shocked if I were capable of so *bourgeois* an emotion. H'm!"

Beyond a visit to the private view of the Royal Academy, Mrs. Wardour had not penetrated into pictorial circles, and faintly, through the impression, volubly audible, of Silvia and Nellie talking together, Peter heard his father leading up to the series of war-cartoons suitable for mural decoration. As regards that, he went walking in the wet woods, as aloof from his father as from any other magnificent self-advertiser. He had heard Mrs. Wardour's promise to go to the studio next day and to bring Silvia, and he thought that very probably the relations of Great Britain with foreign countries might struggle through a free hour without his co-operation. Meantime Nellie seemed to be talking secrets to Silvia, and he sat, nursing his knee, a little aloof from either group. Presently Nellie would go back to her seat in the stalls, and his father would do the same, and then he would hitch his chair a little forward again....

People began to troop back into the stalls; obviously a bell had rung announcing the imminence of the second act. Nellie recognized that, and got up. As yet she had barely spoken to him.

"I must get back to my Philip," she said very properly. "Good night, darling Silvia."

Peter had gone to open the door for them.

"Come to the flat, Peter," she said, without turning her head, as she passed him. "I shall go straight home."

The words were just dropped from her, as if by accident or inadvertence, but the moment she had spoken them she knew that this had been in the main the object of her visit to the box: it was this which she had primarily wanted. The merest hint of an affirmative nod on Peter's part was sufficient answer.

The play came to its happy concluding treacliness, and they went out. Philip and Nellie, of course, were among the first into the vestibule, where he instantly caught his footman's eye. The Wardour group must have left their box slightly before the end, for Peter was seeing them into their motor, thanking Mrs. Wardour for "such an awfully nice evening" and excusing himself from being given a lift, as after a day in the office he liked walking home—yes, all the way to South Kensington. How nice it would be to see Mrs. Wardour at his father's house next day.... He lingered a moment on the pavement, and as Nellie passed him on her way to the motor, just nodded again, without seeming to see her.

Philip's first concern, as they slid off into the traffic, was that there should be air, but no draught for Nellie. Perhaps if he put her window quite up and his half down.... Was that comfortable? And a match for her cigarette? After which he slipped her hand into his, and after a moment's delay she returned the pressure.

In a flash of general, comprehensive consciousness Nellie was aware how comfortable and well-ordered the whole evening had been, and realized that all days, evenings and mornings and afternoons alike, would to the end of life, owing to the very ample "settlements" which she understood to have been made, be padded and cushioned like this. She was conscious at the same moment that her appreciation of that lacked acuteness; she would just as soon, to take an example, be walking with Peter along the pavements, where nobody cared if she felt a draught or not, as be having it all her own way in unjostled progress.... The flash of this perception was instantaneous, measured only by that moment's delay in response to Philip's hand, for he instantly began to tick again, as she put it to herself, a pleasant tick, a good, reliable, firm tick.

"A charming play, was it not, dear?" said he. "And that delicious humour of his."

Well, if Nellie was going to be comfortable all her life, it was only fair that she should contribute, should put her penny into the placid bag.

"Delicious," she said. "I am sure it will have a great success. And how interesting to be there on the first night."

She broke off suddenly, and clasped Philip's arm.

"Ah—we nearly ran over that man," she cried.

Philip remained quite calm. He would obviously be an admirable companion in a shipwreck or a thunderstorm or a railway accident. This was, delightfully, a new point about him, and Nellie found, on the discovery of it, that she must have been collecting his good points, for with the collector's zeal she hastened to net it and add it to her specimens.

He pressed the hand that she had laid on his arm, and looked out of the window which he had opened on his side of the motor.

"My dear, there is nothing to be alarmed about," he said. "The man is quite safe, and has not forgotten his usual vocabulary. You need never be afraid with Logan; he is the most careful of drivers, and has an extraordinary command of the brakes."

Nellie collected this new genus *Philip*; sub-species *Logan*. It added a little bit to the completeness.

"Logan is quite trustworthy," he went on; "you need never have a moment's qualm when he is on the box. We were discussing the play. I should like to see it again. Does not that strike you as the true criterion as to whether you have essentially enjoyed a play? If there is only mere glitter, one does not want to repeat the experience. But there was gold, I thought, this evening."

He was silent a moment, patting her hand, and Nellie divined his mind with a rather terrible distinctness. She had been very considerably agitated for that moment, and he assumed (how wisely and how consciously) a complete oblivion of that. The best method of reassuring her after the little testimonial to Logan was to be unaware of any fluttering incident. A manly calm was the efficient medicine for feminine alarm. He went on talking about the play as if nothing agitating had occurred....

Swiftly as the car slid down Piccadilly Nellie's brain was just a little in advance of it, and before it slowed up at the house of flats she was mentally on the doorstep. Earlier in the evening she had contemplated Philip's admiring ascent with her in the lift, her own surprised recollection, on their emergence, that her mother would not yet be in. But now that picture had been whisked off the screen altogether; there would be no ascent with Philip, no sudden remembrance of her mother's absence. A subsequent engagement, not so conventional, had been proposed by her and assented to with a nod so imperceptible that it had been repeated.

Philip had so often spent a final half-hour like this, that, as the motor stopped, he almost assumed it.

"And may I come up for a few minutes?" he asked.

She laid her hand on his shoulder as if to press him back on to his seat.

"Don't find it horrid of me, dear," she said, "if I say 'no.' I am a little tired, do you think? But what a lovely evening we have had. You come and fetch me in the morning, don't you? Good night, my dear."

The most ardent of lovers could hardly have insisted, after this little collection of sentences, each unmistakably clinking with some sort of final "ring," and it was out of the question for Philip to repeat a request which, in any case, had habit rather than craving to back it. He would certainly have liked to sit with Nellie and her mother—so he supposed—for a quarter of an hour, discuss the play a little more, quietly sun himself, contentedly basking in Nellie's presence, and consider himself a very fortunate fellow; but if she was a little tired, it would have been unthinkably intrusive to beg her to take a part and let him take a part in a *séance* that she had no wish for. But she lingered a moment yet in order to give no impression of being in any hurry; then, forbidding him to get out of the motor, she disappeared, with a final gesture as of but a short separation, into the house.

Her mother, as Nellie knew would be the case, had not yet returned from her card-party, nor would she be likely to do so for a full hour yet, and her absence, in relation to the visitor she now expected, took for itself a totally different aspect. She had limitless opportunities and facilities for a *tête-à-tête* with Philip, and her mother's absence, if it had been he who had come admiringly up with her as she managed the lift, would in no way have been a special, even a desirable, condition. She and Philip were so often alone together, and, before many days were passed, would be so exclusively alone together, that the gain of another such hour was, frankly, quite imponderable. But for the last fortnight she had scarcely had a private word with Peter, and whatever it was that she had to say to him in this visit she had bidden him to, and whatever he had to say to her (that he had something to say was probable from his reiterated acceptance of her request), it was quite certain that these things could not be satisfactorily said, even, perhaps, be said at all, before any audience whatever.

Nellie had no definite knowledge, in any detail, of even her own contribution to the coming interview; all that she knew was that when, half an hour later or an hour later, she would click the door on his departure, she must somehow have looked minutely, with his eyes to help her, at the antagonism which had so odiously flourished. She intensely hoped that it could be rooted up altogether and put on to the rubbish heap of mistakes and misapprehensions; but whether her hope had much of the luminosity of faith about it was not so certain. Too much depended on what he had to tell her, and she did not fall into the error of forecasting the upshot before she knew what contribution he was to make towards the preliminary process.... Then, with an internal vibration—partly of suspense, partly, she admitted, of eager anticipation—she heard the faint tingle of the electric bell. The servants, no doubt, had gone to bed, and she went to the door herself.

"Hullo!" said Peter.

He stood there a moment, after the door was opened, without moving, his eyes agleam, and a smile hovering over his mouth. Often and often had they met in precisely similar fashion, he, as he passed the door on his way home, giving one discreet little ring, which Nellie would answer if she felt disposed to see him. Sometimes her mother would be in; but oftener, if in, she had gone to bed, and the two would sit over the fire, or, on hot nights, seek the window-seat and spend an hour of desultory intimacy, as two boys might, or two girls. But to-night there was some little effervescent quality added to the meeting; the spice that a combined manœuvre, however innocent, brought with it. Both realized, too, that a talk, which must attempt to readjust their old relations or fit them into the changed conditions, lay ahead, and, for the moment, each brought gaiety and goodwill to the task. The best evidence for that was the assumption of the old relations pending the readjustment....

"Peter! How lovely of you!" she said. "Come in."

"Is she in?" he asked, putting down his coat and hat.

"Mother? No; she's at a harpy party. Four women rooking each other at bridge. They'll all be trembling and being frightfully polite by this time. Peter, bring your hat and coat in with you. If mother sees them there she will think Philip's here and will come in to sit with us."

"And if she thought they were mine — —"

"She would come in twice. But if there are no signs of anybody she will probably go to bed and not interrupt us."

The night was hot, with a thundery, overcast sky, and they sat together again in the window-seat. A hundred feet below the street was roaring and rolling along, thick with the discharge from theatres and music halls.

"The clever one! And how did you get rid of Philip?" asked Peter.

"Lied, darling," said Nellie, succinctly.

"Did you, indeed? Nellie, I don't think you're getting on very well with your determination to be conventional."

Nellie blew reproach at him in the shape of a ragged smoke-ring.

"I never heard anything so unjust," she said. "Oh, Peter, it was just here we sat when I told you I was going to be quite conventional. Wasn't it? Don't say you don't remember. Well, I'm being the model of conventionality."

"Pleasant, is it?" asked Peter, in a wonderfully neutral voice. He did not yet quite know why Nellie had summoned him here, and he was greatly aloof still.

"Don't make slightly acid comments," said she, "about conventionality. It's a fortnight, more than a fortnight, since I saw you last. Oh, I don't count balls and that sort of thing. Your friends are invisible at balls. You can only see your acquaintances. What's the use of just seeing a friend? You've got to be alone with a friend in order to see him."

Nellie was still unaware of what course she was really meaning to steer. It was to be a safe course, anyhow, avoiding shoals and avoiding icebergs. Just at present Peter was making himself an iceberg. She went on, talking rapidly and quite naturally, with a view to bringing Peter out of his frozen aloofness.

"But my scheme for conventionality never went so far as to exclude my seeing my friends altogether," she said. "And if, in order to see a particular friend, I have to tell lies to one person and — and tell the other not to leave his coat in the hall, that's not my fault. It's mother's fault for not having gone to bed yet; it's Philip's fault for proposing to drop in."

Peter's smile hovered over his face again, not quite breaking through.

"Brutes," he said. "Perfect brutes."

"I'm not sure that you aren't the worst of them all," remarked Nellie.

His smile broke through at that, and he laughed.

"You may be quite sure I'm not a brute," he said. "But I should like to know why you think so."

Nellie was sincere enough in her desire to re-establish a genuine, friendly relationship with him again. At present their grip on each other was clogged and rusted. If this rather unconventional meeting was to be of any use (what use she did not clearly define), the first essential was to wipe the wheels clean.

"You know perfectly well," she said. "Ever since my engagement you have taken yourself completely away. You have shut yourself up. You have bolted your windows and barred your doors to me. Haven't you?"

Peter weighed this accusation. It might possibly be true; but it contained an arguable point, which was easy to state.

"I never bolted the windows and barred the doors," he said. "It was you who did that. I didn't arrange that you should marry Philip. That's what shut me up, if you choose to put it like that. I told you at the time that our relations must be changed."

She shook her head.

"No relations that ever existed between us need have been changed," she said. "You speak as if we had been in love with each other."

"Not at all. We never were in love with each other; that we both know. But——"

"What then?" she asked.

"I'll take your simile," he said. "My windows and doors were open to you. I might easily have fallen in love with you, or, for that matter, you with me. Our relationship, and the possibilities it held, were just those of open doors and windows. Then you came round and shut me up. And Philip drew the curtains."

She took this in and turned it about before she answered.

"By which you mean," she said, "that whatever our relationship might have ripened into, I nipped it off—like a frost."

"Yes," said he. "A latish frost."

She got up and moved about the room, patting a cushion here and setting a chair straight there. Peter did not move; he did not even turn his head; but he was quite aware of her pondering restlessness. He was aware, too, that so long as he held his tongue he had the whip-hand. The evidence for that was soon apparent.

"I didn't know that my engagement would have that effect," she said. "I think it is unreasonable that it should have that effect. If you had been in love with me it would have been different; in that case I could have understood it. But, as it was, why should it have made any change in our friendship?"

"What's the use of asking me?" said Peter, with a sudden touch of irritation. "I can't tell you why. I don't know the 'why' of anything under the sun. But put it the other way about. Suppose that it had been I who had got engaged to some girl, wouldn't that have made any change in your sense of our friendship?"

Peter had spread himself a little over the window-seat when she got up. Now when she came back to her old seat she pushed his encroaching knee aside.

"That's not the same thing," she said. "A girl can't be a very intimate friend of a married man in the same way that a man can be a very intimate friend of a married woman."

"I won't ask why," said Peter gently, "because I'm aware that you don't know."

"What I say is perfectly true, though."

"Not in the instance of you and me. You knew quite well that I wasn't going to give myself a free rein to fall in love with you after you had settled to marry someone else. Besides, it you come to think of it, a man dangling after a married woman is just as ridiculous as a girl dangling after a married man. I don't see why a man shouldn't be allowed to retain his self-respect as much as a woman."

Though, as far as the spoken word went, they had arrived at no agreement, no compromise even on which agreement could be based, they both felt that somehow in the region of unspoken treaties the ground had been cleared. Though the wheels did not yet revolve again, rust had been wiped off them. And in Peter's next speech the scouring of the wash-leather was busy.

"You mustn't think that I don't regret what we're suffering under, Nellie," he said. "I regret it most awfully. I've been saying, and I stick to it still, that you are responsible for it. It was you who closed my windows and bolted my doors. It would be simply silly of me to pretend that I was broken-hearted about it, for that would imply that I had been or was in love with you. But that doesn't prevent my being sorry, or my missing, which I acutely do, our old relationship. I don't know if it's any use trying to recapture it. 'Trying,' probably, hasn't much effect on what you feel. It's no use 'trying' to feel hot if you happen to feel cold, or trying to feel ill when you do feel well— —"

"My dear, it makes the whole difference," said Nellie quickly. "Will you try to—to feel yourself back in your relationship with me? I want it, too, Peter."

She pulled back his encroaching knee which just now she had pushed away and kept her hand on it. The very fact that this triviality was so instinctive constituted the significance of it.

"I hadn't reckoned with losing you," she went on. "No, I don't excuse myself or account for myself. Probably I should have done just the same if I had reckoned with it. Probably, if it was all to do again now, I should do the same. Don't let us labour the point; if you'll try, that's all I ask. I'll try, too, if that will be of any use. I put my nose in the air just as much as you did, as if my nose wasn't sufficiently in the air already. But it always turns up at the end."

"Not to matter; don't mention it," said Peter.

"That's the old style, Peter," she said. "Keep it up; run with it till it works on its own account. Motor-cycle, you know."

They were looking at each other now with something of the alert unconsciousness of two old friends alone together. But certainly the machine required running with at present.

"They're heavy things to push when they won't get going," said he.

"How odious you are!"

"Hurrah for that word!" said Peter.

"Why?"

"I wonder how often we have told each other we were odious."

Nellie was silent, and in that moment's pause Peter was conscious that, real, no doubt, as had been her desire to uproot the antagonism that had grown up between them, that process had been no more than preliminary to something that should follow. The ground had to be cleared first, but the clearing of the ground was not her ultimate objective. The moment he perceived that at all, he saw how obvious it was; how her appearance suddenly in Mrs. Wardour's box that evening gave a clue to the nature of the further development. Then, quick as an echo, she began to reproduce the thought in his mind.

"Let's pick up the thread again," she said. "I can give you my weavings very simply. Trousseau, Philip; Philip, trousseau. How lucky men are! When a man is going to be married he doesn't have to spend his days in buying things. He doesn't have to buy anything."

"Wedding-ring," said Peter, in parenthesis.

"Yes; but you can't have occupied yourself with that unless you have had a private marriage behind the locked doors and curtained windows. We were telling each other what we had been doing in this long interval. It was your turn."

"Oh, usual things," said he. "Foreign Office, dinner; breakfast, Foreign Office."

"And how's May Trentham?" asked Nellie, wheeling in smaller circles round this objective. "You've left her out; she wouldn't like that."

"She left me out to-night," said Peter. "She had that immense box for the play and never asked me to it."

Nellie folded her wings and dropped.

"But you got there all right," she said. "She saw you, too, sitting with Mrs. Wardour, who hasn't asked her to the party for the Russian ballet. Blood, my dear; there'll be blood over that. Do you know, I think Silvia is one of the most attractive girls I have ever seen."

As she spoke there came from outside the tingle of the front door bell. Nellie got up with a finger on her lip.

"Who on earth can that be?" she whispered.

"It may be anybody," said Peter, very prudently. "You can't tell till you go and see. Perhaps it's Philip; we may have got hold of each other's hats by mistake, and he's come here — —"

Nellie suppressed a laugh.

"Probably mother," she said. "She forgets her latchkey when she thinks she'll be late home. I shan't say you're here, or she'd come in and spoil our talk."

"Oh, what a tangled — —" began Peter.

Nellie took the additional precaution of turning out the lights in the room where they were sitting and leaving the door open. Close outside was the entrance door from the stairs into the flat, and Peter, sitting in the window-seat, heard with an amusement that dimpled his cheeks Nellie's unhesitating account of herself. It appeared that she had just come in and was just going to bed; she had already put out the lights in the sitting-room. There followed a triumphant announcement of her mother's winnings, an affectionate good night, and the closing of a door down the passage. Sitting there in the dark Peter drew the conclusion that Nellie put a high premium on the pursuit of the conversation in which, as he infallibly conjectured, she had just got down to the bone. She would scarcely, for the æsthetic delight in tortuosity, have concealed the fact that he had dropped in, as he had done a hundred times before, for a few minutes' chat on his way home. She wanted to talk about Silvia. For his part he was perfectly ready to talk about Silvia.

Just before the closing of the door, which must certainly be that of Mrs. Heaton's bedroom, Nellie had said: "I'll put out the lights; good night, dear. What a lovely last rubber," and Peter, feeling his way, so to speak, into Nellie's mind by the analogy of his own, knew exactly what she was doing. In a moment now there would be the click of the extinguished light in the hall, and she would very softly rustle back in the dark into the room where he was sitting, close the door of that, and then, perhaps, turn on the light inside again, or, as likely as not, shuffle back into the window-seat. So often had they sat there talking in the dark.

And as he waited for those five or ten seconds to pass, he was invaded by a sense of passionate rebellion against himself. There was the girl, whom for the last two years he had been interested in, fond of to the practical exclusion of anyone else, and now, at this moment she, engaged to a man whom she did not ever so remotely love, was presently stealing back, on the eve of her marriage, to spend a more than midnight hour with him. He ought to have been a balloon, rising into some stratum of sunlight high above the twi-lit earth, and instead he was bumping heavily over uneven ground, quite unable to get into the air. No matter what the ballast of worldly consideration he threw out, he could not feel himself lifting, and Nellie, when she came back, would only add to the weight.

His expectations were ruthlessly, even ruefully, fulfilled. She stole in, invisible in the darkened oblong of the doorway, closed it, and without turning up the light, established herself in the window-seat again.

"Mother's gone to her room," she said. "I did it so cleverly, Peter. I said I had just come in— —"

"I know; I heard," said Peter. "Brilliant."

"Wasn't it? Now we can talk without any fear of interruption. Where had we got to? Oh, I know. I think Silvia is perfectly fascinating. Don't you?"

Here was the bumping process, the added weight. Eager though Nellie had been to re-establish old relations between herself and him, there was a livelier eagerness to ascertain anything about new relations between himself and Silvia. If Nellie, as he had affirmed, had shut his windows and bolted his doors for him, he now made a tour of the secure premises to see that she had done her work thoroughly.

"I don't know if I should say perfectly fascinating," he said.

"But you like her, don't you?"

"Extremely, but — —"

Nellie waited to hear the qualification. She liked the fact that there was a qualification, though at present she did not know what it was. As nothing further came, she spoke again, quite in the old style.

"Oh, it's so rude to say 'but,' and then not go on," she said.

Peter jerked back his head.

"Let me be polite, then," he said. "One can always observe the small decencies of life. What I nearly said was: 'But I'm not in love with her.' I stopped myself, Nellie, if you want to know, because it seemed to me very vividly that it wasn't your business."

There was an illumination cast on to her face from the street lamps from below. To his intense surprise he saw that her eyes, wide and unfocused, grew suddenly dim.

"That's just what I, too, am beginning to realize," she said. "Whatever you do now is none of my business. I've got a separate establishment. I'm bound to say that you have quite realized that. You haven't asked me a single question about what goes on in mine. It doesn't concern you any more; therefore, you don't care. I shall learn to respect your privacy, too, Peter. Another snub or so will teach me."

"That's nonsense!" he said quickly.

"It isn't nonsense. You treat me like a stranger because I happen to be marrying someone else. If you had been in love with me— —"

"We've had that already," said Peter.

"Then listen to it this time. You've absolutely been turning your back on me. You are piqued—horrid word—because I don't want to remain an old maid for your sake. Mayn't I feel interested in you without your resenting it? You object to my marrying Philip when you could have made it perfectly clear— —"

"What could I have made clear?" he asked.

"You could have made yourself indispensable to me," she said. "A single further turn of the screw— —"

Again she broke off.

"No, I'm wronging you," she said. "That final turn of the screw must be made mutually. It never came to us, though I was there, wasn't I, with my screwdriver, and you with yours? It just didn't happen. Let's make the best of what remains. A good deal remains after all. We have everything that is of value between us, except that final turn of the screw. Good heavens, Peter, how I wish I adored you! I do all but that. And you do the same for me, darling, when all is said and done. If only you were masterful and masculine, or if only I were, the thing would be solved. As it is, we are like two oysters in the flow of the tide, just gaping at each other."

Nellie's ultimate objective, unless Peter had completely misunderstood her, had sunk out of sight for him.

"And all the time the tide is flowing," he said; "that's so maddening of it. I mean that the days and weeks and months are passing, and one doesn't even think, still less does one feel; one only exists. I am an oyster, it's quite true. But I don't make pearls. Pearls, I believe, are only pieces of grit which the clever oyster covers up with iridescent stuff. All that stuff comes from the oyster's inside, somehow. I can't *make*; I can't manufacture like that. The clever oyster does it, or the normal oyster, somewhere in the South Seas. I suppose I'm a northern oyster—only meant to be eaten. Just to be eaten. I really want somebody to come along and gobble me up. I'm nothing but a small piece of food."

Nellie found herself hugely interested in this. It gave her what she wanted to know—namely, Peter's own personal estimate as to how he stood to Silvia. He had defined it negatively when he told her that he was not in love with her; but here was a more intimate revelation—namely, that of his willingness to be absorbed. There, too, was the difference, vital and essential, between herself and him, for she never contemplated the possibility of being absorbed by Philip. There would certainly be no absorption there on either side; he, so she judged, was as little likely to make that surrender as she.

For a moment she thought over what he had said, instantly finding herself unable to accept it.

"I can imagine your being very indigestible," she remarked. "I don't really think, nor, perhaps, do you, that you will allow yourself to be assimilated. I can't imagine you giving up your wet woods."

"I shall always remain selfish, you mean," said he. "Self-centred; whatever you like to call it."

She frowned over this.

"What I suppose I really mean is that I don't understand you," she said. And, getting up, she fumbled for the switch of the light by the door. "Let's throw some light on you."

He got up, too.

"I must go to bed," he said. "It's any hour of the night."

She stood in front of him, stretching her arms, which were a little cramped with leaning on the window-sill, and looked at him gravely.

"You're going to ask Silvia to marry you, then?" she said.

"I am, as soon as I think she will accept me."

Nellie received this point-blank. She had fully expected it, and now, when it came, there was nothing in her that ever so faintly winced. Then she took two steps forward, put her hands on his shoulders and kissed him.

"Peter, darling, what good friends we've been," she said, "and we'll carry all that forward into the future. There's no one like you. That's just what I meant by kissing you, that, and to wish you all good luck. Perhaps your son will marry my daughter; wouldn't that be nice; and then we can envy them both, and be wildly jealous. As for asking Silvia—well, what about to-morrow? Perhaps it's rather late to ask her to-night."

He tiptoed his way out, and Nellie closed the door very cautiously behind him. At that moment, when she kissed him, she had given him all of the very best of her. She exulted in having done it, but assuredly virtue had gone out of her. Restless and unquiet in her bed, she thought over what was left for her.

CHAPTER VII

John Mainwaring had prepared his studio for the visit of Mrs. Wardour and Silvia next day with the utmost dramatic completeness, employing for their reception the scenery and the setting which suggested itself as being most likely to impress and astound. With this end in view he had littered the room with all possible properties, bringing down from the attics stacks of his own pictures, which he disposed in careless profusion round the walls. Sketch books and paint boxes littered the tables, lay figures peeped from behind easels, robes trailed over sofa-backs, and he, when his visitors were announced, had designed that he himself should be found, in his oldest velveteen coat and morocco slippers, at the top of the step-ladder which he had put into position again in front of the great canvas representing Satan odiously whispering to the German Emperor. There, absorbed in his inspired labours, he was to be giving the last, the crowning, the positively final terrific touch to it as his visitors (and, as he hoped, his victims) entered.

Since the work had actually been finished at least a month ago, and on that occasion had been toasted in glasses of port wine by himself, his wife and Peter, he had thought it prudent to inform her that more last touches were to be applied to it again to-day. Visitors, he had added, were dropping in that afternoon, and she would, no doubt, be sitting upstairs in the drawing-room when they arrived, with tea prepared for their refreshment. When the time came he would yodel for her, and she would come down, be presented to Mrs. Wardour and her daughter, and would scold him for keeping these ladies looking at his stupid pictures instead of bringing them up to tea....

Such was the general idea of the opening of a manœuvre from which he, with a quite incurable optimism, expected very gratifying results. Peter had already alluded to the surprising dawn of Mrs. Wardour on the town, and he himself, at the play the night before, had paved the way for a commission to execute a portrait of Silvia. He had no idea whether or not Mrs. Wardour inserted any of these golden tentacles with which, like an octopus, she appeared to be enveloping London, into the domain of art, but it was worth while hoping that her sense of completion would not be satisfied unless she had Silvia's portrait painted. That, so he had ascertained, had not been done, and he had, so to speak, left a card "soliciting the favour of a call." The call certainly was to be made that afternoon, and his imagination now, bit in teeth and wildly galloping, foresaw another possible commission in the portrait of Mrs. Wardour herself. Perhaps—here was the rosiest of the summits yet in view—he might profitably dispose of that great cartoon which Mrs. Wardour would so soon be privileged to see receiving its finishing touches. Farther than that his vision did not definitely project itself, but in sunlit and shining mists he could vaguely see himself working for all he was worth (and for much of what Mrs. Wardour was worth) at more of these stupendous canvases, and berthing each, as soon as possible, in the same remunerative harbourage.

The ring at the bell of the street door warned him to scamper up his step-ladder, and absorb himself in finishing touches at the top of the thundercloud of war. In due time the studio door opened and Burrows, announcing his visitors, had to raise her voice to the pitch of a vendor of street-wares and recite the names again before she was so fortunate as to attract his attention. Then Mr. Mainwaring turned slowly round with a dazed expression and, shading his eyes, perceived the expected presences. Then with brush in one hand and palette in the other, he gave an ecstatic cry of welcome (not to be confused with the yodelling summons for his wife), and came bounding down the step-ladder. Divesting himself of his palette and brush, he held out both hands.

"Ah, my dear friends," he said, "but this is charming. I am ashamed of myself to be found in such dishevelment, but—well, we artists are like that, silly donkeys as we are, and I had forgotten, for the moment I had forgotten the advent of my delightful visitors."

He held a hand of each of them for a moment, with pressure and expression, and then withdrew his left hand, holding it to his forehead.

"A finishing touch," he said. "I was at that very moment putting the last touch of paint on to my canvas. Let me forget that: give me a moment to forget it. You are here, that is the great point."

He made a splendid obeisance, and as he recovered thrust back his hair, and embarked on a period.

"You find me, dear Mrs. Wardour," he said, "in a moment of triumph, of jubilation even. Little as that can possibly mean to others, this is one of my red letter days. A moment ago my brush touched my canvas for the last time. My picture is done, all but for the obscure initials, which, in vermilion,

I shall humbly inscribe in the corner. Would it, by chance, be of the smallest interest to you to see that little rite performed? I take my brush then, I squeeze out a morsel of paint, I trace those obscure initials."

No inspiration could have been happier. Mrs. Wardour's eye was already travelling over the huge canvas with rapture and astonishment, and it was thrilling that she should have come just in time to see the artist testify in vermilion that this great thing was of his own creation. Naturally she could not be expected to know that if she had arrived half an hour ago, or had not arrived for half an hour to come, she would have been just in time for this ceremony. She turned to Silvia.

"Well, if *that* isn't interesting, Silvia," she said (as if Silvia had denied it). "Weren't we saying to each other as we came along that perhaps we should find Mr. Mainwaring painting? And what a work of art too! My!"

John Mainwaring having recorded himself as creator, became showman and spectator in one, and moved the step-ladder aside so that he should both get and give an uninterrupted view. Then, losing himself once more as spectator, he propped his chin on his hand and gazed at the work.

"Finished! Finished!" he said with a magnificent detachment. "Now let us see what we think of it."

Mrs. Wardour gazed too, and the more she gazed the more powerful—that was exactly the word she would have used—appeared the significance of this tremendous presentment. She had no great taste for pictures, but if you were in pursuit of pictures (and pictures had certainly been the objective of this expedition), here was what she meant by a picture. Not long before his death her husband had bought what he called "a picture or two," destined to adorn the walls of the gallery which was so great a feature in the castellated residence which he had built on the ridge of Ashdown Forest. It ran the whole length of the house, and when complete as to embellishment, was to be a lane of pictures from end to end hung on red Spanish brocade. To her mind, no less than his, real pictures, true pictures, pictures worth looking at, were brightly (or sombrely) coloured illustrations of famous personages, of well-known places, or told a story; best of all were those that told a story. A few such had already been plucked and gathered there; there was a very splendid record of the coronation of Queen Victoria, the rock of Gibraltar, with a P. and O. steamer to the left and a sunset to the right, an execution of Mary, Queen of Scots, and, in lighter mood, a delicious immensity called "Knights of the Bath," in which a small boy and a large puppy shared a sponging-tin. Here then and now the image of the walls of the great picture-gallery, at present insufficiently clad, and crying out for covering, like a bather who has lost his clothes, flashed into her mind. The image was not sufficiently clearly realized to admit of a definite association of ideas between it and the allegory at which they were all gazing, but certainly as she looked at the size—particularly the size—of Mr. Mainwaring's masterpiece, the gallery at Howes occurred to her. If there were to be pictures, here or elsewhere, she liked to know what such pictures were "about," and she instantly perceived what this one was about. Now that the war was won, and the German Emperor, for all practical purposes, annihilated (he had served his turn because the destruction of ships by his submarines had brought her so excessive a fortune), she could, perceiving the message of the picture, unreservedly gloat over the realism of it.

"If that isn't the German Emperor," she loudly enunciated, "and if that isn't Satan whispering to him about the war. Satan's saying that he would help, and, to be sure, he tried to. I do call that a picture. And there's the war coming up behind, like a thunderstorm. There's a subject for a picture, and how beautifully you've done it, Mr. Mainwaring."

He leaned his chin still more heavily against his hand.

"Ah, you think so?" he asked. "I wish I thought so!"

"But what is there to want?" asked Mrs. Wardour. "It's all as clear as day. We saw nothing so striking at the Royal Academy, did we, Silvia, even at the Private View."

"The Academy? The Academy?" murmured Mr. Mainwaring, as if he wondered whether he had heard that name before. Then he shook his head gently, as if abandoning the attempt to remember what the Academy was.

"And I see lots of guns and bayonets underneath the thundercloud," said Mrs. Wardour unerringly. "They're coming up."

The artist still gazed, and, smoothing his chin with his hand, he repeated:

"Yes; they're coming up, coming up."...

He gave a great start, and seemed to shake himself like a big retriever emerging from the water, where he had brought some thrown token to land. He did not know of the great gallery at Howes, which starved for decoration; but even if he had, he would have bounded out of the water just like that.

"*Basta! Basta!*" he cried. "I am boring you, dear ladies, I am wearying you, I am making myself a most unutterable tedium for you. Where is my wife? Why is she not here to tap me on the shoulder and say 'Tea'?"

He gave the preconcerted signal of a yodel, and opening the door of the studio, repeated it. A faint cry from upstairs answered him, and on the heels of that cry Mrs. Mainwaring came downstairs. The introductions were floridly effected, and she shook her finger at her husband, and explained her reproof to her visitors.

"I always tell him that when he is at his painting he never knows the time," she said. "John, it is very wrong of you to have kept Mrs. Wardour and Miss Wardour down here."

She turned to Mrs. Wardour, as her husband vented himself in contrition and apology to Silvia.

"Of course I'm no judge," she said, "for I always think that everything my husband does is so striking. But is not that a wonderful thing? The Emperor, Satan. Yes. Such expressive faces! Now I must insist on your coming to have a cup of tea. I always have to drive my husband away from his easel. Look at him in his old coat, too. John, I'm ashamed of you! Go and put on something more tidy."

Silvia felt somehow, as Mrs. Mainwaring gave this skilful rendering of the general hints that she had received, as if she was listening to some automaton wound up to emit through a mask-like face certain words, certain sentences that formed its accomplishment. That was the immediate effect, but immediately afterwards followed the conjecture that it was not a mere automaton that spoke. It said, so she seemed to gather, what it had been told (or thereabouts) to say, but probably Mrs. Mainwaring was capable of saying and doing things for herself. Though she had been pulled through the funnel of Mr. Mainwaring's personality, she had not lost her own individual self. But what that individual self was she could form no conjecture. It was as if a voice came from inside a window over which a blind had been completely drawn. She could arrive at no perception of *who* it was who talked behind the blind, nor was the room lit within so that, at the least, there came a shadow on the blind, suggesting features. All this was no more than the details of the first impression made by a new acquaintance, her instinctive valuation of her hostess, something to work upon provisionally. Mrs. Mainwaring was only repeating her lessons, which she seemed to know so excellently well; she gave at present no indication of what she was like when her lessons were over. But that she existed Silvia had no doubt whatever. There were people like that, people who had an aloof, sequestered life of their own. Then, without being conscious of the transition, she knew that she was thinking of Mrs. Mainwaring no longer, but of Peter.

More yodelling proclaimed that the artist had put on his tidy coat, and he pranced back, and led the way upstairs with Mrs. Wardour, saying that he was as hungry as a hunter, and hoping that his wife had provided them with a good tea. Mrs. Mainwaring, on the other hand, seemed a little to be detaining Silvia; she pointed out other of the works of art that so plentifully bestrewed the room, and this struck the girl, somehow, as being part of a manœuvre in no way connected with the lesson she had so faultlessly repeated. The blind had been ever so slightly pushed aside; someone was looking out.

"Yes, there's a picture my husband painted of my son last year," she said. "I think you've met Peter, haven't you, Miss Wardour? That was considered to be very like him. I hope he will be home for tea; he said he thought he could get away from the Foreign Office early to-day. Very interesting for him to be in the Foreign Office."

Silvia said something amiable about the portrait, which was quite recognizable.

"So pleased you think it like," continued Mrs. Mainwaring. "Yes, Peter is at the Foreign Office all day, and he is generally out in the evening. I do not go out very much. I sit at home mostly in the evening and read."

Silvia welcomed a new topic. Though the blind had been distinctly twitched aside she could not see in; she was only conscious of being observed. But this seemed an encouraging opportunity of getting a glimpse.

"What do you read most?" she asked. "Novels? Memoirs?"

"No, what I like reading about is places I have never been to," said Mrs. Mainwaring. "I wonder, when I read, what life is like in those places, and how I should enjoy it."

If that was a glimpse for the girl it was a very momentary one, lit, so to speak, not by any clear illumination, but rather by some vague dim phosphorescence. Silvia, by some whimsical association of ideas, found herself thinking of a phosphorescent match-box; if you felt for it in the dark, you might find matches there which would produce something more illuminating.

"Ah, I, too, love new places," she said. "I love waking in a new place, where I have arrived after dark, and wondering what it is going to be like."

The glimpse grew a little more definite.

"I should like that, too," said Mrs. Mainwaring. "But my husband's work keeps him in London, and I do not get away very often. Shall we go upstairs to tea?"

As they turned, Mrs. Mainwaring cast one glance at the great cartoon. For the moment, infinitesimal in duration, her neat smooth porcelain face grew hostile and malevolent.

No sooner did Silvia appear in the doorway of the little drawing-room facing the street, than Mr. Mainwaring, to her immense surprise, bounded from his seat, chasséed across the room to her, and fell on his knees before her.

"Behold me in an attitude of abject entreaty!" he said. "Your mother, subject to your acquiescence, dear Miss Silvia, has asked me to attempt to use my best endeavours, feeble as they may be, to render you the eager homage of an artist's skill. She has asked me, subject to your consent, I repeat, to paint your portrait for her."

Even as he spoke there came the quick light step on the stairs, the identity of which Silvia, seldom as she had heard it, knew with a certainty that surprised her, and Peter came in.

"Kneel, Peter, my dear," said his father, enjoying himself tremendously and putting up hands of supplication. "Maria, my angel, I beseech you to kneel too. We are entreating Miss Silvia; we are urging the sacred claims of Art."

Silvia gave a laugh of sheer amusement at this ludicrous situation. Amusement was the only possible solvent for it.

"Oh please, let nobody kneel!" she said. "And you, Mr. Mainwaring, please get up. Yes, of course, if my mother wishes it, and if Mr. Mainwaring will be very patient and tell me what to do——"

He bounded up again, ecstatic at the granting of his petition.

"To do?" he asked. "Dear young lady, you have only got to be. Be! Be just as you are now."

Again he supported his head on his hand, as when he gazed at the cartoon, and with the other shaded his eyes, staring at her in an embarrassing manner. He gave a gay yodelling cry.

"I see it—I see it!" he announced. "My superb picture is already flaming in my brain. Madam"—he turned to Mrs. Wardour—"you shall have a masterpiece, and I, John Mainwaring, will have created it."

He took his hand from his forehead, and made a movement as if to cast something away.

"Enough!" he said. "Let us descend to earth again. My angel, give us our tea. We are exhausted by our adventures."

Peter, so Silvia noticed, was looking at his father with eyebrows ever so little raised, as if in contemplation of some phenomenon that, however familiar, was still remarkable, and his lips were faintly smiling. When he turned to Silvia, as he now did, that expression still remained there, and she felt that, wordlessly, he had somehow taken her into his confidence. Certainly his father amused him; his raised eyebrows and half-smiling mouth told her that. And was there a touch of indulgent contempt in it?

John Mainwaring continued to claim the attention of the little party in a boisterous rollicking fashion; it was like being out in a high wind, where shouting was the only means of communication. He assuaged the hunger which he confessed was prodigious, with incredible quantities of tea-cakes; he ate cherries backwards, beginning with the stem. He roared with laughter at his own jokes, he apologized for his boyishness, and whispered to Mrs. Wardour that he was "in for" a scolding afterwards from his wife for making such a noise.... And there, all the time, far more potently vital was Peter blowing off no steam like his father, but quietly, self-containedly reserving it. There was something inscrutable about that smooth handsome face, though now and then, as their eyes casually met, Silvia felt that she was looking into clear dark beckoning water, and if her eyes could not fathom it, that was no fault of his transparence, but only of her own purblind penetration....

Mr. Mainwaring was, just now, launched on a story, the very recollection of which made him laugh in anticipation of what was coming, and Silvia could let her eyes roam at will. She looked at her mother, at the narrator, at Mrs. Mainwaring, all in turn, in order, for the purposes of strict impartiality, to look at Peter as well. Mrs. Mainwaring with wifely and domestic devotion had managed to attach to her face some faint semblance of interest in the story, as if it were new to her. Then came Peter's turn, and that handsome inscrutability suddenly seemed to Silvia to be like a reflecting surface, which, when you looked at it, showed you not itself, but presented your own image. She saw not at all how he stood to her, but how she stood to him. Her own subjective relation, the image of herself regarding him was flashed back at her. Looking at him, in some mysterious way, she saw herself. His dark clear water gave back to her her own soul.... She whisked her eyes away, forgetting the impartiality of her rotation, and found herself met by Mrs. Mainwaring. And there, so it seemed, she found comprehension of this bewildering impression. As regards Mrs. Mainwaring herself, the blind was still drawn, but from behind the blind Silvia heard inwardly and unmistakably that quiet, precise voice saying, "The girl's in love with my Peter." Mrs. Mainwaring, by some divination as mysterious as herself, was in possession of that; she and Silvia shared the secret knowledge. And then, before the girl's eyes could shift themselves to Mr. Mainwaring, who, it seemed clear, from his thumping with his fist on the tea-table, was now at the climax of his narrative, there peeped out from his wife's face that same secret malevolence, with which, as they left the studio, she had looked at the great work of art that hung there, while she admitted that her husband's work kept him and her in London.

The point of Mr. Mainwaring's story entailed the use of the falsetto voice, and Peter at its conclusion got up on the pretext of handing cigarettes, and reseated himself next Silvia.

"It is good of you," he said.

That was fragmentary enough, undetached from any context, but Silvia found herself understanding him perfectly.

"My mother and Mr. Mainwaring arranged it," she said. "I couldn't very well say no, could I? Not that I wanted to; I don't mean that."

"My father's delighted," said Peter.

He paused a moment.

"He's in great form," he added. "You've delighted him. Aren't we a weird family?"

There seemed no direct reply possible to this. Silvia could not imagine herself assenting, and it seemed banal as well as untrue to say, "No, you're quite ordinary." But she found herself not wanting and not even needing to reply at all. She wanted, and for that matter she needed no more than to have Peter there and be wonderfully happy. He shifted himself a little in his very low chair as he turned to get a match for his cigarette, and she again just found herself noticing little things about him. His fingers were very long and smooth, the nails very neatly sheathed in the skin that held them: they grew beautifully. Best of all was the short, closely-clipped hair which, when he bent his head forward towards the match, stopped just above his collar.

"You needn't answer that," he said. "Tell me, instead, what you thought of the play last night. Are people sentimental—girls particularly—like that when they are really moved? I should have thought that emotion killed sentimentality. But it may be different in Scotland."

Peter, at the conclusion of this ridiculous speech, suddenly found himself in the dilemma of talking nonsense without the co-operation and backing of the person whom he was talking nonsense to. Silvia, at any rate, did not contribute any soap-bubbles of her own, and, quick to perceive that, he turned to his mother.

"What sort of hotels are there in Scotland, mother?" he asked. "Oh, I must explain to Miss Wardour. My mother loves reading the advertisements of hotels in Bradshaw. It gives her the sense of travel, doesn't it, mother?"

He paused no more than infinitesimally and went on again in the same breath.

"I love the sense of travel, too, and I got it by going to the Foreign Office. Guatemala has been my *après-midi*."

Silvia triumphantly applauded his quickness. She had seen on Mrs. Mainwaring's face a protest at the invasion of her privacy; but Peter had done more than merely see it, he had slammed the door again with allusions to himself and Guatemala. That, somehow, a perception as quick as intuition, seemed to her extraordinarily characteristic of him. There was no stumbling, no hesitation, where she would have drawn attention to a similar mistake by a bungling silence. His mind was like the hair on his neck—abrupt and crisp.

The ball was with Peter again.

"I nearly fell asleep over Guatemala," he said. "Surely Guatemala is very remote; there are many things more immediately interesting. Nellie's wedding, by the way. It's less than a week ahead, and every young man I know is buying new pocket-handkerchiefs to weep into. I've bought an extremely large one. There'll be room for you to cry into one half of it, Miss Silvia, while I cry into the other. They promised to send it round on a hand trolley, like a sack of coals."

Silvia laughed.

"Ah, I shall want some of that handkerchief," she said, "but not to cry into, only to wave. She is going to be tremendously happy, isn't she? What's he like? I hardly know him."

Peter considered this.

"He's like—he's like a very tidy room," he said. "Solid furniture and not a speck of dust."

"And the person who sits in it?" asked the girl.

"Nobody sits in it. At least I never found anyone there. Philip is the room. There's *The Times* warmed and folded; there's letter-paper, big and little, and envelopes, big and little. Perhaps Nellie has found someone there. Philip may get under the sofa when anybody else comes in."

"And she's very much in love with him?" asked Silvia.

"You ought to know. She takes you out to Richmond Park and sits on the grass with you all afternoon."

Silvia wrinkled up her eyes as if she were focusing that afternoon.

"Nellie dazzles me," she said. "She's like the sun on water. I expect she'll make his room, that tidy room, look lovely. But I shall never understand what Nellie does. I shall only understand the effect of what she has done. She has a spell. She makes you see what she has seen."

She was conscious now of receiving from Peter a more direct answer of eyes than she had ever done before. She knew they were talking about the same things now. They might, each of them, though they were talking of Nellie (superficially the same thing), have been regarding her, have been framing their remarks about her from different angles. Given that, as Silvia had said, she was a dazzle of sunlight as well, one of them, owing to the prismatic process, might have been seeing blue, another seeing yellow. But Peter's answer convinced her that they were both seeing Nellie from the same standpoint.

"That's hit her," he said. "Nellie says and does nothing trivial; one is continually discovering that. She waves her fingers, and she mutters, and then, afterwards, you find she has been making a spell. Isn't she uncanny? Or she tells you something about yourself that you didn't know, or scarcely knew, and you find that it is quite solidly true. Is she a witch, do you think?"

Silvia leaned forward towards him. It was impossible not to "close up" with this.

"That's just what I said to her once," she said. "I said that she was a witch. She told me something about myself that I never had known. It was true; it had been true all the time. But, literally, I had never had the smallest notion of it till she told me."

Indeed, as Silvia acknowledged to herself, the truth of what Nellie had said on that occasion was receiving a firm endorsement at this moment. Etched and bitten-in to her consciousness from the moment of that prophetic babbling had been the image of herself in love, singing, so Nellie had said, in a boy's key; eager to be allowed to give homage rather than receive it; eager to be allowed to love rather than permitting love with whatever ardency of welcome. And here was Peter repeating on general grounds exactly what she had found, and in especial was finding now, to be magically true.

"Since we both agree she is a witch," said he, "we ought surely to collect evidence against her. What was it she said to you, that something unknown to you, which you found to be true when she said it? I have evidence also; she said something to me last night which I didn't know, but which——"

What went through his brain at that moment, with the sureness of a surgeon's incision, was just that which Nellie had said when he told her that he was intending to ask Silvia to marry him. He had hedged that with the reservation that he would do so when he thought that he had a chance of success, and witch-like, with swift incontinent prophecy, she had told him that it was rather late already as regards to-night. The prophecy had been encouraging at the time, but not convincing. Now he suddenly felt himself convinced. Why or how—their conversation had only been about Nellie—he did not know. But it seemed that Nellie had penetrated where he had not....

There was his father sitting on the sofa beside Mrs. Wardour; there was his mother veiled and shrouded from him as she had ever been, doing something with a teapot, doing something with crumbs left on plates, for which she made some concoction, placed in the balcony outside, for birds.... Had he been alone with Silvia, he would have proposed to her, fortified with Nellie's encouragement, fortified even more by his present sense of its reliability, then and there. But unless he knelt on the floor to her, as he had found his father doing when he came in....

"Oh, what did Nellie say to you last night?" asked the girl. "Let's collect evidence, as you say."

"And have her burned outside St. Margaret's, instead of letting her marry Philip inside?" suggested Peter.

Silvia gave a parenthetic gasp.

"I suggested that she ought to be burned, too," she said. "More evidence, please."

Peter found her entrancing at that moment. There was some keen boyish kind of frank enthusiasm about her that attacked and challenged instead of merely provoking. She asked for no effort: you only had to allow yourself to be caught up.

"But it's your turn," he said. "You first suggested that Nellie told you things you didn't know."

"No; it was you who said that."

"It may have been; but it was you who suggested the witch-like quality. You said that she makes you see what she has seen. You know you did."

Silvia, ever so slightly, withdrew herself.

"Did I?" she asked.

"Of course you did. Now do be fair. You began, and therefore it's your turn to bring out the first piece of evidence. It was in Richmond Park, you know, and she told you something about yourself which you didn't know."

Peter put his hand in some judicial manner through that short crisp hair above his neck.

"I am prepared to hear your evidence," he said. "You're on oath. Get on, Miss Silvia. Don't keep the court waiting."

Silvia shot a chance arrow.

"If I promise to tell you," she said, "will you promise to tell me your evidence?"

Peter laughed.

"I think we're both better at cross-examination than at confession," he remarked.

"Oh, but that's no answer," she said.

"I know it isn't. It wasn't meant to be."

"Then be serious. Will you tell me your evidence against Nellie in her character of a witch?"

Peter, quite clearly, let his eyes rest on the other occupants of the room. One by one he looked at them.

"No!" he said. "I suppose the trial is adjourned owing to the inexplicable coyness of the witnesses. So there we are. Nellie will marry her Philip without a stain on her blessed character."

In his glance round the room Peter had observed that Mrs. Wardour was trying to catch Silvia's eyes. She would certainly succeed in doing so before long, and then, as her custom was, she would make some faint little clucking noises, like a hen that mildly wants to be let out. She was incapable of going away, however much she wanted to do so, unless Silvia took the initiative. She clucked, and then Silvia said that it was time to go....

But Peter did not want Silvia to go just yet; on the other hand, if they were all to sit here until the clucking became perceptible to Silvia, their visitors might just as well, for any practical purpose, go away at once. Besides, it was impossible to forget that Nellie last night had prophesied, and it had struck another as well as himself, that she was a reliable seer.

He got up rather slowly, rather tentatively, and fixed in his mind was the idea that Silvia would make some sort of initial step. It seemed to him that they were both hand in hand: it was just a question of who lifted a foot first....

Silvia did not turn her head to look at her mother. If she had, she would have been bound to attend to the cluckings; but what she wanted, more precisely what she needed, was to get away from a masked fire of elderly eyes and, with Peter of course, just to be natural. There was smouldering in this room some ember of supervision; she felt herself (and him) under a magnifying glass being looked at, being noted, being examined. It would answer her need perfectly well to go with him on to the balcony outside the room, to see if the evening was likely to be fine, to be sure that the motor was waiting.... Here, there was Mr. Mainwaring visualizing her portrait; worse than that, here was the more gimlet-like attention of his wife, who, ostensibly, was making a sloppy saucer of food for the London sparrows. Certainly she would sooner go out on the balcony alone than remain here, but when she thought of that it did not in the least satisfy her. After all, she did not want to "sit out" alone. What girl would want that? But she wanted to sit out.... There was no sort of embarrassment in her voice when she spoke to Peter.

"May we go down to your father's studio again?" she asked. "I haven't seen all I wanted to."

Surely his glance met hers with a comprehension that seemed immeasurably marvellous.

"Yes; do come down," he said.

The clucking became inarticulate.

"We ought to be going, Silvia," said her mother.

Peter took this up.

"Oh, you must give Miss Silvia five minutes, Mrs. Wardour," he said. "It's only fair that she should know the sort of thing that father's going to make of her."

Mr. Mainwaring gave a great shout of laughter.

"The impertinence of youth!" he cried. "Peter, I disown you. I would cut you off with a shilling if I had one!"

The two went down the stairs in silence. In silence also they came into the studio. The huge cartoon filled up one end of it; on the other three sides was the stacked débris from the attics; landscapes and portraits and sketches littered the tables.

"That's rather jolly," said Peter, pointing to one at random. "And, O Lord, my father has brought out a thing he did of me last year. Rather like a hair-dresser."

"Not a bit," said Silvia. "But it's very like you."

Peter wheeled about and faced her.

"Evidence!" he said. "Do you know what Nellie said to me last night? Of course you don't, but I'll tell you now. We were talking about you. She said—she encouraged me to think I had a chance——"

Silvia stood stock still, every fibre of her stiff and arrested.

"About you. A chance," said Peter again. "Is it true? Was she right? Was she being a witch?"

Silvia had been looking at him when this spell of stillness struck her. Now her eyelids fluttered and drooped, then once more she looked at him as steadily as before.

"All true," she said. "And Nellie told me something. She said that when I loved anybody, I—I should love just as I love now. Just as I love now, Peter."

CHAPTER VIII

Silvia was sitting in Mr. Mainwaring's studio one Saturday afternoon, waiting, without impatience, for the arrival from the Foreign Office of Peter, with whom she was motoring down to Howes, there to spend the Sunday. Silvia was perfectly capable of humour with regard to Howes, for she called it "the family seat." This indeed it was, since her father had bought the Norman ruin some twenty years ago, and quite unmistakably it belonged to the Wardours. He had made it habitable while Silvia was still a child, and during the war, when he became quite fabulously rich, he made it abominable also. To that period belonged the great picture gallery.

The gathering there for the week-end was, though small, a rather crucial one. It was to introduce to each other the families which would be brought into alliance over her wedding. Henry Wardour, Silvia's uncle on her father's side, was to be ponderously there, and his wife elegantly so. Then there was to be Aunt Joanna Darley, Mrs. Wardour's sister, and her husband. He, Sir Abel Darley, was a round pink profiteer, who in recognition of the considerable fortune he had made for himself by overcharging the Government for millions of yards of khaki, had been made a baronet, presumably in order to stop his mouth if he felt inclined to brag over the gullible Government. Then there was Mr. Mainwaring to represent Peter's side of the connection, but he was to sustain his part alone, since Mrs. Mainwaring, with an impregnable quietness of negation, had absolutely refused to take part in this reunion of families.

"You'll be eight without me, Silvia," she had said, "and eight's a very good number. I shall stop quietly in London and think of you all enjoying yourselves."

Silvia's sense of humour prevented her from forming any tragic anticipations about this party, though, as she would have been perfectly willing to confess, she did not suppose that the meeting of the clans would lead to any instinctive blood-brotherhood. But Peter would be there, and she would be there, and however outrageous and incompatible the rest of them proved themselves, they would be like the heathen "furiously raging together," but unable to disturb seriously the foundation fact of that. She trusted to her own sense of humour and to Peter's, to enable them both to be indifferent to what happened outside their own charmed corner. Uncle Henry and Uncle Abe, and Mr. Mainwaring and Peter would form a very curious company after dinner that night, when she and her mother and Aunt Joanna and Aunt Eleanor had left them to "punish" — as Uncle Henry would undoubtedly say — the 1870 port of which he was so inordinately fond, while the ladies would form an equally inconceivable committee upstairs. But since these things were to be, there was no use in imagining impossible situations. Somehow she conjectured that Mr. Mainwaring would impress himself more strongly on the circle downstairs than either of the uncles; he had more exuberance.

If Silvia had been set down to construct an incongruous party of eight, she could not by any fantastic selection have bettered this gathering. Aunt Joanna, for instance, nourished an ineradicable hatred towards her sister for having married Silvia's father, and for being so much richer than Sir Abe, and even Sir Abe's rank and her own were powerless to compensate her for this. Rich, immensely rich, Sir Abe certainly was, but she could not bear that her sister should be so much richer. Aunt Eleanor, on the other hand, Mrs. Wardour's sister-in-law, had only reverence for Mrs. Wardour's wealth, but what she thoroughly despised her for was her truckling (so Aunt Eleanor put it) to the smart world. Aunt Eleanor had been present at the great party, where the Russian ballet entertained the guests, and the presence of so many distinguished people made her feel perfectly sick. The true diagnosis of her indisposition, however, was that since she had tried to do for years without a particle of success what Mrs. Wardour had so brilliantly accomplished in a few weeks, it was only reasonable that she should have a violent reaction against that sort of thing. If, instead of marrying Peter, Silvia had been about to wed a peer, or somebody of that kind, Aunt Eleanor would certainly have felt it her duty never to speak to either her or her mother again. Indeed, she would never have accepted Mrs. Wardour's invitation at all, so she had made quite plain, unless she had felt it her duty to take an interest in her husband's relations.

Silvia was conscious of a vein of caricature in this flitting survey, but ridiculous people made caricatures of themselves without the collusion of the observer. Mr. Mainwaring was a caricature too: she could not think of him quite seriously. Probably most people, if you regarded them from a strictly individual standpoint, had a touch of caricature about them, for if you rated yourself as a normal person, everybody else must be a little out of drawing. But she looked at the caricatures with the friendliest amusement; she loved them (and here in particular was her mother included) for being so entirely different from her—for being, in fact, precisely what they were. Humorous observation was, with her, less a critical than an appreciative process, and now, as she waited for Peter, she wanted definitely to include Mrs. Mainwaring in her fascinating gallery. But for this last fortnight, since her engagement to Peter, she had found herself increasingly unable to give her this genial amused observation. More and more did Mrs. Mainwaring baffle and elude her. There was, so far as Silvia could notice, nothing humanly ridiculous about her, and, what was even more disconcerting, the girl found herself ever more incapable of attaching herself to her. To attempt to do that resembled, in some uncomfortable manner, the notion of attaching yourself in the dark to a hard smooth surface; you could nowhere get hold of her or find projection or crevice in which to crook or to insert a finger tip. The more closely Silvia looked at her, the more strenuously she attempted to get into any sort of psychical contact with Mrs. Mainwaring, the more directly was she baffled. She could not, for herself, give up as insoluble the mystery of that lady's mental and spiritual processes; there must be, if you could only lay your hands on it in the dark, some key to her future mother-in-law, something that explained, for instance, her unwearied study of the advertisements of hotels. No one could be as completely tranquil and emotionless all through as Mrs. Mainwaring appeared to be. Twice only had her mind slipped for a definite instant into the open, like a lizard emerging into the sunlight and flicking back again; once when, on the first visit that Silvia and her mother had paid to the house, Mrs. Mainwaring unveiled a glance of malicious hostility in the direction of the great cartoon. Less definite, but like in kind, was the habitual, though veiled, hostility with which Silvia felt that Mrs. Mainwaring regarded herself. It did not flame, but she knew that she was right in conjecturing that it incessantly smouldered. And that enmity, to Silvia's sense, was of the same quality, though smouldering, as that which had leaped in that swift little tongue of flame towards the cartoon: what puzzled her was the kinship between the two. From the context of that moment in the studio, it seemed to be Mr. Mainwaring's work which kept him in London (and her therefore with him) that had kindled that odd swift spark. Or was the origin of it a little deeper down than that? Did some shut furnace of impatience at her husband, so floridly symbolized there, some deep-seated core of incompatibility suddenly flame out then? If so, what was the kindred nature of her hostility to the girl? Was it that she was taking Peter away from the home which his presence there just rendered tolerable? But apart from those two "escapes," so to speak, of genuine feeling, the origin of which, after all, was only a matter of conjecture, Silvia had no clue to Mrs. Mainwaring at all; she was practically featureless and even without outline. She could not sketch her at all, or delineate from her as model, one of those genial caricatures, such as her friends so freely supplied her with material for. Such features and such outline as she could perceive were tinged with bitter suggestions....

Silvia did not find the waiting for Peter in any way tedious; there was plenty in the studio to furnish a larder for thought, though what most occupied her was her alert attention for the sound of his light footstep coming down the passage. But apart from that food for reflection was abundant. To-day the end of the studio where the cartoon had hung was empty, so that if Mrs. Mainwaring's resentment was inspired purely by that work of art, she might now regain her tranquillity again. Silvia would see it this evening, for her mother, following up the idea with which it had first fired her in connection with the empty walls of the picture gallery at Howes, had a few days ago made a purchase of it.

Mr. Mainwaring had been very glorious on this occasion; at first he had hysterically refused to part with it. It was his *chef-d'œuvre*, and while he had a couple of pennies in his pocket, he was, though poor, too proud to think of selling it. Then, lest that refusal should be taken too seriously, he almost immediately declared that it should be his wedding present to Silvia. He let himself be hunted out of so untenable a magnificence, and finally he so far humiliated himself as to accept a fancy price for it. As Mrs. Wardour knew (he reminded her, to make certain) that it was the first of a series of six, upon which he was contented to stand or fall in the verdict of posterity, it seemed probable that, at some future time, the walls of the picture gallery at Howes would be far less empty than they were to-day.

On an easel near where Silvia sat was the portrait of herself now approaching completion. To her there was something uncanny and arresting about it, for, by accident or design, the artist had caught some aspect of her which secretly she recognized as a piece of intimate revelation. She herself inclined to an accidental derivation, for certainly in all but one point it was a flamboyant and uninspired performance, a chronicle of a green "jumper" and a scarlet skirt, a haystack of dyed hair, and a rouged, simpering mouth. Her head was turned full to the spectator, looking over the shoulder, in precisely the same pose (a favourite trick of the artist's) as that in which the German Emperor listened to Satanic counsels. But in the eyes, in the badly drawn outstretched hand, clumsily posed, Silvia saw some unconscious rendering of the "boy's key." She acquitted Mr. Mainwaring of all intention and of all inspiration; he had certainly not meant that. He had, through faulty drawing, given a certain brisk violence to her hand, a certain domination to her eyes.

And then she heard the click of the street door, and the quick light footstep for which she had been waiting. She wondered if she could ever get used to the mere fact of Peter's return from however short an absence.

He kissed her, holding her hand for a moment.

"It's too bad of me to have kept you waiting," he said. "I couldn't help myself. There was a messenger starting for Rome. Haven't they brought you tea?"

"No; I thought I would wait and have it with you."

Peter rang the bell.

"And my father's gone?" he asked.

"Yes; mother called for him and drove him down. I've brought my little Cording car for us."

"Just you and me? That'll be lovely," said Peter. "Do I quite trust your driving, though?"

"You may drive yourself, if you like," said she.

"No, thanks; I trust that far less. I must see if my bag is packed. Tell Burrows we want tea at once."

"Can't I help you to pack it, if it isn't done?" asked Silvia.... Somehow she would have liked to do that, to fold his clothes, to squeeze out his sponge.

"No; it's so sordid," said Peter. "Besides, it's probably done already."

"If it isn't, call me," said she. "No man has any idea of how to pack."

"And you want to teach me?" asked Peter, lingering on the stairs.

Silvia hesitated only for a moment.

"No, you darling," she said. "I don't want to teach you anything. I just want to do it."

"Why?" asked he.

She came closer, raising her face towards him, as he leaned over the banisters.

"Your things," she said. "Your sponge, your coat...."

That pleasure was denied her, for Burrows had already bestowed Peter's requirements in his bag, and he came downstairs again. Silvia had given his father a sitting for the portrait this morning, and he stood frowning in front of it.

"Trash! Rubbish!" he said at length. "And the worst of it is that he has got into it some infernal resemblance to you. It's a caricature."

"Oh, we're all caricatures to each other," said she, "with just a few exceptions."

"What a heathenish doctrine. Why am I a caricature, for instance?"

"You aren't. You're one of the exceptions. But tell me what your father has caricatured of me in that?"

Peter looked from her to the portrait and back again.

"All of you," he said. "The reality of you: the rest is quite unlike. You haven't got mouth and nose and forehead and hair and chin the least like that. But the person inside is horribly like you."

Silvia put her arm through his.

"Horribly?" she said. "Thanks so much."

"I didn't say—just then—that you were horrible," said he. "I said horribly like you, your parody, your caricature. I wonder how I dared ask such a masterful young woman to marry me."

"You knew it would be good for you," said Silvia. "It was far more daring of me to accept you."

"There's just time for you to remedy your mistake," said he. "Positively the last chance."

This frank kind of chaffing talk, as between friends rather than lovers, had grown to be characteristic of their privacy. Silvia delighted in it: it had the charm of some cipher about it; the blunt commonplace words held for her a secret meaning known to the two utterers of them, which was only to be expressed by these symbols. When she feigned to misunderstand Peter, and thanked him for calling her horrible, there lay below her foolish words a treasure which words were quite powerless to express. Or when he just now wondered that he had dared to ask her to marry him, she felt that he conveyed something which no amount of impassioned speech could have indicated so well. From the hilltops there flashed the signal that no voice could convey. Then sometimes, as now, she had to use another symbol, which again was only a symbol, and with her hands tremblingly, eagerly, shyly clasping him round the neck, she drew his head down towards her, not kissing him, but simply looking close into his eyes.

"Positively the last chance!" she said. "Oh, Peter, what a fool I am about you. Doesn't it bore you frightfully?"

"Frightfully," said Peter, keeping to the first code of symbols.

"You bear it beautifully, darling," she said. "Oh, shall I ever get used to you? I hope so: I mustn't go on being such a donkey all my days. No; I don't think I do hope so. Being a donkey is good enough for me. Hee haw! Oh, let go: here's Burrows coming with the tea. She'll think it so undignified."

It was, as a matter of fact, she who had to "let go," as Burrows entered, followed by Mrs. Mainwaring. Silvia had before now tried to call her "mother," but the experiment somehow had not succeeded. Mrs. Mainwaring answered to it quite readily, but she received it, so the girl thought, much as she might have received an unsolicited nickname.

"Why, Mrs. Mainwaring!" she said. "I didn't know you were in."

Mrs. Mainwaring paused just long enough to let it be inferred that if Silvia had made any inquiries as to that, she would have obtained the information she sought.

"Yes, dear, I have been reading upstairs since lunch time," she said. "I came to have a cup of tea with you before you started. I hope you will have a pleasant drive."

Silvia tried to approach.

"Ah, do come too," she said. "Change your mind, and come with me. Heaps of room."

"Thank you, dear, I think I will keep to my original plan," said she. "I like a quiet Sunday sometimes. I shall go to church, and perhaps in the afternoon hear a concert at the Queen's Hall. The time will pass very pleasantly."

There was an aura of correct armed neutrality about this, accompanied as it was by that cold sheathed glance, furtive and hostile, that caused some half-comic, half-impatient despair in the girl at her aloofness. Mrs. Mainwaring, so it seemed to her, wanted nobody except herself; she wanted just to be let alone.

"Father went off all right?" asked Peter.

"Yes; Mrs. Wardour kindly called for him after lunch. A beautiful car; so roomy. There was another lady and gentleman there: I think Mrs. Wardour said it was her sister and her husband. Your father insisted on going in the box seat with the driver. He made a great noise with the motor horn, which sounded like a bugle. He was in very high spirits."

The neutrality exhibited in this speech was almost too correct to be credible. Nobody could have been so neutral. Even Mrs. Mainwaring could not quite keep it up, and something very far from neutral lay, ever so little below the surface, in her announcement of her husband's high spirits. Her neutrality towards Silvia was not so deadly as that towards her husband....

Peter laughed. There was neutrality there too, but it was more contemptuous than deadly, and quite good humoured in its contempt.

"Oh, they'll have a noisy drive," he said. "And if Mrs. Wardour drives him back on Monday, you'll be aware of their approach, mother, while they're still a mile or two away."

Mrs. Mainwaring had one of those fine-lipped mouths (very neat and finished at the outer corners), about which it is impossible to say whether they are smiling or not without consulting the conditions prevailing round the eyes. But as Peter spoke she very definitely ceased to smile.

"Monday?" she said. "I thought Mrs. Wardour was so kind as to ask him to stop till Tuesday."

Peter got up: he noticed nothing about his mother, having long ago given up any attempt to comprehend her.

"Tuesday, is it?" he said. "I'm back on Monday, anyhow: otherwise what would happen to our foreign relations? Shall we start, Silvia? I'm ready when you are."

Mrs. Mainwaring rose too.

"Yes, indeed, you had better be off," she said. "You won't have too much time. Then I shall expect you on Monday, Peter. Tell your father——"

She stopped.

"That you don't expect him till Tuesday?" asked he, without the slightest indication of any mental comment.

"Yes, I think Mrs. Wardour quite took for granted that he was stopping till then."

Silvia made one further attempt to evoke a touch of cordiality.

"Mother will be delighted," she said. "But it's horrid for you being all alone."

"No, dear, I shall be very happy," said Mrs. Mainwaring with quiet decision.

Howes stood, of course, in a park of considerable acreage, surrounded by a massive brick wall, and reflected its colossal self in the lake that lay below its terraced garden. This lake had been artificially made by the damming up of the stream that had previously wasted itself unornamentally, and the road that had dipped into the shallow valley now ran along the causeway that formed the farther margin of the lake, and gave the visitor his first complete and stupendous view of the house. The wings and galleries that had been built out rendered the original Norman core comparatively insignificant, and the whole resembled an apotheosis of a station hotel combined with a fortress, for the character of the older part was borne out in the battlemented walls that spread so amply to right and left of it. An avenue of monkey-puzzlers led up to the long façade, and the gardens overlooking the lake were like some glorified arboretum, where you might expect tin labels, asking visitors to keep off the grass and not touch the flowers. At intervals along the edge of its immense lawns were aloes in square green tubs, and below the house was a riband border of geraniums, calceolarias and lobelias. Inside, the expectations aroused by this sumptuous exterior were fully justified, for the high panelled hall was peopled with suits of armour, each with its numbered label, so that a glance at the catalogue would put you into possession of interesting information about it. Armour had long been a hobby of the late Mr. Wardour, and he had, very quaintly, installed electric light in the gauntleted hands. There was a passenger lift in one corner, a groined roof, and the famous malachite table. Heads and antlers of stags hung in the panels.

Silvia had rather dreaded this moment. The whole place with its monkey-puzzlers and malachite, its aloes and its awfulness, had been left by her father to her absolutely, and Peter knew (and she knew he knew) that he was making his first acquaintance with what would be "home" to him. She had not seen it herself since the day of her father's funeral, two years ago, and it seemed to her—and how would it strike Peter?—that, though it had the traditional quality of home, in that there was no place, as far as she was aware, in the least like it, its unique fulfilment of that definition was its only merit.

With a sideways glance now and again she had observed Peter's growing awe, from the time they had crossed the causeway (the pride of it!) to their approach through the monkey-puzzlers, and to the final revelation of the malachite table. And there was much more to follow—ever so much more; the Gothic staircase, the blue drawing-room, the pink drawing-room, the picture-gallery, the swimming bath. And it was not inanimate magnificence alone that was to assail him, for there was Uncle Henry and Uncle Abe and

Aunts Joanna and Eleanor. She ought to have brought him down quietly and alone for his first sight of Howes....

Peter had been gazing in a fascinated manner at the malachite table, and even while Silvia was wondering how to convey to him her sympathy and encouragement, he, with one of the flashes of intuition which she adored in him, showed that he had comprehended with unerring accuracy what she was feeling about him.

"But you're going to be here," he said, just as if she had spoken out all that she was puzzling over.

She took his arm.

"Oh, my dear, I promise you that," she said. "And I've got to get used to it, too. But then you'll be here! Shall we butter each other's paws, Peter, until we feel at home? Let's have some more tea, in fact, and find where the rest of them are."

The picture-gallery seemed a likely kind of place, and there, indeed, the six representatives of the families proved to be, and when kissing ceremonies were over for herself and the rite of introduction for Peter, Silvia found herself thinking that it was really all for the best that they should have burst on Peter in one comprehensive revelation rather than that he should have been subjected to a series of shocks and surprises. Already staggered by Uncle Henry, Peter might have been quite thrown off his balance—so flashed the alternative comedy through her head—by Uncle Abe; or what if, reeling from Aunt Eleanor, he ran into Aunt Joanna just round the corner? Silvia had not the smallest inclination or intention to be ashamed of her relations, but it would have shown the joylessness of a Puritan not to be amused at the blandness and the blankness on so many faces (Peter's included) as he was taken to each in turn; it would have shown too an almost dangerous rigidity that her voice should not betray a tremor of suppressed hilariousness.

Aunt Eleanor came first: she looked like a handsome seal with adenoidal breathing. She bowed to Peter with freezing propriety, but when he was moved on to Aunt Joanna her curiosity got the better of her, and she instantly put up her glasses to get a better look at him. Aunt Joanna, large and marvellously bedizened, with flowers in her hat and her bosom and her hand, irresistibly suggested a van going to Covent Garden in the early morning: she, too, had her notions of propriety, and these expressed themselves in a cordiality as warm as Aunt Eleanor's was cold. Then came Uncle Abe, who was so like a fish that it really seemed dangerous for him to be sitting so near Aunt Eleanor. He held out a hand, and took a cigar out of his mouth, which remained open in the precise shape of the cigar: and finally came Uncle Henry, who was busy with "a drop of brandy," because tea, as he instantly proceeded to inform Peter, gave him heartburn. Then all four of them stared at Peter to see how he was going to comport himself.

Peter was never more grateful to his father than when at this embarrassing moment Mr. Mainwaring, who had been mysteriously employed at the far end of the picture-gallery with a cord and a sheet and a step-ladder and three bewildered footmen, gave a loud yodel, set to some words like *mio figlio*, to announce his perception of his son's arrival, and the accomplishment of that on which he had been so busily engaged. "*Ben arrivato*" was the concluding stave of his melody, and he came running up the gallery (there was quite enough space to enable him to get a good speed up), and after holding Peter for a moment in a joint embrace with Silvia, he cast himself down for a moment on a white bear skin at Mrs. Wardour's feet.

"*Ecco!*" he said. "Ladies and gentlemen, when you will distinguish me with the gift of a moment of your leisure, I shall have the honour to show you the first of my completed labours. The picture, the poor suppliant's picture, is on the wall: masked by a fair linen sheet, which, so I fondly hope, is in control of a cord, just a cord, which, when you are ready, I will, in fact, pull. Unless the mechanism which I have been contriving is sadly at fault, there will then be revealed to you that which the sheet, at the moment, is so discreetly veiling. Valour, perhaps, my valour, is but the worse part of discretion"—Peter had heard this before—"but for the moment I am less discreet than valorous. I will show you, complete and materialized, the vision that since August, 1914, has obsessed and dominated my life. I pray you, gentle sirs and madams, to indulge your humble servant, and to take your places, exactly where I shall have the honour to indicate, opposite the discretionary linen which, when removed, will unbare my valour."

He rose from his reclining posture, and after a superb obeisance, placed himself at the head of the procession. Already, as Silvia had foreseen, he was in a position of dominance: Uncle Abe and Uncle Henry obeyed his orders; Aunt Joanna and Aunt Eleanor clearly "perked up" at this ingratiating suppliance. For himself he took Mrs. Wardour's hand, holding it high, as in a minuet, and led the way. He grouped them; he requested them all, with humble apologies, to have the goodness to move a step backwards; he set chairs for them; he put his finger on his lips, and on tiptoe advanced to the dangling end of the cord and pulled it. Up flew the sheet, waving wildly, but eventually festooning itself clear of the cartoon. Then, swiftly retreating, he magnificently posed himself, and gazed at the picture.

For the moment there was dead silence: then vague clickings and murmurs began to grow articulate. The uncles and aunts vied with each other in perception.

"The Emperor," said Uncle Henry. "Good likeness, eh?"

"August, 1914," exclaimed Lady Darley. "Terrible! Wonderful!" And she drew in her breath with a hissing sound. The perception of the date was not so clever, as it was largely inscribed on the frame, and Aunt Eleanor smiled indulgently.

"Yes, dear Joanna," she said, "we all see that. But look at Satan whispering to the Emperor!"

"And the hosts of hell," said Joanna swiftly.

Uncle Abe turned to Uncle Henry.

"A marvellous thing," he said. "Tells its own story. I call that a picture."

Mrs. Wardour merely wore the pleased air of proprietorship. She had seen it all before, and she could see it again as many times as she chose. Mr. Mainwaring, chin in hand, just contemplated while these appreciations were in progress, but now he seemed to wake out of a swoon, and passed his hands over his eyes.

"Was it I who painted that?" he muttered. "I didn't know what I was doing. I didn't know till this moment, when at last I see my work properly displayed, with no discordant note to mar it, what I had done. Does it terrify you, dear ladies and gentlemen? Does it put you in possession of August, 1914? Does it—ah, *Dio mio!*" He covered his face with his hands and shuddered. Then advancing to the picture again, he violently shook the cord, and the two linen sheets (double bed) rolled back into their original places.

"Enough, enough!" he cried. "We will contemplate it more calmly when we have recovered from the first shock of our bleeding hearts. Let us converse, let us smile and laugh again. Let us remember that the war is over. But it is laid on me by destiny to execute five more such pictures, not less terrible. If I live, they shall be done. Yes, yes; I do not falter! But, for a while, let me forget, let me forget."

Mrs. Wardour spaced out the wall with a pleased eye.

"They will just fill the length of the gallery," she said, "if we do not crowd them. Silvia, my dear, you must persuade Mr. Mainwaring.... Well, I'm sure, if that isn't the dressing bell."

A vindictive purpose was weaving itself below the embowering flowers of Lady Darley's hat, and accelerating the heart-beat below the nosegay on her bosom, so that the gardenias were all of a tremble. Lucy might be rich (indeed, it was quite certain that she was horribly rich), but comparative paupers such as herself were not to be altogether trampled upon, and other people beside Lucy had picture-galleries. Apparently the series of these tremendous allegories was not yet painted, was not yet either definitely "bespoken" by her sister, and Joanna, as she waded through the thick Kidderminster rugs that carpeted the Gothic staircase on the way to her room, felt that the only thing in life that was worth living for at this moment was to order a replica of the first, and secure (with an embargo on replicas) the remainder of this series.

Never in her life had she been so artistically overwhelmed as by that prodigious canvas, and if all the rest were going to be "up to sample" she could, as their possessor, scoff at the art treasures of the world. Sir Abe had dabbled in pictures already: he had a Turner sunset which hung in the dining-room, at which he often pointed over his shoulder as a "pooty little thing"; he had a Rembrandt of a very puckered-looking old woman which had aroused the envy of those who were permitted to see it and to be told that it came out of the Marquis of Brentford's collection. These were desirable possessions, but they were jejune compared to Mr. Mainwaring's masterpiece and the masterpieces that were to follow. The war! That was something to paint pictures about....

Her envy of her sister rose to the austerity of a passion when she contemplated the equipment of her bedroom, and that of her husband next door. There was a bathroom attached to each, both fitted with the most amazing taps and squirts, and a little sitting-room attached to each, and a lift of which Mrs. Wardour (showing her her room, and hoping she would be comfortable) explained the working. You pressed a button and were wafted.... The same lift served Aunt Eleanor's rooms, but Lucy and Peter and Silvia used another one.... The lift clinched her resolution, and she conjugally conferred with Sir Abe. He, to her delight, was as much impressed with the passion for "scoring off" Lucy as with the merits of the cartoon, but his business habits had to make hesitations and conditions, not "do a deal" blindly.

"Well, my lady," he said, "you shall have the pictures if they're to be obtained reasonably. What shall I offer, now? Most striking that one was, and that and similar are worth paying a pretty penny for. What did your sister give for that one? Then, if reasonable, I don't mind if I add twenty-five per cent. more, and secure the lot. They'll be something to point at. Get along and let me have my bath. You try to find out what your sister paid, and then we'll know where we are, my lady."

She noted with pleasure that he relapsed into a cockney accent and a slight uncertainty about aspirates as he spoke. That was a good sign: it showed he was in earnest and interested, for in dalliance of light conversation Sir Abe was "as good at his h's" as anybody.

It was not to be expected that the cartoon and the magnificence of its introduction should have no effect on Aunt Eleanor, or that (her general animosity towards Mrs. Wardour being of the same fine order as Aunt Joanna's) she should not have been kindled with ambition to bring off some similar vindictive stroke. But for her the acquisition of these immense decorations was out of the question, for her husband would certainly not pay such a price as she felt sure would be necessary to secure them, and even if he did his house did not contain sufficient uninterrupted wall space, so that to hang them at all she would have to cut them up into sections and paper several different rooms with them. But Mr. Mainwaring had said something about the original sketches for them, which had suggested an idea that took her fancy at once. The sketches were, after all, the "originals," the significant buds from which these over-blown blossoms had developed, and the sketches would be far more manageable, both from point of view of hanging, and from that of purchase. There was a subtlety, a refinement in possessing "originals" that these acreages of paint could not compete with. Her powerful imagination pictured herself exhibiting them to envious friends.

"Yes, my sister-in-law, I believe, has copies, on a large scale," she would say, "of my series. These, of course, are the originals. Such freshness, such power, all quite lost in the later and larger version." And she held her seal-like head very high, and snorted through her nostrils as she sailed into the pink drawing-room just before the dinner bell rang. She was the first to come down, and had time to examine with pain and disgust the photograph of a royal personage, with a crown on its frame, that stood very conspicuously alone on the table by the sofa where she seated herself.

Mr. Mainwaring's star continued to be violently ascendant all evening. His harangues, his humour, his habit of pausing in the middle of one of his interminable stories, until complete silence had been established round the table, dominated dinner, and when the ladies rose to leave the gentlemen to their cigars and wine, Mrs. Wardour addressed him directly and laid upon him not to permit them too long a sitting. This gave him the rank of host, and developed his social horse-power to so high an efficiency that on rejoining the ladies he sang the Toreador's song out of *Carmen*. Then after that had been repeated he permitted the uncles and aunts to indulge themselves with bridge, and since wives partnered their own husbands, this gave scope for some pleasant family revilings, in which the ladies came off far the best. Having thus arranged for their pleasure, Mr. Mainwaring grouped himself with his hostess, Silvia and Peter, and grew patriarchal and full of sentiment over the charming family party of parents and children. On Mrs. Wardour's going to bed, leaving the bridge-party jealously over-calling their hands, he conducted her once more to pay homage to the cartoon, and remained there in meditation.

Silvia and Peter had wandered out on to the dusky terrace. A twilight of stars lit the still night, and she drew long breaths of restoration from the exhaustion of these stupendous hours. Once clear of the house, and leaning over the balustrade above the lake, she gave way to hopeless laughter.

"Peter, darling, are my relations more than you ought to be asked to stand?" she said. "Did you know there were such people as Uncle Abe?"

"Did you know there were such people as my father?" said Peter.

"Oh, but he's your father," said Silvia quickly. "You mustn't bring him in."

"Why not? After all, it's he who brings himself in. There's only one word for him. Bounder. Uncle Abe isn't a bounder exactly. Uncle Henry isn't a bounder."

"No, he's just a cad," said Silvia enthusiastically. "I love people being themselves, whatever they happen to be. I should enjoy them much more, though, if you weren't here."

"I can go to-morrow morning," said Peter.

For one moment she thought that he spoke seriously: the next she laughed at herself for having been hoaxed by his assumed sincerity of voice: "assumed" it just had to be.

"Ah, you said that beautifully," she announced; "and all the evening, do you know, you've been saying things beautifully, with your mask on, too, your best and smartest mask. I've been listening to you, and never for a moment could I catch a word or a silence on your part to show that you weren't thoroughly amused and interested by the aunts. You behaved as if they were just the sort of people you were accustomed to meet, but rather more charming. You have been convincing, and you were convincing just now when you suggested going away to-morrow."

Peter had not, of course, meant to convey that he really could go away to-morrow, but it had been quite easy for him to render his seriousness plausible, since, though impossible, this was a most agreeable project. But what rendered that project so attractive was the escape not from the aunts and uncles, with whom he was quite as willing to be diverted as their niece, but from his father. His father, in this *milieu*, with his bounce and his bounding, his general "make-up" of the large-souled, childlike artist, now humbly bespeaking the indulgence of his patrons, and immediately afterwards behaving as if he was Michael Angelo, was intolerable. His gaiety, his singing, his family grouping, with himself as aged and contemplative parent, while the moment before he had been twirling his moustaches and bellowing out the song of the toreador, were indecencies for a son's eye. If only he had been slightly fuzzy and intoxicated with many liqueur brandies like Uncle Henry, that would have been a palliative: as it was he was only intoxicated with himself....

Peter recalled himself from these impious meditations to the needs of or (if not the needs) the appropriateness for the immediate occasion. Silvia and he had contrived a lovers' interlude under the stars.

"Will you always be as charitable to me as you are to my father?" he asked. "When I am absurd and annoying, will you just be amused?"

The question seemed to him well framed: it led him and her away from all these nonsensicalities into the region where the simple things abided. He expected some pressure on his arm, some little deprecation of his silliness, some whisper to inform him that he was a goose or an idiot. Instead, Silvia's hand slackened in the crook of his arm and withdrew itself.

"Oh, Peter, what a thing to ask!" she said. "As if I could be 'charitable' to you as long as you loved me, or as if I could find you annoying so long as I loved you. You're pretending not to understand. Don't pretend like that any more."

Peter's quick brain was alert on the scent. He had meant his words to be construed into a lover-like speech, and had completely thought that they could be interpreted thus. But her answer convinced him that to her they were not construable at all, but only gibberish. Before he could emend himself, or even quite follow her, she flashed out her full meaning.

"Anybody else in the world except you can be annoying," she said, "and I hope I can be charitable to anybody else in the world except you. But how can I be charitable to you? Or how can you be trying to me? Don't you know that I *am* you? For a month I've ceased to be myself at all. There isn't any 'me.' It isn't 'me' you think you are in love with; it's—it's just the completion of your own wonderfulness. And as for their being any 'you,' why, you've ceased long ago. I've absorbed you. I've—I've drowned you in myself and in my adoration. I'm round you. I crush you and I worship you— —"

Silvia broke off suddenly as there appeared at the drawing-room window a black tall silhouette yodelling and crying, "Coo-ee. Children!"

"Oh, damn that man," said she. "Sorry, Peter, but, well, there it is."

CHAPTER IX

Peter was sitting (so superbly that it might have been called lying) on a long dream-provoking chair set outside the south façade at Howes. For the moment he was alone, and he surprised himself with the unbidden thought of how seldom he had been alone during the last fortnight—since the day of the wedding, which had taken place in the unfashionable early days of September. This constant companionship of Silvia, their motor drives, their golf, their fishing in the lake, their long sittings with books or newspapers of which but little was read, had seemed to him as he looked back on them (conglomerated and coagulated, like little drops of mercury running together to form a globular brightness) to have been wholly delightful and satisfying. These days had been for him, in fact, a soft luminous revelation of how completely pleasant days could be. Without a touch of complacency he could not help knowing how every word and every whim of his had seemed adorable to Silvia, and he knew that, search as he might (he did not propose to search at all), he would be able to find no movement or mood of hers that he could have corrected or rectified. She had taken possession of him tenderly, and, as if with held breath, watched, beautifully bright-eyed, to discover and anticipate the moods of his desires; and in answer he had given her not acquiescence alone, but the eager consent of every fibre of his being. It seemed perfect that she should be like that.

Silvia had just left him to meet her mother, who, at the expiration of their uninterrupted fortnight, was coming down to Howes that day; and Peter, alone for an hour on this September afternoon, let the hot sunshine, fructifying and caressing, melt the marrow of his bones, the impressed records on his brain, into definite consciousness. The bees humming over the flower-beds, the red-admiral butterflies opening and shutting their vermilion streaked wings, the swallows not yet gathering for their autumn departure, all conduced to leisurely summer-like meditation, and he found himself in possession of propositions and conclusions which he had scarcely known were his. This supreme sense of content came first; that, like a wash of warm colour, underlay the details that now began with a finer brushwork to outline themselves, and each of them appeared equally admirable, equally germane to the values of the emerging picture.

Mrs. Wardour's arrival was an important touch; it might almost be called a fresh wash of colour. Out of numerous reflections, considerations, weighings of this and that, each of them at the time too liquid and inconclusive to call a plan, a plan now had certainly crystallized. They, the three contributory contrivers of it, had, so to speak, pooled the London house and this, making two houses for the three of them. Peter would be returning to his work in Whitehall next day, and since no sane being would wish to remain in London in these mellow radiances of September and October for longer than was absolutely necessary, he would, as a rule, flow up in the swiftest of cars in the morning, and stream back again in the late afternoon. For one reason or another, again, he might find himself wanting or being obliged to spend a night in town; he would be away all day, anyhow, and what could be more convenient than Mrs. Wardour's perfect willingness to establish herself for the present at Howes, where she would supply companionship for Silvia, and find it herself? Silvia again might want to spend a day or two in town, and her mother could please herself as to whether she joined her or not. From such a germ the idea of keeping both houses pooled and permanently open for any or all of them had easily developed. Headquarters for the present would be in the country, and London, to Mrs. Wardour's notion, would be something of a picnic, with the house half shut up. But with four or five servants there, there would, she hoped, be no angles of real discomfort.

Mrs. Wardour then, to all intents and purposes, was to live with them; but Peter, so ran the deed, was "master" at Howes; while in London he and Silvia would have the wide licence of guests peculiarly privileged, at liberty to ask friends there whenever they wished. The crystallization of it, the definite statement and treaty, after infinite probings and testings on her part into Peter's most intimate feelings on the subject, had been entirely Silvia's. It had been she who had finally suggested it, with the proviso that anybody—by which she undoubtedly meant her husband—was to tear up the treaty without any possibility of offence, if he found it unworkable or unsatisfactory; but, as he thought over it now, he was frankly surprised at himself to find how eminently satisfactory a fulfilment of it he augured. Silvia had suggested it (there was the great point), and though he felt that he could not himself have conceivably presented a treaty like that to her for her signature, he applauded her insight in so doing. A man could hardly have suggested that to the girl he had but lately married; it would have savoured, would it not, of his considering that the ideal arrangement did not procure for them their own undiluted companionship? But she had known that he would not put such a construction on her proposition. She did not, in fact, let an attitude which would have been typically feminine deter her from adopting this more sensible and more manly pose. But that was Silvia all through: there was a robust quality about her, an impotence to harbour littlenesses....

They expected another visitor that day in the person of Peter's father, who had, in a letter which was no less than a bouquet of flowering eloquence, indicated that for the due, the supreme, the sublime execution of the second cartoon, it was necessary for the artist to soak himself once more in the contemplation of the first, so as (this was rather involved) to catch to the fraction of a tone the key in which it was pitched. There had to be a gradual crescendo, a deliberate tuning up and up, a continual ascent throughout the series.... Shorn of the mixture of metaphor, he wanted to study the first cartoon before plunging, with the aid of his sketches, into the remainder. These sketches, he added, were, as soon as he had finished with their use, to pass out of his possession, for the charming Mrs. Henry Wardour had induced him to let her purchase them at a figure which convinced him that they would find an appreciative home.... Then the letter became slightly mysterious. The projected series of cartoons, he had reason to know, was exciting stupendous interest in artistic circles. Flattering—perhaps a man who was proud of his work ought not to say flattering—evidence of that was to hand, evidence substantial and conclusive. He had not made— this was lucky, since he would not have dreamed of going back on his bargain—he had not made any contract with Mrs. Wardour—to whom all salutations—about the rest of the series, and thought himself fortunate in not parting with them for a comparative pittance. He did not (mark you, my Peter) complain of the price she had paid him for the first of them, and he was quite sure that, with Peter's assistance, everything would be arranged quite satisfactorily.

Peter had read this letter, which he must talk over with Silvia on her return, with the detachment of which he was so terribly capable, and had come to the conclusion that his father had somehow induced a deluded Crœsus of some sort to offer a higher price per cartoon for his future perpetrations than that which his mother-in-law had, no doubt, already given him for the first. For this deduction he had the most cordial welcome. As long as his father was dumping his "beastly" goods—so Peter was now at liberty to think—on the picture-gallery at Howes for fancy, if not fantastic prices, he could not in mere pious decency put it to Mrs. Wardour that she was paying, as he supposed, heavily, for colossal rubbish. But his father's letter, maturely considered, made it quite certain that somebody was willing to pay more for rubbish than Mrs. Wardour. Already the general question had received his attention: Mrs. Wardour was, so he supposed, under contract to buy those melodramatic daubs for the decoration of a house that belonged to Silvia, and of which he, by attested treaty, was master. So long as his father could profitably dispose of this rubbish here, Peter was filially prohibited from any protest, but when once his father announced that he was receiving a mere pittance, though without complaint, for what he would in another market receive a less despicable dole, his son, surely, was free to welcome his taking his wares elsewhere. His son, in any case, was heart and soul allied to the new enterprise, for already Peter had experienced a vivid distaste of the fact that he countenanced, by mere acquiescence, this further decoration of Howes. He knew that if the artist had not been his father he must have already protested against the bargain which perhaps was not yet complete on either side. His acquiescence, in fact, had brought home to him that his father was profiting by his marriage....

Then, so swiftly and involuntarily that he had not time to stop the thought on the threshold, there burst into the door of his mind the inquiry as to whether he, too, as well as his father, was not unloading rubbish at a high price. And the price that he, Peter, was receiving for his rubbish was infinitely the higher. His father received, no doubt, a substantial cheque; he himself received, as far as the material consideration went, an immunity from the meaning of cheques, and, in a standard immeasurably higher, some sort of blank cheque which, as Silvia told him one night (or was in the middle of telling him when his father made that flamboyant interruption), would be honoured by her to any figure he chose to fill in, and yet leave her richer, in such standard, than ever. There, in that immortal bank, he divined then, and knew now her illimitable credit. Whatever she paid out, by that, in the royal mathematics of love, was she the richer.

The impression made by that unsolicited thought was to him like having seen some pass-book of the soul which was hers. It had blown open in front of his eyes, and before he had, so to speak, time to close it, he had caught a glimpse of sums so vast that they exceeded his powers of realization. His eye, in that involuntary survey, had received no impression of *his* payments into her account; the credit side was but a catalogue of her own inconceivable affluence. Every moment, it seemed, she was giving, and every moment her bounty flowed back to her. It was with some kind of sceptical envy that, in that glimpse, he realized this omnipotent finance. It was not so marvellous that love should be stronger than death; the miracle was that it could be so much stronger than life.

It was at this moment in Peter's reflections, a moment that, only half realized, he was glad to get away from, that an interruption, reasonably claiming his attention, occurred in the shape of a little old butler, who had been drafted down here from London in view of Mrs. Wardour's advent. He was black-eyed and grey-headed, and "perky" in movement to an extent that fully justified Peter's exclamation of "The Jackdaw," when he had quitted the scene last night, and now the Jackdaw's immediate mission was to hand Peter a couple of letters on an immense silver salver, and inquire where Mr. Mainwaring, who, so the Jackdaw understood, was to arrive that evening, should be "put." He should be "put" clearly, in the place that would please him most, for this was Peter's undeviating creed when self-sacrifice was not involved, and beyond doubt the state-rooms, so called, would please his father inordinately.

The state-rooms had been insisted on in the rebuilding of the house by his father-in-law, in a rich vision, so Silvia had half piously, half humorously intimated, of royal personages being sumptuously housed there. There was a tremendous tapestried bedroom, *en suite* with a second bedroom, a breakfast-room, a sitting-room, all tapestry and oak mantelpieces and silver sconces. Yes, the state-rooms for Mr. Mainwaring. Silvia (they were on humorous terms now about Peter's father) would enjoy that immensely.

Peter took his letters from the Jackdaw, as the latter gave a pleasant sort of croak in answer to this order, and remembered how Nellie had once said that wealth was not an accident, but an attribute, a quality. He had been disposed to dispute that at the time, but somehow his own allocation of the state-rooms to his father confirmed the suspicion that she was right. He himself, for instance, was clearly a different person in the eyes of his father now, when he could gloriously endow him with state-rooms, from what he had been when he, as on that same occasion he told Nellie, only lived in the beastly little house off the Brompton Road because free meals and free lodging were a consideration to his exiguous purse. You were different— Nellie was right—when you could dispense material magnificence instead of accepting a tolerable shelter, where, though the rain was kept out, the odour of dinner, with that careless Burrows, could not be kept in.

Still fingering his letters, and trying to insert a thumb into a too honestly adhesive envelope flap, Peter slightly amplified by corrobative illustration this thesis. How often had he, so to speak, "sung for his dinner," accepting and welcoming such invitations as Mrs. Trentham extended to him, by which, for the pleasure of comfortable, decent food, he had gladly spent an insincere and boring evening! It had not quite been greed combined with moderate penuriousness which had enjoined that: it was the natural thing to do, if you were young and poor; to dine, that is to say, comfortably, and by way of acknowledging your indebtedness, to be towed about for the rest of the evening by a foolish, married, middle-aged woman who, for some inscrutable reason of her own, wanted to present her unblemished reputation in some sort of compromising limelight. But now, on this opulent sunny afternoon, Peter tried in vain to recapture the mood, once habitual to him, of accepting any invitation merely because it implied a good dinner and perhaps a good supper, with a boring opera in between. Certainly it had been easy for him to fulfil his part of the bargain in these evenings: it was natural and also habitual for him to make himself pleasant, to look handsome, to tell Mrs. Trentham that she had never been so marvellous, so chic, so smart, so entrancing generally. But now the mere notion of such an evening seemed foreign. If he wanted to dine at the Ritz and go to the opera and have some supper, he could do it, and secure as guests just those with whom it was pleasant to spend an evening. Henceforth if he wanted to do that he could, vulgarly speaking, "pick and choose" the recipients of his bounty.... Stated like that the whole thing sounded rather sordid, but it seemed to him that, for himself, he had got rid of that sordidness, the "court-fool-touch" which compelled you to make jokes in payment for your dinner, or (which was worse) to talk to your hostess in the serious, wistful note of an adorer, or at any rate of a dazzled and delighted guest. To be host, to pay the bill, provided you had plenty of money, was far the easier part.

There it was then: he had no longer to be asked to dine at the Ritz, and to go to the theatre or what not afterwards. He could bid to his feasts, and no more consider the expense than in the old days he would have considered whether he could afford a bus fare. Whatever enjoyments of that kind the world had to offer were his for the mere formation of his inclination to enjoy them.... And then, suddenly as a blink of distant lightning, and, so it seemed, wholly independent of his own brain, there came the question as to what he had paid for these privileges. And remote as drowsy thunder, the question supplied its own indubitable answer. He had somehow—the thing was done—convinced Silvia that he loved her. He had, at any rate, given her the signal of response that had ecstatically, rapturously contented her, when, below her breath, as she accepted him as her lover, she had whispered, "Ah, just let me love you, all I want is to love you, to be allowed to love you."... He had known quite well what that "allow" really implied. He had to be on the same plane of emotion as she; else, to her understanding of it all, they could never have arrived at this.

All the time (he knew that then, and knew it infinitely better now) her level shone in sunlight like some peak far above the clouds, compared with his little wooded hill that drowsed in the grey day below them. Round him there was no gleam of that ethereal brightness in which she walked, or, at the most, through some rent in the clouds, he caught a glimpse of her. She, at present, so it appeared to him, was so encompassed with brightness that, dazzled, she took for granted that he was with her, and indeed, by some device of desire and of cleverness on his part, he could convince her that through the clasp of their hands there throbbed the sweet entanglement of the soul. She interpreted his lightest action, his words, his glances, by some magic of her own; but already he knew that he, though with consummate care, was "keeping it up." There was no element of difficulty about it, any more than there had been any difficulty about behaving to the complete satisfaction of Mrs. Trentham at her Ritz-Opera entertainments. But in both rôles, as guest at the Ritz and as "master" of Howes, there was an inherent falsity. In both he was dressed up for the part. The difference between the two situations was that in the one Mrs. Trentham was dressed up too, and in the other Silvia was not.

Peter was quite ruthless in tearing off the motley from himself, and contemplating with the candidness of a true egoist the revealed deformities. He never cultivated illusions about himself, nor strove to soften down his own uncomeliness. There he was; that was he, to make the best or the worst of. He did not on the other hand, try to depreciate his assets; he tried, in fact, to make the most of them and use them to the utmost possible advantage. He was, and knew it, a marvellous physical type, handsome as the young Hermes, and crowned with the glory and flower of adolescence. He surrendered to Silvia all that physical perfection; he gave her the wit and charm of his mind; and he was aware that with these he dazzled her much in the same way as Nellie had dazzled her. The use and the enjoyment of them, utterly at her service, was responsible for the splendid success of this solitary fortnight.

In spite of the divine conditions of these golden country days, he knew that he was not sorry to be enjoying the last of them. To-morrow he had to get back to his work, and this sword of his, body and mind, would be sheathed for intervals of absence. And then, with the sure certainty of apprehension that had stamped out these conclusions, he knew that it was not for these alone, or even for these at all, that Silvia had loved him. At the most they were for her the bright-plumaged lure, to which her attention had been originally attracted. But even in the first moments of this attention she had divined something in him, below the feathers and the fur, which she sought. Her quest had gone deeper than skin and conversation, than glances and smiles and level shoulders and firm neck, and quick response, and humour and all the lures of the male for the female. She had claimed and clasped him for something other than what certainly appeared to her as mere appurtenances. And what on his side had he looked for in her? Nothing, so he branded it on himself, except her mere physical attraction, her mere mental charm and freshness and her wealth.

But the admission of this was a branding: the hot iron hurt him, and, not liking to be hurt, he recollected the letters which, a few minutes ago, the Jackdaw had presented to him, and which—the first of them, upside down in his hand—was so honestly gummed that he could make no insertion into its flap.

He turned it over and saw the handwriting of the address. He managed then to open it.

"Isn't it delightful to be married?" wrote Nellie. "I didn't write to you at first, Peter, because you wouldn't have enjoyed anything that came from outside. But after a fortnight, you ought to be able to be congratulated. Before that it would have been merely impertinent (and probably is now); but your friends have to take up the threads again some time. All we blissful people, in fact, must remember that we are human beings, after all, and break ourselves into 'behavin' according' (Mrs. Gamp, isn't it? No, I don't think it is). Anyhow, we shall all meet again, shan't we, and buzz about in London, and ask each other to our lovely country houses. We've got to go on, Peter; the world has got to go on. Hasn't it?"

Peter turned a page, and began to be quite absorbed in this new but familiar atmosphere. He slipped out of his present environment under some spell which lurked in these trivialities.

"I'm getting on beautifully," so began the second page, "for Philip and I understand each other so well, and it's tremendously comfortable. We seem to want just the same sort of thing. He's awfully keen about birds, for instance, and I am becoming so. We go out with field-glasses, and see willow-wrens, and yesterday we saw a marsh-warbler. Then I like golf— you always hated it, I remember—so Philip is learning to like it too. He nearly lost his temper yesterday when he missed a short putt, and that's always a good sign. We don't quite agree about motoring, because I always want to go as fast as the machine can manage, and he always wants to slow down when there's a cross-road. He talks to the chauffeur through a beastly little tube, and it's like a funeral.

"Peter darling, what rot I am writing. Fancy my writing such rot to you. It's the wrong sort of rot, isn't it? There are rots and rots. You and I always used to talk rot, but it wasn't about birds and golf. (I'm having a new sort of mashie.) But, bar rot, when are we going to meet again? Isn't the country a sleepy place? Do come up to town soon, and Philip and I will come up, too. (You and Silvia, I mean, of course.) I want to be in the silly old thick of it again. Because when you're in the thick of it you can make privacies, but when you're in the privacy of the country you can't make a thick, except when you have a great house-party, as we're going to have next week, and that isn't really a 'thick': it's only partridges. The men go out in the morning, and the women join them for lunch, and then the men come home in the evening, and the morning and evening are the first day. But it's all extremely comfortable—that's the word I come back to. Mother has been here for the last three weeks, and she's almost ceased saying that she must go away the day after to-morrow. I suppose that's because she's tired of hearing either Philip or me murmur something about its being such a short visit. P. and I really both like her being with us: it isn't half a bad plan, and I expect she'll stop till we go back to town again.

"I want you and Silvia to come over here on November 10th for the week-end. There will be hosts of rather nice people here: so many, in fact, that you and I can steal away without being noticed, and have a scamper through the wet woods (they are sure to be wet in November) and wave our tails and congratulate ourselves on being settled for life. We've both of us got somebody to take care of us (Yes, I mean that), and if you're as pleased with the arrangement as I am, why, we're very lucky people. You and I, you know, if things had been utterly and completely different, would have quarrelled so frightfully.... I saw two cats yesterday sitting with their faces within an inch of each other, scowling and screeching at each other in a perfect tempest of irritation.

"Here's Philip come to take me out. He will sit in the chair there waiting quite placidly till I have finished this letter, not reading the paper or doing anything at all, but just waiting. He knows where there are a pair of golden crested wrens. Isn't that exciting?... Oh, I can't go on with him sitting there. Good-bye, my dear. Mind you and Silvia come on the 10th."

As Peter read, he heard, by some internal audition, Nellie's voice enunciating the sentences with that familiar intonation of light staccato mockery. The written words were but like a prompter's copy which he held and glanced at; it was Nellie who stood there and said the lines. He would have liked to argue a point or two with her, but he knew that there was between them that deep fundamental agreement and comprehension without which argument develops into mere contradiction....

Peter thrust the letter into his pocket as steps sounded on the gravel just behind him.

"Been sitting here ever since I left you?" asked Silvia. "Oh, Peter, without your hat in this hot sun!" She picked it up and perched it on his head.

"There! Oh, dear, what a nuisance it is that this is your last day here. But what a last day. Any letters?"

Peter's hand fingered Nellie's letter.

"Yes: one from Nellie," he said. "She wants you and me to go there for the week-end on November 10th. Shall we?"

"Oh, how unkind of her! What are we to do? Shall we say that mother will be here for that Sunday? It will be quite true in its way, though it won't mean precisely what she thinks it means."

Peter looked at her below the rim of his straw hat. She had placed it rather forward over his forehead, and as she stood beside his chair he had to incline his head sharply back, so that the muscles at the side of his neck stood out below the sun-browned skin. She came a step closer and held his throat between thumb and fingers.

"What shall we tell her?" she asked. "Speak, or I'll strangle you."

"Strangle away!" he said.

"I would sooner you spoke," she said. "I don't want to murder you just yet. So unpleasant for mother."

"Whether it's unpleasant for me or not doesn't seem to matter," said Peter throatily, for Silvia increased the pressure of her hand.

"Not a bit, darling," said she. "I shall squeeze tighter and tighter until you tell me what we shall say to Nellie."

"Brute!" said Peter. "Don't do it, Silvia. You're hurting me frightfully."

He wrinkled up his forehead and drew in his breath quickly, as if in great pain. Instantly Silvia took her hand away.

"Oh, my dear, I haven't really hurt you?" she asked with compunction.

"Once upon a time," said Peter, "there was a woman who believed every word that her husband said."

Silvia sat down on the edge of the long chair.

"Was? There is one," she said. "If you told me you hated me, I should believe you."

"I hate you," said Peter promptly.

"You didn't say that," said she. "Your mouth said it. What are we to tell Nellie? Seriously, I mean. It will be nearly our last Sunday here, if we go to London in December."

Peter made a short calculation.

"Dear Nellie," he said, "we are so sorry we can't come, because November 10th will be our last evening but twenty-one alone here, as we go up to town the next month.' Will that do?"

"It sounds perfectly sensible," said Silvia. "She'll understand: it wasn't so long ago that she was married. Then you'll write that, will you?" she added hopefully.

"I will if you really wish it," said he; "but it's not very sane. You see ... well, some time we've got to begin behaving like ordinary human beings again. And, after all, Nellie is a very old friend of mine, and a very intimate one of yours. She'll think it rather odd."

Silvia sighed.

"A whole Saturday to Monday," she said. "How selfish Nellie is! I never knew that before. But perhaps we had better go. Shall I answer it for you?"

Peter got up.

"No; I must write to her in any case," he said.

"What else does she say?" asked Silvia. "No message for me?"

Peter could not definitely remember any, but there was sure to have been such.

"Of course: all sorts of things. Come for a stroll, Silvia. I'm getting chilly in the shade of my straw hat. There's another thing I want to talk over with you. Let's go down by the lake!"

"Hurrah! I love being consulted. What is it?"

"It's about my father. Oh, by the way, the Jackdaw asked me where he should be put, and I said the state-rooms. Is that all right?"

Silvia pinched his arm.

"When are you going to understand that you are master?" she said. "Oh, Peter, it will be lovely for him having the state-rooms. He'll like it tremendously. Won't he? I wish I had thought of it. It wasn't that, I hope, that you wanted to consult me about."

"No. Now, before I consult you, I want to ask you a question or two, which you must promise to answer not tactfully, but truly."

"Not even a little tact, if I find it necessary?" she asked.

"Not an atom. Do you like that cartoon of his?"

Silvia glanced sideways at him.

"Well—I don't find I go and look at it for pleasure," she said. "Not often at least, not every day. Do you like it?"

"I think it's the largest piece of rubbish I ever saw. Now try again to express your opinion."

Silvia gave a sigh of relief.

"Oh, I do agree!" she said. "It's *the* most appalling. Now, isn't it?"

"Question number two," said Peter. "Do you think you will like the others any better? Do you, in fact, look forward to seeing the whole wall of the gallery covered with allegorical Mainwarings?"

"Not in the very smallest degree. But we've got to have them, haven't we?"

"I don't think so," said he. "In fact, from a letter I have received from my father, I gather that he doesn't consider he made a contract for them at all. It's clear from what he says that somebody else wants to buy them at a higher rate, considerably higher, than your mother paid for the first. In fact, he alludes to the price she paid for it as a pittance. By the way, what did she pay for it?"

Silvia looked sideways at him again.

"Do you really want me to tell you?" she asked.

"If you don't mind."

"Well, she gave him a thousand guineas for it, Peter. I rather wish he hadn't called it a pittance; it makes mother seem mean. He was quite willing to accept it. And I don't suppose—do you?—that he sells much at that sort of price?"

"And the rest of the unspeakable six at the same price?" asked Peter.

"I suppose so. Mother understood so," said she.

"And does she want to have them?" asked Peter.

"No. I don't think she does, very much," said Silvia. "She spoke to-day of 'my cartoons'—wasn't that darling of her?—when I said your father was coming this evening. But I think I could explain to her that she needn't have them; if I do it the right way, she won't think she wants them. But what about the one we've got?"

"Sell it back to him at the price she gave for it," said Peter.

Silvia seemed to consider this simple proposition rather intently.

"Yes, perhaps she would do that," she said, without much conviction as to its probability. "Oh, Peter, haven't we got rather odd parents?"

"I have; but why have you, except in so far that it was odd to give a thousand guineas for that monstrosity? I'm delighted at the prospect of getting rid of it, not only, and not chiefly, because it's an atrocious object, but because I hate the idea of my father imposing upon your mother and then talking about a pittance. He would have jumped at selling it in an auction room for a quarter of what she paid. I wonder who can have offered him more for it. Oh, by the way, Aunt Eleanor has bought his sketches for the cartoons."

Silvia burst out laughing.

"Then Aunt Joanna has bought the cartoons themselves," she said. "But don't suggest that to mother. Or rather, if you want me to talk about it all to her, I won't. Aunt Joanna, you see, wants to, what they call wipe mother's eye. I'm quite certain of it. And if mother got wind of it, she wouldn't part with that wretched picture for a million."

"But how odd — —"

"Yes; that's her oddness. I said we had got odd parents. And I doubt — at least, there's no doubt about it at all — whether she will let your father have back the one cartoon that she has got for what she paid for it. She doesn't want any money, and she's as generous as she can be, bless her, but she won't be 'done.' The picture is hers, and she won't let him have it back at a penny less than he is going to receive for it. Oh, let's talk about something more interesting. Anyhow, you and I don't want the cartoon we've got, or any more like it. But people are so queer, and I love their queernesses: they are part of them. After all, the queernesses in people are exactly what makes their individuality. You're queer, I'm queer."

"Why am I queer?" demanded Peter.

"I've told you so often," said she.

Peter guessed at that what his imputed queerness was. It was true that she had told him often, but it was true also that there was a thing which a lover was never tired of repeating.

"Never: never once," said he.

"As if I wasn't doing it all day," she said. "Taking advantage, I mean, of your queerness — not merely telling you about it directly, but being so much more direct than just telling you. What's your queerness, indeed, if it isn't that you allow me to be queer, just because you are?"

"You've changed the subject," said he. "You're talking about your queerness now."

"It's all the same queerness," she said.

Peter could squint more atrociously than most people, and now, looking at Silvia, he allowed himself to contemplate the end of his nose. Silvia couldn't stand this trick, and a nonsensical ritual had built itself up upon it.

"Oh, Peter, put your eyes back!" she cried.

"I can't. They've stuck. Push them back for me."

He shut his eyes, and Silvia stroked the lids from the nose outwards.

"They will stick some day," she said," and then I shall divorce you."

Peter looked at her straight again.

"Go on about the queerness," he said.

"Yours or mine?" she asked.

"You said they were the same."

"They are in a way. But your queerness is much the queerest. For it was I whom you loved. What I did wasn't queer; anything else would have been not queer, but imbecile.... Peter, don't ever be tired of knowing how awfully I love you. If you're not there, the thought of it frightens me; there's something crushing about it. But when you are with me, the only thing that frightens me is the thought that it shouldn't be so. But why on earth you're like that—like me, I mean—that's what is so incomprehensible. Me, you know: this bit of nothing at all."

Peter became aware, more consciously than through the hints he had previously been cognizant of, how, though Silvia's level was some sun-basked plateau far above him, he welcomed and spread himself in the gleams that came to him. There was a splendour in being loved like that, and at this moment the inherent falsity of his position was just burned out by that consuming ray. Her love, not in the least masculine, was yet male in its adoring self-surrender; his, as regards her, though not in the least feminine, was female in its reception of it. There was an ecstasy in being adored by so magnificent a lover. Even as in material ways, she showered herself on the Danae for whom, in their drama, he was cast, so in the subtler and splendid beauty of the soul, she poured herself out in a love that passed the love of woman. And that very quality, here triumphantly shining, drew out the essential fragrance of his.

"More," he said, "more nothing at all."

She seemed to step from her height at that, diving down to him, entrancingly tender.

"That's all there is, my darling," she said. "If you want more than I've got, you must teach it me. Now I won't be absurd any longer. Look, there's a moorhen!"

This was quite in the habitual manner. Like a lark, she sang for so long as she was in the air, then folded her wings and dropped to her nest. The singing was over, and it left her panting with the ecstasy of it. But Peter, to continue that metaphor, received something of a shock; he had not known she would so swiftly come to ground. Yet that sudden dip was equally characteristic of him; he probably had shown her the trick of it, for often he had done just that. The sky, after all, extended to the actual ground: there was no intermediate element.

"It's a coot," he said.

"I don't care. I only hope it's happy," said she. "Oh, my dear, there's the bell for lunch, and we're half a mile from the house. The Jackdaw will peck us for being late."

"Not our fault. The lake shouldn't have been so long."

"We might fill some of it up," said she. "Let's talk sensibly. What were we saying before you began to talk nonsense? Oh, yes, pictures, pittance— —"

"Papa," said he.

"Peter.... I can't think of any more."

"Peter's papa purchases the picture he sold for a pittance," said he. "American headlines. Make another."

This sort of monkey-gymnastics of the mind, at which Peter and Nellie and all the rest of them so fluently excelled, was always productive in Silvia of an intense gravity; she made her contributions with effort, struggle and bewilderment, amazed at how quickly everybody else—everybody else was so clever—made words out of words, and reeled off the names of eminent men which began with an X....

"Something about mother," said she with knitted brows. "I must manage—oh, Peter, isn't that good?—I must manage to make mother— —"

Peter giggled.

"That's not the right form," he said. "You must get the right form. Let's see. 'Millionaire mother manages to make—to make—oh, yes—money on Mr. Mainwaring's monstrosity,'" he finished up in a great hurry.

"Oh, Peter, how lovely!" said she. "How do you do it? And why can't I?"

Mr. Mainwaring rose magnificently to his tenancy of the state-rooms, feeling that it had been a very proper arrangement to put him there. Here was the father of the master of Howes paying a visit to his son; here, too, in the same earthly vesture, was the creator of the great cartoons which, among all the futile crosses and cenotaphs and hysterical verse and prose, were not unworthy of the heroic history which they commemorated. With the same abandoned thoroughness with which he could be, when suitable, the rollicking, jovial boy, hungry for his tea, or the robust-throated Toreador, so now he saw in the assignation of the state-rooms to his occupancy a very proper and touching homage on the part of Peter or Silvia, or Mrs. Wardour (or more probably on their joint acclamation) to the sovereignty of his Art. These pleasant reflections that accompanied the appreciative exploration of his territory suggested that there was, so to speak, a little state business to be done, the nature of which he believed he had adequately indicated to Peter. Peter, good lad, would no doubt have attended to it, and it would be well for him to give his report.

Probably it was as much the desire of having this conversation with Peter secure from interruption as anything else that caused him to send a message to his son that Mr. Mainwaring would be much obliged if he would spare him a few minutes in the state-rooms before dressing time; but it certainly fitted in pleasantly with his sovereignty that Peter should be requested to present himself, and that Mr. Mainwaring should be set on a throne of Spanish brocade.

He waved Peter to a seat. Peter seemed to prefer to perch himself on the tall steel fireguard. He divined with sufficient accuracy his father's pose, and was partly amused, partly irritated. Silvia would have been wholly amused.

"Hope you'll be comfortable here, father," he said.

Mr. Mainwaring glanced round him.

"Yes, indeed," he said. "I shall do very well. Ah, by the way, before we get to business, I have a letter from your mother which she asked me to give you. Perhaps you would hand me my despatch case.... Here it is."

Peter was lighting a cigarette, and spoke between the puffs.

"Right. I'll take it when I go," he said. His father looked at the tapestried walls.

"My dear boy," he said, "I don't know if I am right to allow you to smoke here."

Peter dropped his match on the carpet. He did that on purpose.

"Oh, don't bother about that," he said. "I allow myself. Now I suppose you want to talk to me about that cartoon?"

"You got my letter? You have arranged what I indicated?"

Peter felt his irritation gaining on him.

"Well, your letter was rather—rather involved, rather vague and magnificent," he said. "What Silvia and I made out of it was that you had been offered a higher price for work that Mrs. Wardour had commissioned you to do for her, and wanted to call it off. That seemed to be the general drift of it."

"No; there was no definite commission," said he. "I mentioned that."

"Mrs. Wardour was under the impression that there was. But that, I think, can be arranged, for the series was intended—commissioned or not doesn't matter—to hang in the gallery here. This is Silvia's house, you see, and in a way mine, so that if we consent there will be—under certain conditions—no difficulty with my mother-in-law. Silvia has talked to her about it. We cordially consent, father. We are both quite willing that you should paint the rest of the series for somebody else."

Mr. Mainwaring could find no fault with the substance of the speech; indeed, it gave him precisely what he was wanting. But, in spite of Peter's neutrality of statement, he found it dealing some dastardly wound to his vanity.

"Ha! You and Silvia, it appears, don't want the great series," he remarked.

"But apparently somebody else does," said Peter. "And you said in your letter that they were exciting a stupendous interest in artistic circles. That's all right, then; we are very glad."

"Yes, glad to get rid of them," said the insatiable one.

Peter practically never lost his temper. He used it as a stored-up force. But certainly the sight of his father on the Spanish throne, looking like Zeus, did not predispose him to exert his habitual pleasantness.

"You are, of course, at liberty to make any comments you choose," he said. "You are vexed with me because I give you your way quite willingly instead of reluctantly. By the way, don't tell me, and in particular don't tell Mrs. Wardour, whether the 'artistic circles' is another expression for Lady Darley. If it is, I think it highly probable that she would refuse to let you have back the first cartoon, if that is part of your plan. You would, in that case, I suppose, have to copy it if she allowed you to."

Mr. Mainwaring rose to a splendour of pomposity.

"Copy?" he said. "And could I copy the fiery execution of it? You speak of pictures, my Peter, as if they could be produced like boots or hats. The intending purchaser—I do not say whether or no I refer to Lady Darley—

wants no cold replica. She insists on the one that came hot and terrible from the furnace of my imagination."

"Then on certain conditions," said Peter, "Lady Darley—I mean the purchaser—may have it."

"Name them," said his father, looking like a captive king.

"The first is that you completely withdraw, and if possible regret, the use of the expression 'pittance,' in connection with the price you received for it. There's an implication of meanness about it with regard to Mrs. Wardour."

Mr. Mainwaring clicked his thumb and finger as if to say, "*That* for what I sold it for."

"I make no such implication," he said. "Mrs. Wardour or anybody else is well within her rights in acquiring fine work at such prices as the artist is obliged from straitened circumstances to accept."

"The point is," said Peter, "that you hadn't often, if ever, been obliged to accept a thousand guineas before for any picture."

"And may not an artist, after years of unremitting endeavour, be allowed to come into his own and enjoy the appreciation he has long merited?" asked Mr. Mainwaring.

"Certainly he may: we are all delighted. But when he does—when, that is to say, you at length receive a high price for a picture, you shouldn't, because you are offered immediately afterwards a higher price, talk of a pittance as applied to the first. You thought yourself, father," continued Peter pleasantly and inexorably, "remarkably fortunate to get a thousand guineas."

Mr. Mainwaring, at this, displayed the versatility of a quick-change artist. It was pretty well demonstrated that Peter was not impressed by the majestic attitude, and he yodelled and burst into a laugh.

"Well, well, my Peter," he said, "you shall have it your own way. It was no pittance. I ought not to have called it a pittance—*mea culpa, mea maxima culpa*. Pittance it is—let us distinguish, my dear—when I contrast it with the subsequent offer that has reached me, but at the time a thousand guineas seemed to me a very fair remuneration. I had been too modest about my value, it appears now. Ah, yes, but recognition is pleasant enough, and when the brush slips from my hand, and my spirit flies" (he made a circular motion of his arms as if swimming) "to join the mightier dead, the Mainwaring estate will be found not too inconsiderable to place beside the fortunes of the Wardours. But that will not, I hope, be for a long time yet," he added, as the notion of picturing himself in front of some great canvas with the brush slipping from his nerveless hands, supported by Silvia and Peter, occurred to him with an almost ominous vividness.

"Quite," said Peter in general acknowledgment of this magnificence. "There remains then one thing to settle, and that is the price at which you repurchase the cartoon of which Mrs. Wardour is the present possessor."

Mr. Mainwaring did not for the moment see the bearing of this, and remained splendid.

"I should not dream of repaying her one penny less than what I received for it," he said. "The full price, Peter: assure her of that."

Peter thought it better to let another aspect of the case strike his father, without suggesting it, and was silent till Mr. Mainwaring spoke again.

"H'm. I see what you mean," he said.

"I hoped you would, because really there doesn't seem to be any reason why she should let you have for a thousand guineas a thing which is now indubitably hers, and which you will immediately sell for a considerably higher sum."

Mr. Mainwaring began to regret that he had said quite so much about the utter impossibility of recapturing the fire of the original in a copy.

"You would be offering her, you must remember," Peter added, "a pittance for her picture."

"You think I ought to give her what I shall receive for it?" asked Mr. Mainwaring.

Peter kept steadily before him his distaste of his father "scoring off" Mrs. Wardour. The whole thing, though humorous, was rather sordid; but he knew that he rather liked himself in the part he was playing in it.

"I think the justice of that view will appeal to you," he said. "You couldn't very well do otherwise."

Mr. Mainwaring was silent a moment, and then decided to be completely superb.

"I have no experience in business or in bargaining," he said. "If you tell me that is right and fair and proper, I yield."

"I think it's your only means of getting the picture," said Peter. "So that's settled, is it? Oh, the letter from my mother. Thanks. Dinner at half-past eight."

CHAPTER X

Peter, as he strolled down the corridor, knew that he had been rather signorial—if that was the word—and designedly so, in this interview. In spite of Mr. Mainwaring's magnificent occupation of the state-rooms, for which, after all, he had his son to thank, Peter was pleased to feel that he had been putting his father in his place. It had certainly been with this object in view that he had smoked his cigarette, and dropped the expired match on the carpet, not exactly calling attention to his position, but casually assuming it. Again, in the matter of the picture, he had, ever so quietly, ever so indulgently, just hinted at the right course, and like a lamb—a great vain rococo, farcical lamb—his father had bleated his way into the proper fold.

Peter confessed to himself—he seldom confessed to anybody else—that the motive which inspired these manœuvres was an unamiable one. He might easily have obtained the results that he now, together with his mother's unopened letter, carried away from this interview, by tact, by pleasantness, by the general small change of sympathy. Hitherto he had been accustomed to use such lubrications to make the wheels of life run smoothly in domestic dealings; but now that no further domestic lubrication was necessary on his part (his father, it is true, might have to flourish the oil-can with desperate agility, if he was to ensure smooth working) Peter knew that he had just driven ahead and let the wheels, if so they felt disposed, squeak and squeal, and grind and grumble. While that small, smelly house off the Brompton Road had been his home, it had paid to make the bearings run easily; but now, when he thought with incredulous wonder that he could have "stuck" all that small stuffiness so long, he detachedly admired his own past deftness and patience in dealing with the daily situation there. He saw in the mirror of his own vanity the incomparable crudeness of his father's, and discovered, almost with a sense of shock, how cordially he disliked him.

For the present his sense of humour with regard to him was in total eclipse; the type of quality which Silvia hugged as being the lovable queerness which makes for individuality, he saw only as tiresome and contemptible eccentricity, a thing to be contemplated baldly without comment, whenever contemplation of it was necessary, and to be dealt with summarily. The vexing affair was that Peter caught some broken image of himself in all this. One glimpse of himself in especial was irritating; that, namely, in which he looked with great distaste on his father's profiting by the wealth of the Wardours without giving a due return for his depredations on it.

It was natural that when, as now, he was so acutely aware of his father's unique capability for rubbing him up the wrong way, he should wonder afresh at the placid, unruffled tolerance that had enabled his mother to spend a quarter of a century with him. Women, of course, so ran his reflections, have a greater gift of patience with men than a man can be expected to have. Sex, no doubt, had something to do with it, for on the other hand men were more tolerant of a tiresome woman than other women. Yet that could not wholly explain his mother; she was quite inexplicable, for Silvia even, gifted as Peter ever so cordially recognized with the power of putting herself into the position and realizing the identity of other people, had fallen back like a spent wave from the hard, smooth impenetrability of his mother. She had confessed herself baffled, had no idea whether there was something, somebody, hermetically sealed up behind that neat porcelain face by the inexorable will of its occupant, or if there was nothing beyond that blank imperturbability that cared only whether the door at the head of the kitchen stairs was "quite shut" and had no desire except to be left alone and allowed to read advertisements of hotels in railway guides. Had his mother been driven into that small, but apparently impregnable fortress by his father's colossal and ludicrous personality, or was there indeed no one there at all, no beleaguered garrison grimly holding out?

Peter wandered on to the terrace for a minute of composing dusk and quietness. He half expected to find Silvia there, and felt a little ill-used that she was not. She knew what was the nature of his interview with his father, and Peter would have welcomed the warmth of her applause at his masterly conduct of it. But in her absence he could read the certainly placid communication from his mother. She would hope he was well, she would hope Silvia was well, she would let it be assumed that she was well. She would certainly also say that she was so sorry she could not come to Howes with his father, but that she hoped to do so some time during the autumn. She would undoubtedly wind up by saying that it was nearly post time, and that she had other letters.... Peter drew the letter from his pocket, and prepared to let his eyes slide smoothly over the lines of it. She wrote a wonderfully clear hand: you could take a whole sentence in at a glance.

"My dearest Peter,—I am sending this letter to you by your father, because I want it to reach you without fail. Letters by post go wrong sometimes, and I don't want this to go wrong. When I have finished it, I shall put it into his despatch-box myself.

"When your father comes back from his visit to you and Silvia, he will not find me here. It is no use mincing words, so I will tell you straight out that I can't stand him any longer. It would not have answered my purpose just to go away from him for a month, for I should have felt all the time that at the end of a month I should have to come back; I should have been on the end of the string still. As it is, I shall stop away just as long as I choose. I shall be free. I want a holiday without any tie whatever. When I mean to come back (if I do) I shall write to him and ask him if he will take me back. I don't know how long it will be before I want to. It might be a fortnight, or it might be a year, or it might be never. I shall simply stay away from him, at some pleasant place which I have selected, until I feel better.

"While you were living with your father and me I could just get along; but since you have gone I can't get along at all. We weren't much to each other, for all my individuality—isn't that what they call it?—had long ago been hammered back into me. I was like a small person in a large suit of armour. But somehow you were a part of me, and while you were there I couldn't go away.

"I ask you, my dear, not to make any attempt to find me, and I want you to persuade your father not to. I shall be quite comfortable, and as I am never ill I don't see why I should begin to be so now. I shall go to a nice hotel, where I shan't have to order lunch and dinner or add up bills. It is astonishing how many nice hotels there are, quite moderate in price, which will just suit me.

"Now this may seem unkind, but the fact is that I don't want to hear a word from either you or your father. You and I have nothing in common; in fact, I have nothing in common with anybody, and I only want to be left alone in peace, and not to be reminded of the last twenty-five years of my life at all. I want not to be bothered with anybody. I want to get up and go to bed when I choose, and go for my walk, and read my book, and play patience. You and I have never loved each other at all, so there's no use in pretending to be pathetic over that now. Before you were old enough to understand, I hadn't got any feeling left in me, or, at least, it was hammered right inside me. If any time during these last ten years I had died, you wouldn't have missed me, though if you had died I should have missed you to the extent, anyhow, of your absence making my life with your father quite intolerable. I don't bear him the slightest ill will, and I hope he'll bear me none. He has excellent servants, and they will make him quite comfortable, which is all he wants. But I've got too much sense to remain with him any longer.

"He has been saying great things lately about the immense sums of money he will get for his series of cartoons, so that I have no scruple in withdrawing from him the £600 a year which is my own income. I can't be certain, of course, whether he has not been multiplying everything by ten, in order to glorify himself, but I suppose there is some truth in it all. Anyhow, he has got a cheque from Mrs. Wardour for a thousand guineas, because he showed me that. He was in great spirits that night, dancing round the table and singing and drinking quantities of port. And that, it appears, is nothing to what he is about to get for the rest of his great series."

Peter took his eyes off the neatly written sheets for a moment and gave a great gasp. The figure of his mother, as he was accustomed to behold it, veiled and still, and sitting in shadow and never giving a sign of individual life, had suddenly cast off its concealment and tranquillities, and stood out violently illuminated. That smooth, polished object which had lain inert so long in the midst of railway guides, had proved itself to be a live shell which, without any warning or preliminary sizzling, had exploded. He himself was unhurt, though immeasurably astonished and startled, and he exulted in the fact that the thing had been alive after all, carrying within it such store of devastating energy. His own marriage, his departure from home, had set off the fuse; he had been, all unconsciously, the controlling agent.

He dived again into this most lucid report of the explosion, observing with regret that there were but a couple of pages more. At the moment Silvia appeared at the door from the terrace into the drawing-room close behind where he sat.

"Peter, is that you?" she asked.

"Yes; one minute. Or come here, Silvia. Take these sheets and read them without saying anything till I've finished. It's a letter from my mother."

He buried himself in the remainder of the letter, hardly hearing Silvia's gasp of surprise as she came to the second paragraph.

"Now I want you," the narrative continued, "to consider this before you pass any judgment on what I have done. I am injuring nothing and nobody, except your father's vanity, and I have no doubt he will find some explanation of my leaving him which will quite satisfy him. He will not be the least less happy without me, nor will you. I have got no friends, for I am not the sort of person who can make friends or wants them; I have been hammered, as I have said, into myself, and I break no ties the severance of which is painful for others any more than for me. I see so few people, and those so very occasionally, that there need be no scandal of any kind; your father will only have to say, about once a month, that I am on a visit in the country, which is quite true.

"My solicitor knows where I am, and from time to time he will let you have a note from me, saying how I am. As for news, I shall have none; I shall take my walk, and read my book, and entertain myself very well, and I shall be very happy, because I shall be free. I rather believe that you are sufficiently like me to understand that, for you have always kept yourself independent of everybody.

"Finally, I leave it to you (no doubt you will consult Silvia) as to whether you let your father find out that I have gone when he returns home, or whether you tell him. I think personally that it would be wiser to tell him, because when he got home and found the few lines (not like this long letter) which I have left for him there, just to say I have gone, he might make some dreadful scene and upset everybody. But that I leave entirely to you.

"All the wages and books were paid up to the end of last week. The bills, with their receipts, are in their place in the third drawer of my knee-hole table.

"Your affectionate mother,
"Maria Mainwaring."

Peter thrust the remaining pages into Silvia's hand, and waited till she had come to the end. Then they looked at each other in silence.

"I'm going to laugh," said Peter at length.

"No, please don't," said Silvia. "If you do I shall cry."

Peter tapped the sheets that lay in her hand.

"But it's gorgeous," he said. "I should laugh, if I did, not from amusement—though there are amusing things—but from pleasure. Every word in that letter is true; that's something to be pleased about, and, what's more, every word in it is right. But the surprise, the wonder of it! There's a splendour about it!"

Silvia shuffled the sheets together, and, giving them back to him, leaned her forehead on her hands.

"Ah, haven't you got any tenderness?" she said. "Don't you see the bitter pathos of it? Your mother, you know!"

"But she says there is nothing pathetic about it," said he.

"And that's just the most pathetic thing of all!" Silvia said.

Peter puzzled over this a moment. He understood Silvia's feeling well enough, but he understood equally well, and with greater sympathy, the answer (the retort almost) to it.

"But if she sees nothing pathetic in the situation, and I quite agree with her, what's the use of trying to introduce pathos?" he asked. "Pathos painted on—like a varnish—ceases to be pathos at all; it becomes simply sentimentality."

Silvia turned to him like some patient affectionate teacher to a child who pretends only not to know his lessons.

"If the absence of love in relationships like these isn't pathetic," she said, "love itself is only sentimentality."

Peter again saw precisely what she meant; he knew, too, that what she said was true. But he knew that he, for himself, did not realize it with conviction, with a sense of illumination.... The statement of it was just an instance the more of Silvia's shining there aloft of his confining cloudland. The thought of that dealt him a stab of envy, and under the hurt of it his spirit snapped and snarled, and retired, so to speak, into its kennel, leaving his mind outside to manage the situation.

"Well, then, it's pathetic," he said, "but it has been pathetic so long that one has got used to it. I know you're right, but what you say hasn't any practical bearing——"

"Ah, my dear, but it has," said she. "It has all the practical bearing. It is up to you, practically, to handle it in hardness in—in a sort of ruthlessness, or you can, recognizing what I say, deal with it tenderly."

"By all means; but the facts aren't new. Leave me out: let's consider my father and mother only. There's the practical side of it. He's got to be told— at least, I suppose so. There's no new pathos there. They've both been aware of lovelessness for years. If my father takes the wounded, the pathetic pose, it will—it will just be a pose. Frankly, I'm all on my mother's side. By one big gesture she has explained herself; she has made a living comprehensible reality of herself. The Bradshaws, the railway guide advertisements—good Lord, we know what it has all been about now! There's flesh and blood in it! I always respect flesh and blood!"

"But her way of doing it is an outrage," said Silvia. "She's your father's wife, after all: she's your mother. Take your mother's side by all means— we've all got to take sides in everything: nobody can be neutral—but take his side in her manner of doing what she has done. Sympathize with him in that! That letter, too—will you show him the letter? The hostility of it, the resentment!"

Peter sat still a moment fingering the leaves of the letter.

"It's not so much resentment," he said, "as repression. She has been hammered back into herself all these years. Oh, I understand her better than you. It *had* to happen this way. What else was she to do? Could she go to my father and say, 'If you can't put some curb on your egoism and vanity, if you continue to be such a bounder (that's what bounders are) I really shall have to leave you'?"

"You want to score off him, Peter," said she. "That's the hardness, the ruthlessness. And you aren't hard, my darling. Who knows that better than I?"

"Are you sure I'm not?" he said.

She did not answer this directly.

"You've got to be gentle," she said.

Peter's fingers closed on the letter, hesitated, and then tore the sheets in half. He tore them across yet again. "Well, he shan't see the letter," he said. "It was written to me and I've destroyed it. But if, when I tell him, he becomes melodramatic how can I *help* being what you call ruthless? He's so vain: you don't know how vain he is. This will be a brutal outrage, an attempted assassination of his vanity. But it won't injure it. The dastardly blow will glance aside, and he'll put an extra bodyguard round his vanity for the future. He's a ridiculous person, Silvia," said Peter in a loud, firm voice.

Silvia gave a sigh.

"Ah, that's better," she said, "for you've torn the letter up, anyhow, and when you said he was ridiculous, you said it, my dear, as if you were justifying yourself rather than accusing him. Oh, you said it firmly and loudly, but—will you mind if I say this too?—you didn't say it so spitefully. Now, let's be practical. You always used to be practical, Peter. When are you going to tell him?"

Peter looked at his watch.

"That means that if I say that I haven't made up my mind," he said, "you will certainly let me know that there is plenty of time to tell him before dinner. You want me to tell him now: that's where we are. You call me practical: who was ever so practical as you, when it comes to the point?"

She did not challenge that, but rather proceeded to justify Peter's opinion for him.

"My dear, you can put off pleasant things if you like," she said, "because you enjoy the anticipation of them. But where—where is the use of putting off unpleasant things? That only lengthens a beastly anticipation."

"He'll make a scene," said Peter. "I hate scenes."

There was nothing to reply to this: it all came under the advisability, which she had already expressed, of not putting off unpleasantnesses. So she made no reply, and soon, for the face of her continued to push him, he got up, still wondering if she would prefer to tell his father herself. How strongly she wanted to do that, and how, more strongly, she refrained from doing it, he had no idea. Her inclination, that which she combated, was simply to go straight to those voluptuous state-rooms; but her will, her convinced sense of what was right, of what was Peter's own duty and development, kept her silent.

"Oh, I am sorry for you," she said at length, as he turned to go into the house. "But don't forget to be sorry for him, Peter."

His only answer to that was a just perceptible shrug of his shoulders (comment on the futility of her sympathy), and he walked away across the crackling gravel.

Silvia knew how Peter's mere presence stifled her power of judgment with regard to him. Often and often she had to cling, desperately, to a mental integrity of her own, in order not to be washed away by the mere tide of her devotion to him. Her desire, not only the flesh and the blood of her, but her very spirit, would always have surrendered to him, would have given up herself, whole and complete, to what pleased him, to what made him comfortable, content and happy. But somewhere between these two apexes of physical and spiritual longing there came another peak, a mental and judicial apex, so she framed it to herself, a thing solid and reliable, a kind of bleak umpire that gave inexorable decisions.

Already in their fortnight of married life it had several times asserted itself—it was her will, she supposed, clear-eyed and unbribable, which was as distinct from the blindness of love as it was from the abandonment of physical desire. Peter had suggested, for instance, that he should "chuck" his work in the Foreign Office (this was the most notable of these instances) and live, just live, now at Howes, now in London, always with her. They would travel, they would entertain, they would have plenty of interests to keep him busy enough. He had urged, he had argued, he had appealed to her for her mere acquiescence, willing or not, and she had steadily and unshakably refused to give it. Here, to-night, was another test for this umpire of the mind. It would have been infinitely easier for her to tell Mr. Mainwaring herself, and she knew quite convincedly that she would have proved a far more sympathetic breaker of shocking tidings than Peter would be. Peter would now, on his way to the state-rooms, be framing adroit sentences, be schooling his anticipatory impatience at a melodramatic reception of that news by his father into tolerance and gentleness. But she had as little temptation to be intolerant or ungentle, as he had to be the reverse; she would naturally have stood in an attitude which Peter would find it gymnastically difficult to maintain. But he had got to do his best, not to let her do so infinitely better.

It took but a moment's stiffening of herself to baffle any inclination to follow Peter and shoulder his mission for him, and her thoughts went back to Mrs. Mainwaring's letter and its startling effect (or want of effect) on Peter. That had produced, so she found now when she was no longer under the spell of his presence, a certain incredulous dismay. "You aren't like that," she had assured him, but now she found herself saying, "He *can't* be like that!" He appeared to have received this intelligence with a savage, or, if not a savage a wholly unpitiful comment. He had seemed, and indeed seemed now, to have applauded this tragic sequel to years of resentful companionship. He had confessed to a desire to laugh (this was the ruthlessness). It might be that the logical result of such years was that Mrs. Mainwaring, given that she retained any independent identity of her own, should have been goaded into this assertion of it. It might, in the ultimate weighing of souls, be better that she should have cut the knot like this, rather than have been strangled by it. It was all very well for Peter to take her side, but to take her side competently included an appreciation of what she had suffered, and what she had failed in. Anyone could form a fair idea of what she, as exhibited now, had suffered by the smallest recognition of what it must have been to be tied to the present occupant of the state-rooms, and the same exhibition showed exactly her tragic failure in allowing herself to be driven into this hermetical compartment, where all that reached her was the contemplation of her escape, as shown by her study of hotels. But Peter turned over all this, which was the root of the matter, as he might turn over the leaves of a dull book, and only saw a dramatic comedy in it, deserving of applause for its fitness, of an exclamation, "Serve him right!" or a laughing, "Well done, mother!" ... You couldn't deal with people like that; at that rate the whole world would become a relentless machine, always grinding, always seeing others ground, always being diverted at the pitiless revolution of the wheels. Compassion, tenderness, these were the qualities that just saved and redeemed the world from hell, or at least from being a wounding comedy, at which no human person could laugh for fear of crying instead.

Silvia got up from the seat where she and Peter had read his mother's letter, definitely desiring to avoid the conclusion to which her thoughts were leading her. He had wanted to laugh—that was certain, but she must forget that. Probably he had not meant it; it was only incongruousness and surprise (like funny things in church, which would not be in the least funny elsewhere) which had made a spasm.... Peter assuredly was not like that really, and the loyalty of love derided her for supposing it. He was (her heart insisted on that) all that her love adored him for being.

The dressing bell had already sumptuously sounded from the central turret, and, still quite ignorant of what had been the result of the disclosure, but conscious of a yearning anxiety to know, she went up to her bedroom. She was not so much anxious to know how Mr. Mainwaring was "taking it" (how he "took it" seemed to matter very little), but how Peter had done his part. Between his dressing-room and her bedroom were a couple of bathrooms, and she heard, with a certain clinging to the usualness of life, splashings and hissings of water coming from one of these. Whatever had happened, there was Peter having his bath, and soon, most likely, he would tap at her door, barefooted (he never would wear slippers as he paddled about between his room and hers) with the blue silk dressing-gown tied with a tasselled cord about his waist. Peter had a wondrous ritual for his bath: he had to immerse himself first of all, and then stand on the mat while he soaped himself from head to foot. Then, still slippery and soapy, in order to get cold and heighten the enjoyment of the next immersion, he turned on more hot taps, and put spoonful after spoonful of verbena salts into the water. Then he got in again, and stewed himself in this fragrant soup. When he was too hot to bear it any longer, he retired into a small waterproof castle at the end of the bath, and turned on all the cold water douches and squirts and syringes. Then, without drying himself at all, he put on the famous blue silk dressing-gown, which had a hood to it, lit a cigarette, and tapped at her door, to ascertain whether he could sit and finish his cigarette there. Silvia, by this time, knew precisely the interpretation of these splashings and hissings of water, and she would hurry up her own dressing, or slow it down, so that she could admit him. Fresh from his scrubbings and soapings, with the glow of the cold water on his skin, he was paganly sensuous in his enjoyment of the physical conditions of the moment, and, sitting by her dressing-table, talked the most amazing nonsense. He dried his feet on the tail of his dressing-gown, he rubbed his hair on the hood of it; there was the scent of soap and verbena and cigarette, and more piercing to her sense than these his firm, smooth skin, the cleansedness and the freshness of him.... At such chattering undress séances she was most of all conscious of him to the exclusion of herself; for whereas his kiss, his caress, united her with him, and she had part in it, when he came in thus, rough-haired, bare-legged, wet-footed, with a smooth shoulder emerging from his dressing-gown, while, enveloped in it, he rubbed himself dry, she felt herself merely a spectator of this beautiful animal.

But if he came in now—he might or might not—she knew that to-night she would be involved, so to speak, with him; his character, the essence of him, as exhibited in such account as he might give her of the interview with his father, would come like a cloud or a brightness that would obstruct this purely spectator-like view of him. He would not only be the clean, lithe animal, which, for these few minutes, she could look at without passion, without love, without friendship even, and be absorbed in the mere joy that there should be in this world so young and wild and perfect a creature....

There came his knock, and the usual inquiry, and he entered while her maid, with chaste, averted face, rustled out, not waiting to be dismissed, through the other door. He sat down in the big low chair by her dressing-table.

"Oh, the simplest pleasures are so much the best," he said. "Just washing, you know, just being hungry and sleepy. I never enjoy a play or a book or a joke nearly so much as a bath and food and getting my head well down into the pillow. But I hate sponges. Why should I scrub my nose with a piece of dead seaweed?"

Listen as she might, with all the delicacy of divination that love had given to her ear, she could find in his voice no inflection, no hesitation, nor, on the other hand, any glibness (as of a lesson learned and faultlessly repeated) that showed that he was speaking otherwise than completely naturally. The topics of bath and dinner and bed came to his lips with quite spontaneous fluency, as if he had not in this last hour been the bearer to his father of a tragic situation—one that, at least, must wound the vanity which was so predominant a passion in him. Or had Mr. Mainwaring taken it with the same ruthlessness, the same cynical amusement as Peter had appeared to? Silvia could not believe that: he must have been hurt, been astounded. But why, in pity's name, did not Peter tell her about that interview? He must have known how she longed to be told, whether there was good or bad to tell....

"A revolving brush covered with wash-leather," continued Peter, "like a small boxing-glove. You would cover it with soap and work it with your foot. But a sponge! Odious in texture, dull in colour, and full of horrible dark holes which probably contain the pincers of defunct crabs and the fins of dead fish.... Oh, by the way, I quite forgot! I did really, darling; I was thinking so much about substitutes for sponges."

Silvia could not doubt the sincerity of this: he had been thinking about sponges; there was the full statement of the case. And with his acknowledgment of that, his mere physical presence, the mere glamour of his radiant animalism, which, after all, was part of his essence and his charm, captured her again, whisking away for the moment all possibility of criticism, or of wishing that he could be other than he was. She knew that her misgivings—they amounted to that—would come flooding back, but just for the moment they were like some remote line of the low tide, lying miles away across shining levels.

"Oh, Peter," she cried, "if you can design a small revolving wash-leather boxing-glove to use for a sponge, I'll promise to have it made for you. But you must explain just how it's to work...."

She broke off.

"And about your father?" she said.

"Yes, I was just going to tell you when you interrupted about the sponge-plan," said he. "By the way, I'll draw you the revolving boxing-glove. A foot-pedal below—below, mind—the water, so that your foot doesn't get cold. And, of course, you hold the socket of the boxing-glove—the wrist, so to speak—in your hand, and it goes buzzing round as you work with your foot, and you apply it, well soaped, to your face. No more dead seaweed and lobster claws! My father now!"

Peter gathered up his knees in his arms, and sat there nursing them. His dressing-gown had fallen off his shoulder; he looked like some domesticated Satyr, wild with the knowledge of the woodland, but tamed to this sojourn—enforced or voluntary—in human habitations.

"I went to him, as you told me to do," he began.

Silvia interrupted him. She wanted him to do himself justice.

"No, my dear; you went quite of your own accord," she said. "I never urged you."

Peter's eyelids hovered and fell and raised themselves again. Often and often had Silvia noticed that shade of gesture on Nellie's face; but never, so it struck her, had she seen a man do just that. The gesture seemed to imply acquiescence without consent.

"Well, I went anyhow," he said. "I tapped on his door, and as there was no answer I went in. He was standing in front of that big Italian mirror in—well, in an attitude. He is intending to paint his own portrait, when he has finished that daub of you."

Silvia leaned forward towards him.

"Oh, don't talk like that!" she said. "Don't be ironical—not that quite: don't feel ironical."

Peter turned on her a face of mild, injured innocence. "I was telling you the bald facts," he said.

"The balder the better," said she.

"I told him I had read my mother's letter," he continued, "and that there was news in it which he had better know at once. I got him to sit down, and I got hold of his hand. And then I told him just the fact that she had gone away."

Peter shifted himself a little further back in his chair and drew his legs more closely towards him, so that his chin rested on the plateau of his knees.

"I am not being ironical," he said. "I am trying to tell you precisely what happened. He made a noise—a gurgle, I think I should call it—and he asked who the damned villain was with whom she had gone. And, to be quite bald, that seemed to me to be unreal. I said that there wasn't any damned villain, and that she had gone just because she felt she must be free. He wanted to see the letter, and I told him that I had torn it up. Then he began throwing his hair-brushes and dress-clothes into a bag, in order to start off and look for her, and asked me where she was. When I told him that I hadn't the slightest idea, he accused me of collusion with her. I merely denied that, and said that her letter was as great a surprise to me as it was to him."

Peter threw away the end of his cigarette.

"Then he began to guess why she had gone. Now the point of my tearing up my mother's letter was that he shouldn't know, wasn't it, darling?"

Silvia heard herself assent. There was a sickness of the heart coming over her, something too subtle for her to diagnose as yet.

"So he began to guess," continued Peter, "and as he tried to guess I was sorry for him—really sorry, you understand?"

Silvia's heart began to thrive again.

"Yes, yes; I knew you would be!" she cried.

"He soon hit on the reason," said Peter quietly. "There could only have been one reason, so he thought, and it filled him with the utmost remorse. He had been too big for her, that was what it came to—too great. He had not, in the exaltation of his art—this is quite what he said—remembered the limitations of—of the rest of us. She had fainted before the furnace of his genius. It was all his fault: he hadn't made allowance for the prodigious strain on her—for the effects, cumulative no doubt, of the high pressure. He strode about the room, he knocked over a chair— —"

Some fierce antagonism to his narrative blazed up in Silvia. She had wanted the facts, and here they were, but she had not allowed for the baldness of their presentation, though she had asked for it.

"Ah, don't talk like that, Peter," she said. "You're not a newspaper reporter."

Peter gave no reply at all. There he sat with his chin on his knees, quite silent.... If Silvia chose to speak to him like that it was clear that she must either go on or draw back; anyhow, the next word was with her. But all the time that he thus tacitly insisted on his rights, resenting what she had said, there was within him some little focus of light breaking through from her sunlit altitudes that illumined and justified her protest. Good Lord, wasn't she right? Wasn't his sentiment towards his father immeasurably ignoble compared to the comprehension of her love? And that very fact—his own unavowable condemnation of himself, that is to say—irritated him. If she was like that there was no use in his continuing his story.

Silvia spoke first. Humanly, she could not bear this silence in which Peter seemed to mock her, but divinely she must be ever so humble.... Humble? How love sanctified humility and transformed it into an ineffable pride. She pushed back her chair and knelt by his. She longed to unclasp the brown lean hands that enclosed him in himself and make them embrace her also. But that might annoy Peter: there was a suggestion of "claiming" him about it. She did not want to claim him.

"I don't know why I spoke like that," she said. "I asked you what happened, and you are telling me. Will you forgive me and go on?"

Peter had never seemed so remote from her as then. In the frantic telegraphy of her spirit, which seemed to be sending all the love that the waves of ether would bear, there came no response from him, in spite of his answer. "I never heard such nonsense," he said. "We should be a pretty pair if we had to forgive. How silly — you know it — to ask me to forgive you."

"Show you do, by going on," she said.

It was clear to him that what she wanted was to know not his father's part in this interview, but his own. Whether she liked it or not, he was going to be perfectly honest about it.

"When he knocked over a chair and strode about," he repeated, "and found out the reason for my mother's going away, I began to be less sorry for him. He enjoyed himself: it was all a tribute to his impossible greatness. From then onwards I acted, because he was acting. The alternative was to tell him that my mother simply found his egoism intolerable. That wouldn't have done any good, so I agreed with him: that was the best thing to do. He is in despair, a rather luxurious despair. I had either to explode that or let him enjoy it. So it was no use being sorry for him any longer."

Silvia broke out again; it was her love for Peter that spoke.

"My dear, you ought to have been a million times sorrier," she cried. "If he had been just simply broken-hearted about it, it would have been so much better. Can't you see that? Can you help feeling it?" She was shedding the gleam on him.

"I know what you mean," he said. "But I'm telling you what happened. I was less sorry for him when he began to console himself. I suppose I'm made like that."

Silvia bit her lip.

"Indeed you are not," she said. "You're making yourself out to be hard and unloving."

At the moment the clang of the dinner-bell from the turret just above Silvia's room broke in.... The whole neighbourhood must know when the family at Howes were warned that it was time to dress, and that three-quarters of an hour later it was time to dine. Peter, on the first evenings he had spent here with Silvia, had asked whether, like a Court Circular, such publicity need be given to their domestic affairs; but Silvia, confessing herself sentimental, had told him that her father had delighted in the installation of that sonorous announcement. The brazen proclamation "hurt" nobody, and "Daddy liked it."... Certainly it served a purpose now, and Peter jumped up.

"Lord, there's dinner!" he said. "And I haven't begun to dress. My father, by the way, wants to dine upstairs. Will you tell them, as you are so much more advanced than I, to send up his dinner? I must fly." Peter stood for a moment looking at her. If a situation between them had not actually laid hold of them, it had thrown a shadow over them, and he wanted to get out into sunlight again.

"Ah, you darling!" he said with a blend of envy and of admiration somewhere gushing up. Envy at her immense nobility—he could think of no other word for it—and admiration at that shrine of love which rose from the ground of her heart. It was so beautiful an edifice: he despaired of being worthy of it, and at times, so he confessed to himself, he wearied of its white stainless purity.... Somehow this evening there seemed to have opened a little crack on its soaring vault, which he must mend somehow.

"Give me a kiss, then," he said.

CHAPTER XI

Peter, though he often hung a veil over the real workings and processes of his mind for the benefit and admiration of others, before whom he was anxious to present a charming appearance, was honest with himself, and found, during the next fortnight, without any desire to dissimulate, that he was distinctly grateful to Silvia's insistence that he should not resign his place in the Foreign Office, for, in the present conditions and environments at Howes, it was certainly preferable to spend the solidity of the day in London rather than enjoy uninterrupted leisure at home. Even then the evenings were full of crashes and crises and intolerable ludicrousness....

His father, who still majestically occupied the state-rooms (and showed no indications of vacating them), moved along peaks and summits of the ridiculous, which his son really believed had never before been trodden by foot of man. That he was enjoying himself immensely Peter made no doubt whatever, living as he did on the heights of egoism, and free to indulge in the most extravagant exhibition of it. His standard (victoriously raised), his principle, his determination (announced with magnificent gestures once if not more, during the evening) was that he would remain rock-like and immovable, fulfilling the destiny of his own supreme will, whatever bombs Fate might choose to drop on him. That his whole soul was bitter with remorse for his failings and failures he did not deny. He should not have isolated himself, as he had done, in the supernal realms of Art; he should have remembered that he was a man as well as an artist, and had a wife as well as the celestial mistress of his soul. He ought to have been kinder, more tender, more indulgent to the frailty and the weakness of his Carissima. But remorse (so waved his standard), if it was the genuine article, must express itself not in idle repinings, but in a manful facing of the consequences of past error. His remorse (the right kind of remorse) did not weaken, but strengthened a man to go forward. He must not lose touch with the joy of life; he must not get from the severe spanking that remorse gave him only a smarting and a humiliation of the flesh. He must draw the lesson from his punishment, and proceed more tenderly but not less sublimely than before....

It must not be supposed that Mr. Mainwaring used such expressions as "spanking" in actual speech, or that the ironical account of his sublimity, as given above, was verbally his. But such, anyhow, was the manner in which these great tirades, delivered to Peter when he went up to see his father on his daily arrival at Howes an hour or so before dinner, impressed themselves on his mind. Usually there was a note for him on the table in the hall, which ran something like this:

"My Peter,—I am very low and despondent to-night, and I do not know if I can face a sociable evening. Come up to see me, my dear, for you are the only link which is left to me of those happy—far too happy—years, and see if your sweet spirit will not, like David playing before Saul, exorcise the demons of remorse and regret which shriek and gibber round the head of your unhappy father. I have tried so hard—ah, so hard—all day not to make myself a burden and a shadow to your dear ones, but I fear I have acquitted myself very ill. Come and cheer me up, Peter."

Peter, to do him justice, always went, and in the majesty of egoism, his father, without any encouragement at all, would talk himself into a splendid courage. At whatever cost to himself, at whatever effort from worn and debilitated nerve-strings, he would show that there was some music yet left in his. He would twang his mental guitar, and if the frayed string snapped— well, his lawyer would know that his affairs were in order.... Then, sooner or later, to Peter's great relief, the sonorous dressing-bell would ring, and he could go and have his bath. As likely as not, before he definitely quitted the room, his father would allude to the magnificent 1896 port which formed so admirable a feature in the cellars of Howes.

Usually after the bath he went in to see Silvia, but, for some reason or other, the spontaneous nonsense of these interviews had wilted and withered. Silvia, so it seemed to him, held herself in reserve, waiting for something from him. Peter would give an account of his day, of his talk with his father, and still Silvia seemed to wait. She was overbrimming with all that she ever had for him, but, to his perception, what she waited for was for him to turn the winch of the sluice.

Once there had been a really outrageous scene with his father, in which, after tears, Mr. Mainwaring had slid from his chair with a groan, and lay, an ignoble heap, upon the floor. Peter on this occasion had given Silvia a perfectly colourless *précis* of the degrading exhibition, and had endorsed it, brought collateral evidence to bear on its nature by the production of one of the notes which usually awaited him on his return from town. He had done that in some sort of self-justification: Silvia could not fail to realize how trying, from their very unreality, such scenes were for him, and he gave her also every evening a very respectable specimen of his patience with his father. And yet he felt that Silvia was not waiting for *that*; it was not how he behaved, how patient and cordial he schooled himself to be, that she waited for. He was patient, he was cordial, and though she often gave him a little sympathetic and appreciative word for his reward, it was no more than a sugar-plum to a child, something to keep it quiet. What she wanted, what she longed for the evidence of, was an internal loving driving force which turned the wheels of the machinery of his impeccable conduct, and that he had not got for her. He spun the wheels with a clever finger from outside.

But usually these wheels went round merrily enough. He reported his father's despondence; he, ever so lightly, alluded to the fact that he had cheered him up, and his estimate was justified, for Mr. Mainwaring, on the crashing of the dinner-bell in the turret, would sometimes announce his progress from the state-rooms by a jubilant yodelling, and would remain for the greater part of dinner in a state of high elation. True, he would have a spasm now and then: if he happened to have his attention called to Mrs. Wardour's pearls, he might for a brief dramatic moment cover his eyes and say in a choked voice: "My Carissima had some wonderful pearls"; but then, true to his manly determination, he would dismiss the miserable association and become master of his soul again.

Peter usually had a second dose of his father's Promethean attitude later in the evening, after Silvia and her mother had gone upstairs.

"Your treasure, your pearl of great price, your angel!" he would ejaculate. "Her sweet pity, her divine compassion! It is she—she and you—who reconcile me to life. But I must not bask too long in that healing effulgence. I must get back to London; I must reinstate myself in my desolate house, and face it all, face it all. I must stand on my own feet again, poor sordid cripple that I am." Then perhaps, if quite overcome, he would bury his face in his hands, but much more usually he would stand up, throw out his chest, breathe deeply, and draw himself up to the last half-inch of his considerable stature.

"Work!" he said. "Work is the tonic that God puts in the reach of all of us. Remember that, my Peter, if grief and sorrow ever visit you. But then you have by your side the sweetest, the most sympathetic woman ever sent to enlighten the gloom of this transitory world. So had I, by God, so had I, and I did not recognize her preciousness and her fragility.... Enough! Silvia! Did you notice her exquisite love towards me at dinner to-day, when for a moment the sight of Mrs. Wardour's pearls unmanned me?"

Peter on this occasion was lashed to the extremity of irritation.

"I don't think I did," he said. "I only remember that she instantly asked you if you would have some more pheasant."

He tried to do better than that. Certainly there was no use in saying that sort of thing.

"But she looked at you, father," he added hastily. "You felt what she was feeling. Was that it?"

His father clasped his hands.

"A divine beam came to me," he said. "A message of consolation. It made me live again. Surely you saw its effect on me?"

Peter, at such moments, longed for his wet woods. He wanted to be by himself, or, at any rate, with someone who could understand and enjoy this stupendous farce. If only Nellie, for instance, had been sitting there with him, how would their eyes have telegraphed their mental ecstasy. Silvia, at this same moment, would not have served the purpose; she might see how ridiculous his father was being, but below her perception of that, which might easily have made her telegraph and smile to him, there would have been that huge, unspeakable tenderness which, when you wanted an answering perception of farce, would have spoiled it all. That universal embracing compassion required salting. Before now she had seen, and communicated to him, her sense of his father's absurdities, but now, when he turned trouble into an empty arena for his posturing, her sense of comedy completely failed her. Or, if she still possessed it, Peter could not get at it. With a flare of intuition he guessed that it might be unlocked to him, if only he could use the right key to it. But the key was compassion, and it was he for whom she waited to thrust it into the wards. If only he loved they could laugh at anything together; without that the gate was locked.

Well, if it was locked, he would enjoy his imperfect vision of what lay within.

"Yes, I saw its effect on you," he said, trying to imagine that Nellie was here, enthralled and wide-eyed, "You amused us all very much immediately afterwards by making that lovely sea-sick passenger out of an orange. Perfectly screaming!"

His father thrust his hands through his hair; it stood up like some glorious grey mane.

"Yes, yes," he said, "I made an effort. I won't, no, my Peter, I will not lose sight of the dear gaieties of life. God knows what it costs me! Even after a little thing like that I was more than ever plunged in the gulf of despondency. I know how wrong I am. I must never relax my efforts; I mustn't give myself time to think. Work and laughter—those divine twins."

He poured himself out a glass of whisky and soda, and chose a cigar with proper care.

"A word or two on practical affairs," he said, "before I go to my lonely and wakeful bed. You will be here, I understand, till early in December. By then I trust (I insist, indeed, on thus trusting) that I shall have schooled myself to face the desolation of my home (what once was home) again. May I, do you think, ask to remain here till then? I look upon your beautiful Howes as my hospital. Soon, still maimed, still limping, still in the blue uniform of pain, I know that I must, indeed I insist on it, face the world again and make the best of my shattered existence. But till then? Silvia, whom I consulted with regard to this matter, told me that you were the master of Howes, and suggested my speaking to you about it."

Peter saw an opportunity. His father, it is true, was an odious infliction of an evening, but there was something to be gained by his own eager tolerance of that, which quite outweighed the inconvenience. But he must do more than tolerate; he must welcome; and Silvia—here was the point—must know how splendidly he had risen to it. Before he answered he made himself remember what the intonation of cordiality sounded like.

"But that is perfectly charming of you," he said. "It's lovely that the suggestion came from yourself. She and I may be away for a day or two in November——"

Peter did not quite know what arrangement he was to suggest about such days when he and Silvia would be away, for instance, on their visit to Nellie. He was spared the trouble of formulating one by his father, who gave a great gesticulation, admirably expressive of courage.

"I will go home—home for those days," he said. "I will, with set teeth and firm mouth, begin to grow accustomed to my desolation and loneliness. I will learn to bear it, taking in long draughts the inestimable tonic of work. Peter, Peter"—and the voice shook—"when will my Carissima come back to me?"

He was unmanned only for a moment, and his mastery of himself returned to him.

"Was ever a stricken man so blessed by the love of his children?" he exclaimed. "God bless you, my Peter. You are going to bed?"

The abruptness of this benediction convinced Peter that his father had got what he wanted and had no more use for him that night, and he went along the corridor to his room and Silvia's. His first impulse was to tell her how cordially, for his part, he had welcomed his father's suggestion; the second and wiser one was to say nothing about it. Mr. Mainwaring was sure to make the most of it to her; he might even attribute to it that force from inside which turned the wheels. Yes, Silvia should learn about it like that.

He let himself very quietly into his room, and undressed and went to bed without going in to say good night to her. If he went in to see her, it was more than likely that she would ask him whether his father had alluded to the question of his remaining with them, and he wanted the information concerning that to be conveyed to her by one who would give him, Peter felt sure, a florid testimonial for cordiality. He had passed, moreover, a monotonous and fatiguing evening, and wanted not to talk at all, but to sleep. His father had been slightly more dreadful than usual, Mrs. Wardour had more than ever been non-existent, and Silvia, so it struck him, had been waiting, had been watching him, not, it need hardly be said, with fixed eye or stealthy glances, but with some steady psychical alertness that was incessantly poised on him. Without looking at him, without any talking to him or talking at him, he had felt all evening—this, perhaps, had been the most fatiguing part of it—that she had scarcely been conscious of anyone else but him. Though her eyes were on the cards, and she ruefully bemoaned that the goddess of piquet, whom she jointly invoked with Peter's father, had been so niggardly in her favours towards herself, it had been no more than an automaton that was thus victimized to the extent of three lost games, including a rubicon.

Peter, as he curled himself up in bed, let his mind stray drowsily over such details of the evening, coming back always to this impression of Silvia's watching him. Whenever he spoke to her of his father she watched him—seldom with her eyes—in just that manner. By aid of his quick perception, that felt rather than reasoned, Peter had, he was sure, arrived at what she watched for then. She watched for some token, she listened for some inflection that indicated tenderness, sympathy, affection towards his father. She could not have been watching for any such token as that for herself, for he gave her those; she knew they were hers. But he had never felt more certain about anything in these dim, vague regions of sentiment and desire than that she wanted something more than that which he gave her, and a certain impatience gained on him. What, after all, had been her own first words to him when he asked her to marry him? Had not her face flamed with the light of the beacon that welcomed him as she whispered that all she asked was to be allowed to love him? At the time that had seemed to him a divine intuition, one that, in a word, precisely defined her way of love and his.

There came at that door of his bedroom which led to her room the lightest, most barely audible of touches; he was scarcely sure whether he had heard it or not. But he did not reply, for either it was imaginary, and needed no answer, or it was Silvia come to see whether he was in his room yet. In that case, even more, an answer must be withheld, for after this evening of strain and high pressure all he wanted was to be let alone and to go to sleep. But underneath his eyelids, not quite closed, he watched the door which was opposite his bed and was dimly visible in the glimmer of starshine that came in through the open and uncurtained window.

Round the edge of the door, though he had heard no click of a turned handle, there came a thin "L" of light, which broadened until, in the shaft of it, appeared Silvia. She held a lighted candle, which she screened from his bed with her hand, the fingers of which, close to the flame, were of a warm transparent crimson. Apparently his clothes, tumbled together on a chair, first caught her notice, and from them she looked straight towards the bed. Her face was vividly illuminated, and when she saw him lying there with shut eyes, some radiant, ineffable tenderness came like dawn over it. Never had he seen so selfless and wonderful a beam; she might have been some discarnate spirit permitted to look upon him who had been the love of her earthly heart. That, then, was how she regarded him when she thought she was unobserved by him; he meant *that* to her. Next moment, round the half-open door, the light narrowed and disappeared, and he was left again in the glimmering dusk. Never had he seen with half such certainty and directness what Silvia was. She had thought he was asleep, and so she could let free her very soul. Neither by day nor night had she come to him quite like that; all other emotions, amusement, interest, sympathy, desire, passion even, had concealed rather than revealed her. They had been webs and veils across the sanctuary, illumined, indeed, by the light that burned there, but still hiding it. Now for one moment Peter had seen her with those veils drawn aside, the holy place of her, and her love was the light of it.

He was sitting next afternoon in his room at the Foreign Office, rather harassed by the necessity of being polite to everybody. The clerk senior to him in his department was on leave, and it happened that an extra King's messenger had to be sent off to Rome, carrying a new cipher. That was a perfectly usual incident in Peter's routine, but this messenger was fresh to his job, and had been in and out of the office all day, fussy and pompous, wishing to be assured that he had got reserved compartments and a private cabin. There was a strike on the French railways going on, and Peter had told him that it might be impossible to secure a compartment farther than

Paris, but all that could be done had been done, and, anyhow, he would find a seat reserved for him. Usually Peter rather enjoyed applying soothing ointments to agitated people, and his skill as a manipulator of pompous and fussy persons was so effective that by common consent (he quite agreeing) tiresome officials were often turned on to him for emollient manipulation. But to-day the telephonings and the interruptions and the pomposity and the prime necessity of remaining dulcetly apologetic for inconveniences which were wholly out of his control had got on his nerves, and when finally, in answer to inquiries, it had been determined that the King's messenger had better, in order to secure a journey probably unvexed by strikes, go round by Southampton and Havre, Peter had been treated to some very acid talk. Of course, the man was an ass, no one knew that better than he, and it was ludicrous to be infuriated by an ass.

About six then, that afternoon, Peter had done all that patience and polite inquiries from French station-masters could do for the ass, and with undiminished civility he had wished him a pleasant journey. In half an hour, or, if he chose, now, since there was nothing more that could detain him, he could telephone for his car and slide down to Howes. He did not in the least look forward to his evening there; it would assuredly be an evening of as high a pressure as the day had been. His father would certainly be voluble with blessings and gratitude, and Peter hated the prospect of these benedictions. Installed as Mr. Mainwaring now was for a couple of months more, he would surely develop the idea which he had before now outlined, when he assured Peter that during his daily absences in London he himself would act as his vice-regent. He had already caused the luncheon hour to be changed in order that he might get an extra half-hour of work into the morning; already he had got the estate carpenter to "knock him up" an immense frame in which he could see his second cartoon, now dismally approaching completion, more satisfactorily displayed. And then Peter thought of that short candle-lit glimpse last night, when Silvia had looked into his room.

For one moment the remembrance of that magnetically beckoned him; the next, as by some inexplicable reversal, the needle of that true compass swung round and pointed in the opposite direction. It no longer gave him his course back to Howes; it steadily pointed away from Howes. But even as he told himself how inexplicable that was, his subconscious self gave a convincing explanation of it. To hurry back to Silvia and her watch of love, to feel that there were veils which only he could draw aside, but which, when drawn aside by God knew what aspirations towards a light he did not comprehend, would reveal to him again the glory of her sanctuary, was a task for saints and lovers. He would rise to it in time, he would learn to be worthy of an ideal that somehow, in spite of its white heat, had the chill of asceticism frosting it; but just now he longed for ordinary, unreflective, unstruggling human gaiety. She—Silvia—lived naturally on those heights, just as his father lived in the cloud—or the shroud, maybe—of his own inimitable egoism.

He was tidying his table, intending to ring up very soon for his motor to take him back to Howes. If he started in half an hour he would have time to see his father before dressing, and to talk to Silvia between bath and dinner. Then he changed his mind and determined not to ring for his motor at all. Instead he would walk back across the park—no, not across the park, but up Whitehall, and so by streets all the way to Piccadilly. He would have time to get a cup of tea at home and start from there immediately afterwards. The rather longer route by the streets was infinitely preferable. There would be crowds of ordinary human beings all the way, people not monstrous on the one hand, so far as he knew, from swollen egoism, nor irradiated by idealisms which made you pant in a rarefied atmosphere. There would be just masses of people, people gay, people sulky, ugly people, pretty people, but above all ordinary people.

At the moment when his tidying was complete, and his table ready for his next day's work, the telephone on his table tinkled. He resigned himself to more inquiries from the incomparable ass, but they could not last long, for his train left Waterloo within a manageable number of minutes. But in answer to his intimation that it was indeed he who waited at the end of the wire, there did not come the voice which he had listened to so often that day, but one quite other and equally recognizable.

"Nellie?" he said.

"Yes, my dear. How lucky I am to catch you. You're in town, then?"

"At the moment," said he. "I'm going back to Howes in half an hour."

"Oh, what a pity! You won't be in town to-night, then?"

"Why?" asked Peter.

"Only that Philip and I were going to the play, and Philip's got a cold and thinks it wiser not to go out. I thought perhaps—just a lovely off-chance—that you might come instead. Oh, do, Peter."

"Hold on. Wait half a minute," said he.

He put the receiver down on the table, seating himself on the edge of it. Here *in excelsis* was precisely what he longed for. Dinner, a theatre, a talk, all with Nellie, who represented to him (though *in excelsis*) the ideal epitome of the world of humanity. He had thought a moment before, with the sense of anticipating a "break," the mere walk through crowded streets. She would in this programme give him all that intimately, she would give also the sense of intimate friendship without effort. They would jabber and enjoy— —

He took up the receiver again.

"Yes, all quite easy," he said. "It's late already, and when it's late and I can't get down there, I can always sleep in town. Silvia and I settled that when I began work again in this doleful office."

Nellie appeared to laugh at that.

"Silvia evidently spoils you," she said. "But it's too lovely to catch you like this. Will you dine with me at the Ritz? Seven? The play—can't remember what it is—begins at eight. So we shan't have to hurry, and can sit with our elbows on the table for a bit and talk."

"Sit with what?" asked he.

"Elbows on the table," said Nellie with elaborate distinctness. "No hurry—talk."

This time he laughed.

"Oh, don't let's go to the Ritz," he said. "Come and have elbows at my great house. I'll go back there now and order dinner. It'll probably be beastly, but it's more private. Shall we do that?"

"Much nicer," said Nellie. "How are you, Peter? Oh, I can ask that afterwards. Seven, then. Wardour House."

"Yes. Give condolences to Philip. Not congratulations, mind."

Peter hung up the receiver, and then took it off again at once in order not to give himself time to think. There would be clamour and argument if he thought, and he wanted nothing of that sort. Ten minutes afterwards he left the office, having telephoned to the Jackdaw that he was detained here and would be obliged to sleep in London.

Two months had passed since Nellie and he had met, but whatever frontier-change of limitation or expansion had been decreed for each severally since then, their meeting to-night had the power to put such aside, and they hailed each other without the embarrassment of altered circumstances. Their compasses were rigidly in accord, and as the excellent impromptu meal proceeded the talk sailed towards northern lights, in the direction of their steadfast needles. Soon they were sitting (at the elbow stage) with their coffee and cigarettes, with a quiet quarter of an hour in front of them before they need start.

"Motor at ten minutes to eight," said Peter to the servant, glancing at the clock. "Tell me when it comes round."

He shifted his chair a little sideways towards her.

"Oh, this is jolly," he said, "for we've gone on just where we left off. You're just the same. It's two months, you know, since I set eyes on you. Do say you've missed me."

"What else did you expect?" said she. "Marriage isn't— — Oh, Peter, what's the name of that river?"

"Thames?" asked Peter.

"No, the forgetting one—Lethe. Because I'm married to Philip I don't forget—other people. But tell me, has Silvia been giving you Lethe to drink instead of early morning tea?"

"Not a drop. She's given me everything else in the world."

Nellie still had that habit of plaiting her fingers together.

"You ought to be very grateful to me," she said. "It was I, after all, one night at my mother's flat, do you remember?"

"I was Jacob that night," remarked Peter.

Nellie frowned.

"Don't tell me how," she said. "I want to see if we think side by side still. Ah, I've got it! Philip was Esau—isn't that clever?—and I told him I was tired, and so you supplanted him."

"Right. Get on," said Peter.

"Yes, about your gratitude. It was that night that I told you to ask Silvia to marry you. Didn't I?"

"Yes. Thank you, dear Mrs. Beaumont," said Peter effusively. "So good of you to tell me."

"It was a good idea, wasn't it?"

Nellie's mind stiffened itself to "attention" at that moment. Before, it had been standing very much at ease.

"The best idea in the world," he said.

"I'm awfully glad," said she. "What you say, too, makes it all the more delightful of you to stop up in town to-night, instead of going back to her."

Though up till now they had fitted into each other with all the old familiar smoothness, it appeared now, when they got near, in their conversation, to what had happened to each of them (not, so he still felt, altering them, but putting them into new cases) that there was fresh ground to be broken; hitherto they had only picked their way over the old ground. Nellie felt this even more imperatively than he. They had got to run the plough (so why not at once on this admirable opportunity?) through the unturned land.... Peter's servant had already appeared in the doorway, announcing the motor, and she had noticed that, but Peter had not. She concluded from that, that he, easy as their intercourse had up till now been, was feeling some pre-occupation. His hesitation in answering her last acknowledgment of his amiability in remaining in town instead of going back to Howes, confirmed that impression. Then, before the pause was unduly prolonged, so as to amount to embarrassment, she put her word in again.

"I appreciate that," she said, "because it shows that the new ties haven't demolished the old. And on my side I admit, far more definitely than you, that if my poor Philip must have a cold, I am glad—ever so glad—it visited him to-night, so as to give me an evening with you."

She swept her plate and coffee-cup aside, to make room for an advance of the elbows.

"Oh, my dear, I have missed you," she said. "Naturally, however perfectly Philip is himself, he couldn't be you. My mind—perhaps you haven't noticed it—has wonderfully improved these last months—I am learning Italian, and we read Dante—but it needs just a little holiday. And I've found out such a lot of things about Philip, and all of them are good, worse luck."

Peter looked up at her with that liquid seriousness of eye which to her meant that he was walking in the wet woods.

"Oh, poor thing," he said.

For some reason which she did not choose to investigate, Nellie found that remark immensely encouraging. Certainly, a few minutes ago, she had tried to provoke him to talk—really talk, but the ironical perfection of his condolence, which, so she felt, saw all round what she was saying, made her more than acquiesce in his listening instead of talking. She felt sure that this beloved Peter understood— —

"I knew you would sympathize," she said; "but there's my tragic prosperity. My Philip isn't lazy or spiteful and inconsiderate or selfish, or bad-tempered or greedy or—or anything at all, except that he knows so much about birds. He has taught me a lot, and he's quite absolutely devoted to me. He never liked anybody so much as me. But do you know, darling, to a woman, at any rate, having a good, nice man quite devoted to her, as far as his affections go, gives her, once in a way, a little sense of strain. She has to find her hymn-book and sing."

"I'll lend you mine," said Peter, speaking without thought, but only by instinct.

"Thanks. When will you want it back? No; I won't borrow it. But the fact is, that an undilutedly good man wants something to make him fizz. You must have humour or a vile temper or cynicism or greediness, or something, to make you drinkable.... My dear, what *am* I saying?"

The clock on the mantelpiece struck the hour at which the curtain of their play rose; but the chimes, eight sonorous thumps, preceded by the quarters, penetrated Peter's brain no more than the announcement of the motor ten minutes ago had done.

"You're talking awfully good sense," he said. "At any rate, you're talking a language I can understand. You always did; we quarrelled and wrangled, but we were on the same plane."

"So we are now, thank heaven," said she. "It's time you gave me some news, you know."

Whatever pre-occupation it was that held Peter, he seemed to shake himself free of it.

"Yes, I've got news all right," he said. "Domestic tragedy."

"Oh, my dear, what?" asked she. "Nothing awful?"

He seemed to know for certain that she was figuring in her mind something about himself and Silvia. So, in the upshot, the sequel, the development, he was. But he tested her, so to speak, over the domestic tragedy itself.

"My mother has run away from home," he began.

Nellie did not laugh. She only bit her tongue with firm purpose.

"Dear Peter!" she said, when she released it.

"She has simply gone," he said. "Round about ten days ago, when father arrived to study his first cartoon, with a view to the rest of the series—Mrs. Wardour bought it, by the way—gracious me, what a lot we have got to talk about."

"Never mind the cartoon," said Nellie with thrilled interest. "Get on with the tragedy."

Quite uncontrollably Peter's mouth began to lengthen itself. He did not quite smile, but the promise of a smile was there.

"Tragedy, then," he said. "My mother sent me a long—oh, such a priceless letter, to say that when my father came home again—his home, I mean—he would find she had gone."

The Dryad, the gay conscienceless Nellie, could not, in spite of her improved mind, quite contain herself.

"But your mother?" she asked. "At her age? How absolutely wonderful of her! Do you know who he is?"

Peter tried not to laugh, and completely failed in that dutiful endeavour. She could but follow his lead, and the two, drawing psychically nearer to each other every moment, abandoned themselves, just for natural relief, to this irrepressible mirth.

"You are such a damned fool, Nellie," he said at length. "Do listen: don't be funny. It's quite different."

"'Pologies," said she, rather shakily.

"It wasn't anything so romantic, but it was just as human," said Peter. "You know how my mother was hammered into herself—that phrase came in her letter, by the way: it's not original."

"But I never guessed there was anything to hammer," said Nellie.

"Nor did I; at least, I only half guessed. But there was. A breaking point came, and she couldn't stick my father any longer. She has just gone away. Do you remember how she used always to be looking up hotels in railway guides?"

"I remember that most of all," said she. "Well?"

"She's gone to one of them. She's just gone away to be free, not to lead somebody else's life any more. When she has got a good breath of air, she may, apparently, come back. But she doesn't promise."

Nellie had grown quite serious again.

"That's even more wonderful of her," she said. "She just went away because she wanted to be herself. My dear, what a mother! And waiting till you were married! And your father? Go on."

This time Peter's mouth strayed beyond the limits of mere reflective meditation, and smiled broadly.

"He has discovered, to his complete satisfaction, why she left him," he said. "He knows—as if Gabriel had told him—that his tremendous personality, his devotion to Art, all that sort of thing, was too much for her. He reproaches himself bitterly—and oh, my dear, how he enjoys it—with having failed to realize the frailty—not moral—the weakness, the ordinariness of other people. She was scorched in his magnificent flames, and escaped from that furnace with her life."

"But how lovely for him!" said Nellie. "Lovely for her, too. But why tragedy? You said it was a tragedy?"

His whole body gave a jubilant jerk. If he had been standing up he must have jumped.

"Ah, you do see that, don't you?" he cried. "I just rejoice in her! At least, I would——"

Nellie divined perfectly well that "if Silvia understood" really completed the sentence. But if Peter wished, for the present anyhow, to leave that unspoken, loyalty to their comradeship prevented her from suggesting it. Another motive, not less potent than that, dictated her silence on the point, for she infinitely preferred that he should volunteer some such information concerning himself and Silvia than that she should give away her knowledge of it. Certainly she longed to know in what real relation he and Silvia stood to each other, but it would be a tactical error (tactical was too businesslike) to let him know that his incomplete sentence gave her so certain a hint.

"I see," she said quickly. "You would rejoice in her if it wasn't for your father."

Until the two ultimate words of that were spoken Peter's eyes had been bright and expectant. He evidently waited for the termination which she had refused to utter. When her sentence was complete she saw, unmistakably again, that his eyes accepted and acquiesced in her conclusion.

"Quite," he said in a level voice. "So for the present my father is consumed with remorse, and is occupying the state-rooms—you've never seen them; gorgeous tapestry and Lincrusta Walton ceilings—till we come up to town. He is painting away at the series of cartoons."

Peter poured himself out a second cup of coffee from the tray that had been left between them half an hour or more before.

"Aunt Joanna!" he said. "You never heard such a plot or saw such a person. She's my mother-in-law's sister, you know. She's 'got at' my father, there's no doubt of it, and she's secured all the cartoons by bribery and corruption, instead of their being painted for the gallery—the Art Gallery, I should say—at Howes. Aunt Eleanor—she's my father-in-law's brother's wife—has secured the sketches for the cartoons. They've been to Howes once, but my father quite dominated them. That was before the crash, so you may judge how much more, with that added string of tragedy to his bow, he would dominate them now. They are more priceless than words can say. There will be a family gathering at Christmas, I understand. Nellie, do come. We would have such a gorgeous time if you were there. We would sit quiet and notice and drink in, and then we would sit over the fire together when Uncle John and Uncle Abe——"

"Uncle Abe?" asked Nellie in an awed voice.

"Yes. Sir Abel Darley, K.B.E., husband to Aunt Joanna. Don't interrupt. When Uncle John and Uncle Abe and Aunt Eleanor and Aunt Joanna have gone, not staggering at all, but 'full up,' to bed, we would have such holy convocations about them."

Nellie had inferred a little more information about Silvia by this time, but what occupied her most was not what she was inferring about anybody. It was quite enough for her to realize that for the duration, anyhow, of the first act of the play which they had meant to see she was in the old full enjoyment of Peter again. They had stepped back into the candour and closeness of their friendship, and though he had not, as she had, confessed that he was having a holiday, it was transparently clear that this was the case. But just there the candour was clouded; she guessed that, even as she was having a holiday from Philip (God bless him), so Peter was having a holiday from Silvia. Only—here was the difference—he did not or would not own up to that. Even in the projected scheme of Christmas-hilariousness at the uncles and aunts, Silvia did not appear as ever so faintly ridiculous, or as ever so faintly partaking in the midnight merriment. Throughout their talk Peter had kept her hermetically apart. Once or twice, Nellie conjectured, he had pointedly enough refrained from introducing her. She could visualize the rest of them down at Howes, but the part that to Peter Silvia played was mysteriously shrouded. When you were laughing at everybody all round, why should you except one person from the compliment of amused criticism? It was clear that Silvia had no applause for the comedy of Peter's parents, for he had so cordially welcomed her—Nellie's—appreciation of it. What, then, was Silvia's line, what was her relation, above all, to Peter?

She decided not to burn all her boats, but to set fire to just a little one.

"Won't Silvia enjoy them too?" she asked.

"Can't tell," said Peter.

If there was a lapse of loyalty there, if, in a minor degree, there was a sense conveyed of disappointment, though of accepting that disappointment without comment, Nellie decided that Peter was not intending to enlarge on it. She still (after that small burned boat) clung to the chance of Peter's volunteering information, but clearly she would not get that just now; and another heavy booming of quarters from the clock gave her an excellent opportunity of abandoning that which, after all, had never been a discussion on her own initiative.

"Good gracious, it's a quarter to nine," she said. "You wretch, Peter! We've missed one act, if not two."

"Let's miss them all," he said, "and have an evening."

That made her pause, but only for a moment. Peter had consistently shied away from that one topic she wanted to hear about, and a break of some sort was much more likely to produce in him the pressure that would eventually "go pop" than if they remained just sizzling here.

"But we absolutely must go," she said. "Philip will ask me about the play, and I couldn't tell him that you and I simply sat talking till it was over."

"Why not?" said Peter.

"Because it isn't done. My dear, you and I have signed on to the conventionalities of life. Come along. A bore, but there it is. Besides, how would you account for your evening to Silvia? Dining at seven, you know. That requires a theatrical explanation."

"Oh, don't be vulgar," said Peter. "As if Silvia wouldn't delight in my spending an evening with you."

"I know that," said she. "Don't lose your sense of humour, Peter. It was a mild kind of joke."

"Come on, then," he said. "And as for its being my fault that we're so late——"

The second act was drawing to an end when they stole into their box. On the stage there was proceeding the most elementary of muddles, to which it was not in the least worth while to devote any ingenuity. It was clear at the first glance that these people who pretended to be servants were really landed gentry, and that just before the end the Earl (who had taken the house) would propose to the cook and be violently accepted. Psychologically they presented no point of interest. Far more engrossing to Nellie was the fact that she had got Peter with her, and the pleasure of that and the general problem it propounded was far more absorbing. Marriage had certainly quickened her emotional perceptions, and she inferred, from the extraordinary delight that it was to be with him again, how much in the interval she had missed him. She had no reason to complain, either, of the welcome he had given her, but it was manifest (how she could not definitely have said) that the quality of that was different from hers to him. To his sense, as he had openly stated, they had taken up the old attitude, the old intimacy, without break, but as she thought over that in the few minutes that elapsed before the act was finished, she found that, for her part, she did not altogether endorse his view. Certainly the old intimacy was there, firm and unshaken, but somehow, hovering over it, like a mist which to her eyes seemed to be luminous with tears, there was some new atmospheric condition, sunny and tremulous.

Peter turned to her as the house sprang into light again.

"Oh, what a waste of time," he said. "We should have done much better to have left our elbows on the table. We're always doing it too. Do you remember the last play at which we met? That time you were with Philip and I with Silvia and Mrs. Wardour. Then we had our talk afterwards; to-night we had it first. I like the other plan best."

Though Peter had here stated several things with which she was in cordial agreement, his tone was not in tune with the old footing, the old intimacy. Not many minutes ago it had been she who, in opposition to his inclination, had insisted on breaking their *tête-à-tête*; now, with all possible lightness of touch, she suggested its resumption.

"I've seen enough," she said. "I can tell Philip all about it. Let's go back, my dear, and have half an hour's more talk. It was my fault that we broke up; but how could I have told that the play would have been as silly as this? We shall talk more sense in five minutes than they'll put into the whole of the next act."

Peter's eyes were wandering round the house. At this moment they were attracted by a feather fan violently signalling from a box directly opposite, and the general buzz of the theatre was quite distinctly pierced with a shrill scream of laughter which came from precisely the same direction as the gesticulating fan. It was hardly necessary to put up his glasses to ascertain the authorship of these phenomena.

"Mrs. Trentham," he said unerringly, "with the usual myrmidons. She has seen us, Nellie. Come round and be conventional."

"Oh, why?" said she. "If she wants to see us she can come here, can't she? But she doesn't want to see us: she only wants to be seen."

She felt that at that moment she was becoming, to Peter, part of the general foreground, a prominent object in it, but still only part of it. His next words confirmed the impression.

"Oh, come along," he said. "Let's embark on the ordinary ridiculous evening. Let's all go back to supper with me. Or perhaps there's a dance going on. Come round and forage, Nellie. I've been in the country for a month, you know. Besides——"

She knew perfectly well what he had left unsaid, and answered it.

"But what does it matter how much she talks?" she asked.

Peter gave her a glance of brilliant surprise.

"How did you know that that was what I didn't say?" he demanded.

"Because it's you, of course. Or, if you like, because it's me."

The fan waved more vehemently than ever.

"We'd better go," said he.

Nellie got up. In the old days she would almost certainly have been able to superimpose her wish over his. Now it was the other way about. She seemed to be in the grip of some internal necessity of doing what he wanted. He had to have his way, not because he had become stronger of will, but because she had lost her power of self-assertion with regard to him. It was not any general debility of will on her part; she had her way with Philip, for instance, with an effortless ease. But then she was not part only of the foreground to Philip, nor to her was Peter part only of the foreground....

CHAPTER XII

Peter managed to get away from the Foreign Office next day, in the absence of anything to detain him, an hour or so before his usual time, and arriving at the gilded gates of the battlemented lodge of Howes while the warm October twilight still lingered in the sky, he got out to walk across the mile of park that separated him from the house. His truant evening in town last night, the plunge into the froth and noise and chatter, had quieted some sort of restlessness, had assuaged some sort of hunger, and he was still licking the chops of memory, content in a few minutes now to "wipe his mouth and go his journey" again. He just had the sense of having enjoyed an evening out, of having lolled in the old familiar tap-room, with the usual habitués, over a pot of beer, while a friendly barmaid (this was Mrs. Trentham) made the usual jokes over the counter as she served him. Some of these seemed to have sounded better by electric light, so to speak, than did the timbre of their memory in the dusky crimson of the dying day, and he recalled the welcome of screams and shrieks she had given to Nellie and himself when, at his insistence, they had visited her in the box opposite. She threatened when she learned they had already dined alone (appearing so very late at the play) to send anonymous letters to Silvia and Philip. There was a judge in the divorce court, she added, who was much devoted to her, and would no doubt give her admission for the two cases when they came on. The robust wit of Lord Poole had ably seconded her.

Then, with the exception of Nellie, who had to go home to put an end to Philip's solitary evening, they had all gone back to Wardour House, where Peter promised some sort of scratch supper, and Nellie, finding that her husband had already gone to bed, joined them again. It had been altogether a pleasant ridiculous evening which had made itself in this impromptu and accidental manner an ordinary human evening. Just twice there had for Peter been a slight check, a signal momentarily against him—once when he found that Nellie had left again, very soon after her reappearance at supper, without a word to him; once when, without warning, it had entered his mind that at just about this time, the night before, he had seen his bedroom door open, and Silvia's face look in on him as he lay with closed eyelids, feigning sleep. That was rather a dreadful thing to have done....

He paused a moment on the bridge that crossed the lake, looking at the image of the house duskily reflected on its far margin. There was someone coming towards him along the path that led by the edge of the lake, and joined the road here, and before his eyes had time to tell him who it was, she waved a hand at him, without the screams, without the violent gesticulations by which Mrs. Trentham the night before had made herself known. She quickened her pace as he answered her signal, and in three minutes more he had joined her.

"The chauffeur told me you had walked from the lodge," she said, "so I came to meet you. You're early."

Peter kissed her.

"I'll go away again, shall I?" he said.

"No; as you've come, you can stop," she said.

"And what did you do with yourself last night? Not all alone, I hope: you found somebody?"

Peter smiled at her.

"Somebody?" he said. "Crowds! First of all, Nellie rang up at the F.O., saying that she had been going to the play with Philip, but that he had a cold. So would I? We dined at home, and talked so long with elbows on the table that we didn't get to the play till towards the end of the second act."

"Ah, that was luck to find Nellie," said Silvia. "I was afraid you might have a horrid lonely evening. And then?"

"Then just one act of *Downstairs*. But one act was better than four. There had been railway whistles and flags waving from the box opposite."

"That was Mrs. Trentham," said Silvia.

"It was. So we swept in her lot—the usual one—with Lord Poole, who told me to kiss you for him, and they all came to supper at home. Really, that plan of keeping the house open was an admirable one. It's awful fun; we talked and smoked and laughed until everyone melted away."

She saw (and loved to see) the brightness and briskness of him; she heard (and loved to hear) his cheerfulness and alacrity.

"Oh, I am glad you had a nice evening," she said. "I nearly telephoned to say I was coming up to keep you company. But then I thought I had better stop and—and try to make myself disagreeable at home."

"Did you succeed, darling?" asked Peter.

Exactly then it struck Silvia that if Peter had dined, had sat "so long" with elbows on the table, and had got to the theatre in time for anything at all, he could not have been detained very late at the Foreign Office. She instantly drew down, with a rush and a rattle, some mental blind in front of that. She shut it out: she did not choose to see it.

"Yes, pretty well," she said. "Mother went to bed at ten, anyhow, which is early for her, so I must have been fairly successful."

"Not proved," said Peter. "She may have been sleepy. It's a sleepy place, you know."

"I know," she said. "Two nights ago I came and looked into your room, as I had not heard you come to bed, and there you were, fast asleep."

"Snoring, I suppose you'll tell me?" said he.

This point about detention at the Foreign Office, with time yet to dine and confabulate and go to the theatre, had struck him too. He had meant it to be assumed that he had telephoned to signify the knowledge that he would be detained, and now by this stupid inadvertence in giving the account of his evening, he had shown, for all who cared to think, that he had not been detained. But Silvia apparently had quite missed that, or she would surely have said something to that effect; as it was, she had passed it by: it was out of sight by now, behind another—well, another misunderstanding.

She proceeded to put a further corner between her consciousness and it.

"No, I don't say snoring," she said. "Oh, Peter, your father has told me how delightful, how angelic you were to him, about his stopping on here till we go back to London. It touched him very much."

She took his arm. "It touched me too, dear," she said, "and I must tell you that it furnished a reason—one out of several—why I came to meet you. I've got a confession——"

Peter guessed what this reason was and what the confession. When he made a plan he was quite accustomed to find it work itself out as he had meant. But now in the very apex of its success he felt ashamed of it. If it came to confessions he could make his contribution. He interrupted her.

"I don't care about that reason," he said. "Tell me the other ones instead."

"The other ones will come afterwards," she said, "if you want to hear them then. This has got to come first, so don't interrupt, darling. I *will* tell you: it's an affair of conscience."

"And I'm a conscientious objector," said he. As it became more and more certain in his mind what Silvia's confession was, the less he wanted to hear it, though he himself, patting his own back for his cleverness, had contrived the plan of which this was the logical sequel. But when he did that he had not yet pretended to be asleep one night nor, on another, telephoned his detention in town.

Silvia went on with a gentle but perfectly determined firmness.

"I've misjudged you altogether, Peter," she said, "and I've *got* to confess. For days now—more days than I like to number—I have been watching you, looking for something I missed in you. I thought you were unkind and sarcastic and cynical about your father, and what he told me of the manner in which you welcomed his proposal to stop on here convinced me how utterly I had been wronging you. It was owlishly stupid of me to suppose you could be like that, and, what was worse, it was brutally unloving."

Peter laughed.

"Any more big words coming?" he asked. "Owlish, stupid, brutal, unloving? That's you all over. Have you murdered anybody?"

She shook her head.

"It's no use making light of it," she said, "It was stupid, it was unloving of me. I thought that because you saw certain absurdities and unrealities about your father, you saw nothing but them, and were impatient and untender with him. Do you forgive me for being such a fool?"

Peter tried to imagine himself telling her that she had been perfectly right throughout: that only a piece of trickery on his part, in getting his father to give an account of the welcome his proposition had met with, had deluded her into thinking she was wrong. But his vanity, the thought of the sorry figure he would present, made it quite impossible to contemplate so fundamental an honesty. Short of being honest, he had better be superb.

He stopped, facing her, knowing well the effect his physical presence had on her.

"You darling, there's one thing I don't forgive you for," he said, "and that is for being such a fool as to think there was anything for me to forgive."

Even as he made this neat phrase, the truth of it came home to him. There was indeed nothing for him to forgive. She gave a long sigh.

"Oh, you must teach me to be generous," she said.

Peter felt himself unutterably mean at that moment. But the thing was done; he had been superb as well as dishonest, and if honesty had been too high for his vanity to attain to, it was just as incapable of demolishing the golden image of himself that he had set up for Silvia. Then there was the point concerning his apparent slumber two nights ago; there was the point concerning his telephone last night.... He wished intensely that she hadn't asked him to teach her generosity.

"Now for the other reasons why you came to meet me," he said. There would be balsam and food for his vanity here. He had the grace to recognize that even while he asked it.

"Because I wanted to see you," said she.

"I like that reason. Have you any more of that brand?"

He knew that the word which took lightly what was so immense would, after her confession, cause her to smile. It was of the species which she had thought cynical, and which she now knew was just the everyday garb in which affection and tenderness clothed themselves.

"Because it seemed so long since I saw you," she said. "Oh, Peter, there's only one reason really which matters. Because I love you."

... And that brought home to him a meanness, a dishonesty against which all the rest was but feathers in a scale weighted on the other side with the world itself. Often before now he had known how unintelligibly great that was; now for the first time he was irritated at himself for his want of comprehension with regard to it. He was accustomed to understand things to which he gave his mind, but here his mind was brought to a dead stop by this great shining wall that was unscalable and impenetrable. But, to be honest, was his irritation quite confined to himself, or did that shining wall from its very incomprehensibility provoke a portion of it?

Silvia seemed to herself to miss something in his silence, but with Peter there, nothing could really be missing....

"How often I say that," she whispered; "but how often I feel that there's nothing else worth saying."

"More of that brand," said he.

"Not a drop. We must go in. You haven't seen your father yet, and after that you must have your bath."

"And after that you must send your maid away, so that we can get a few minutes' sensible conversation," said Peter.

"I'll begin it now," said she. "Sometimes, you know, your bath goes to your head, and you're not quite as serious as you might be."

"Say I'm drunk and have done with it," suggested he.

"Very well; sometimes your bath makes you tipsy. But while you're sober, I want you to promise me something."

"Shall I like it?" asked Peter prudently. "It isn't to spend a week with Uncle Abe or anything of that kind?"

"Nothing of that kind. Poor Uncle Abe! You'll like it. At least, you'll find you'll like it; you'll know it does you good."

"That's not the same thing," objected he. "It does me good to get up bright and early, so as to start for town without hurrying, but I hate it."

Silvia laughed.

"It will relieve you of that to some extent," she said. "Oh, do be quick and promise instead of making such a fuss!"

"Right. But if you've deceived me, I'll never trust you again. I promise."

"Well, for as long as we are here I want you to spend at least one night in the week in town."

"I shall do nothing of the kind," said he. "I don't care an atom about my promise. Pish for my promise! And how will it relieve me? Oh, I see. But I shan't—unless you come too, that's to say."

Silvia stopped.

"Now listen to me," she said. "You enjoyed last night immensely. It's perfectly natural that you should have. I should think you were ill if you hadn't."

"How do you know I enjoyed it? I never said so," said he.

"You did better than that. You beamed all over your atrocious countenance when you told me about it. You were obliged to stop in town, and being obliged you found, and you know it perfectly well, that it was a sort of night out. You saw your friends: you had a beano."

Silvia kept her finger on the cord of the blind she had chosen to pull down in her mind. She refused with a sublime intellectual dishonesty to look at the fact that Peter certainly could have come down here by dinner time if he had time to dine early in town; she would not see it. Already, so she told herself, she had once fallen into an owlishly stupid error and worse, by doubting him, by watching him; now at least she could repair that to some extent by the supreme honesty of trusting him without question. Something had happened to keep him in town, and it was no business of hers to think of that at all. He had said he was detained at the Foreign Office, and, for her, he was detained there. She held her eyes open to the intensest light of all, which was that of her own love, and the more it blinded her to everything else the better. It was only creatures like bats (and owls), things of the night, that were blinded by the dayspring.

"You enjoyed it: you had a beano," she repeated. "Why not say so?"

Peter hesitated, but for a reason that she had refused to entertain the existence of. The fact, now shiningly clear, that Silvia had never so remotely seen that he could easily have got down here in time for dinner, made it unintelligibly and unreasonably needful for him to tell her so. There was something sordid in not doing so. Had she shown the smallest suspicion of it, he would probably have explained it away in some ingenious manner.

"Yes, I enjoyed it," he said. "That was why I did it. I could easily have got down here in time for dinner."

Up went the blind at that with a snap and a whirr, and Silvia's face, beaming and delighted, smiled out at him.

"Oh, Peter, how lovely of you to tell me," she cried. "Of course, I guessed, only I wouldn't guess. There's just the joy of it all."

That came from her like the stroke of a bird's wing, that bore it through the sunny air. With another stroke she returned to him.

"Now you've got no excuse for refusing my beautiful plan," she said. "And it *was* nice of you not to tell me at once: you knew you had to some time, and it was all the better for keeping. My dear, there's the dressing bell. Just go and see your father for a minute: you can talk to him in the smoking-room after mother and I have gone to bed."

As Silvia heard through her bedroom door the splashings and the rinsings and the gurglings which regulated her own speed of dressing, she was absorbed in the perception of the one thing that was great, and its myriad manifestations. Up the trunk of the tree and through the branches and to the remotest ends of the twigs flowed the sap, and all—the firmness of the trunk, the vigour of the branches, the elasticity of the twigs, the decoration of flower and leaf and fruit, which made the tree lovely—were manifestations and embodiments of the sap. If there was a wound in its bark, the sap healed it; if there was a nest among its boughs, an external loveliness of life which visited it, it was still the sap which had fashioned its anchorage. The remotest leaf of that tower of forest greenery was nurtured by it, and all the being and the beauty sprang from it.... There was nothing big or little, if you looked at it in that way, though just now she had decided that only one thing was big and all the rest was little....

Then came a rare, an unusual splash. Occasionally when Peter began to stand up in his bath after the hot soaking, he fell down; his foot slipped on the smooth surface, and this made the rare and enormous splash. This always caused her a certain anxiety: he might hit his head against the edge of the bath....

"Just tap at the bathroom door, Wilton," she said, "and ask if Mr. Mainwaring is all right."... But before the chaste Wilton could get as far as the door, a new splashing began. "It doesn't matter, Wilton," she said.

"Your pearls, ma'am?" asked Wilton.

Then came the tap at the door, and Wilton slid out of the picture.

"I fell down," said Peter. "I might have hurt myself, but I didn't. I wish you weren't so wonderful."

"I can't help that," said she. "You should have thought of it before."

Peter began drying his toes.

"I've had quite a long talk with my father," he said, "and all about you. He thinks you're wonderful, too. He adores you: they all adore you, particularly Lord Poole."

"Peter, don't be tipsy," said she.

"I shall be as tipsy as I like. I want to know one thing. Why weren't you annoyed with me for saying that I couldn't get back last night?"

Silvia held out the pearls for him to clasp round her neck.

"If you don't understand that, you must be tipsy," she said.

"And if I do?" he asked.

She leaned her head a little back.

"Why, then you understand it all," she said. "You understand, for instance, why I insist on your having a night in town every week."

"Yes, I see. Just that you shall get rid of me now and then," he said.

"Quite right. You're as sober as—as a commoner, I suppose."

She moved in her chair, and one end of her necklace slipped from his fingers.

"Am I putting them on for dinner," he asked, "or am I taking them off for bedtime?"

"Whatever you're doing, you are being wonderfully clumsy," said she, as his fingers, warm and soft from his bath, touched the back of her neck.

She was down before him next morning to give him his breakfast, and, waiting for him, strolled out on to the terrace. There had been one of those exquisite early October frosts, and in the air was that ineffable fragrance derived from absence of smell, the odourless odour of frosted dew. The sun was already warm with promise of a hot, cloudless day; but as the heat had not set in motion the weaving of the scents of earth and grass and flowers which would soon decorate and veil the virginal beauty of the morning. Last night, when she and Peter had lingered here in the end of the twilight, the air was not less clear and windless, but it had been charged with all the myriad scents distilled by the hot hours of autumn sun. Now there was a precision, a crystalline quality.... Some such sort of clear sparkle bathed her spirit also: her love basked in some such virginal beauty of young day, flamelike and scentless.

All the evening before, from the time when she met Peter by the lake, she, body and soul and spirit, had been rising towards some new peak of passion, and the true topmost summit seemed to her now to be where she stood in this cool brightness, able to see that the upward path which led here was below her. They had dined after Peter had clasped her necklace for her; there had been the usual piquet for her and Mr. Mainwaring, and for the latter a triumphant pæan of achievement over some effect of lightning in the second cartoon, which positively, as he stood aside as artist and became spectator, appalled him, and before they settled down to their cards he must needs conduct them to the masterpiece in question, and let them also feel the cold clutch of fear.

But whatever Mr. Mainwaring did or said, whatever her mother, it was Peter whom, in this rising tide of flame and self-surrender, Silvia watched, no longer looking for those signs of tenderness and affection which (owlish) she had missed, but in the rapturous contemplation of them. Often she had seen him charming to her mother and to his own father; but always, so she had thought, she could detect in him politeness and amenity, the controlling hand of breeding, the practice of pleasant behaviour. But this evening there had been no "behaviour" about him at all, he had been radiant with them both, divinely natural.... He had sat next Mrs. Wardour on the sofa, as the piquet was in progress, and entertained her with ludicrous but hopelessly recognizable caricatures of her and his father over their cards; he had held a skein of her wool, he had mixed her hot water and lemon juice for her. All these things he had often done before, and they were all trivial enough.... He was the same with his father, looking over his hand when so bidden, dutifully observing exactly how to play that puzzling game; eager to anticipate his wants, chaffing him sometimes, behaving to him—this again was the wrong word—being to him, rather, all that his own sonship implied, fulfilling in every word and gesture the welcome which he had given to the suggestion of his remaining with them till they went to London. And all that was "the world's side" which anyone might see, and behind it in "lights and darks undreamed of" was that other aspect and reality of him, which was hers alone.... She was already in bed when she heard him, after his smoking-room chat with his father, come into his room, and presently, after tapping on her door, he looked in, coatless and shoeless. She pretended—in parody of what happened two nights before—to be asleep, and between her eyelids, nearly closed, she saw a broad smile overspread his face.

"I don't believe a single word of it," he remarked.

All this—all it was and all it meant—Silvia now, as she waited for him, looked at, looked down on even from this crowning pinnacle, as on upward, ultimate slopes. Even, as in the cool scentless air of the morning, the miracle of the sunshine on the windless world was more itself than when its beams had drawn that response of fragrance from all living things, so shone for her, untroubled with passion and desire, the essence itself of love in its own crystal globe. Not less precious, now that it was conveyed to her in no material manifestation, would be the bodily presence of him through whom that essence was conveyed to her, who embodied love to her mortal sense, but for ever far more precious was it now that she, in this pause of content that crowned passion with a royal diadem, could for the moment see that in loving him she loved not him alone, but Love itself that "moved the sun and the other stars," and being all, gave all....

The duration of the moment in which Silvia reached that point, not theoretically, but as a felt and experienced reality, was infinitesimal, just as in significance it was infinite.... At the sound of Peter's step on the bare boards of the dining-room just within, the atmosphere of the summit where she stood grew laden and fragrant with the scents of the world. She did not come down from it: it did not rise up above her. She was there still, but she was there in body as well as in spirit, the fragrance of material sweetness was near her, even as when now she stepped back into the dining-room, a waft of rose-scent from the sun-warmed wall smothered her nostrils.

Peter was poking about among dishes on the side table, and gave her a grunt, neither more nor less, in answer to her salutation. He held that to be in good spirits at breakfast-time was a symptom that could not be taken too seriously. By that test there was nothing wrong with him this morning.

He sat down with an ill-used sigh.

"I've got a headache," he remarked.

"Oh, I'm sorry," said she. "Where?"

"In my left ankle, of course," said he.

Silvia, passing behind him, just tweaked the short hair at the back of his neck.

"Oh, don't finger me," said Peter angrily.

He gave her so quick a glance that she could scarcely tell whether he had actually looked at her or not, and went on without pause and without hurry, clinking out his words like newly-minted coins, separate and crisply cut and hot.

"Just let me alone sometimes," he said. "You know how I hate dabbing and pressing and grasping. You're the limit, you know."

He had got her stiff and staring, and still without pause and in precisely the same voice he went on:

"Don't let me have to speak to you like that again," he said. "And don't be so owlish, but confess that you've fallen into that trap."

Still she stood staring, and he took one step towards her and flung his arms close round her neck, pressing her face to his, and then, more directly, finding and claiming her mouth.

"You utterly divine girl," he said. "I never dreamed I should take you in. I did. Kiss me three times to signify 'Yes,' and three times more to signify that you are a darling, and once more to—well, once more."

"Peter, I thought you were cross with me," said she, when she could say anything.

"How perfectly splendid! That joke did come off, didn't it?"

She could smile again.

"You brute!" she said. "But never take me in over that again, darling. Anything else; not that."

Once more before his motor came round they strolled on the terrace outside. It was thick now with the web of scents, for the sun's weaving was busy. The late roses gave their fragrance, and the verbena and the mignonette, but these were but strung like beads on to the smell of the damp, fruitful earth. By now Silvia could laugh at herself about that fierce phantom moment, for never had Peter seemed more utterly hers. Usually in these early half-hours he was rather silent, rather morose; to-day, penitent perhaps, or consolatory for the fright—it was no less—that he had unwittingly given her, there was something of the bath-intoxication about him.

"If you were in any sense a devoted wife," he said, "you would drive up with me, deposit me at the F.O., and then wait three hours for me in the motor till lunch time. I could give you an hour then, after which you would wait four hours more and drive back with me. Therefore shall a woman leave her father and her mother and cleave to her husband."

"Yes, of course I'll come," said she, "if you want me to. You must just say you really want me."

He took hold of her elbows from behind and ran her along the terrace.

"Motor-bike," he observed. "I'm pushing you till you get your sense of humour working on its own account."

"It's working—I swear it's working," shrieked Silvia. "Don't be such a bully."

A seat on the balustrade of the terrace seemed indicated after this violent exercise.

"There's another thing," said Peter. "My mental power of association of ideas is decaying, which is a sign of softening of the brain. Aren't you sorry?"

"Is that the brain in your head?" asked she.

"No; in the same place that ached when I had a headache. Left ankle. Don't interrupt. But there's something in this house front, and I believe it's the cornice, or whatever they call it, which runs all along there underneath the windows on the first floor, which—that's the cornice—reminds me of some other house."

Peter pointed to the broad frieze-like band which projected some foot or so from the wall of the house. It was of Portland stone, amazingly carved with masks at intervals, and ran, as he had said, just below the first floor windows from end to end of the façade. Then he gave a yodel which, consciously or not, was a hoarse and surprising parody of his father's favourite method of indicating a general sumptuousness of sensation.

"That's done it," he said. "Just speaking of it has reminded me what it was. And there's the motor, bother and blight it, confound and curse it."

"And what is the house it reminds you of?" she asked.

"The flat belonging to Nellie's mother. Just below the windows there ran a band like that. I noticed it one day last summer. She had said something about it, but at that point there's softening of the brain again. All I said about the motor holds, though."

"Send it away. Walk up to town instead," suggested Silvia.

"Likely, with that headache in my ankle. But I would so much sooner sit here with you than do either."

Silvia waved to him as he drove off, and waiting, waved again as he crossed the bridge over the lake. The air was thick with earthy fragrances now, and her mind with fragrant memories, and among them there was some new scent, not quite strange to her, but one from which she had always, whenever it presented itself, turned her head. Now it insisted on being analysed, on being recognized.

When, half an hour ago, she had just tweaked his hair as she passed him, his remonstrance, to her ears, had been wholly instinctive and sincere; he objected to being "fingered." He had piled that up, so she seemed to see, making of it a joke against her, until the joke grew preposterous. Then, ever so convincingly, he had smothered her with kisses. Yesterday evening, too, how convincing had been, on some other plane, his "dearness" — that word must serve — with her mother and Mr. Mainwaring. On one side were bright tokens of affection, and to her of so much more than affection; on the other that one little hot coin that clinked with a true ring before, with admirable mimicry of himself, he had showered out a whole flood of such.

Which was the more real? And where, in these mists, was that austere and shining summit?

CHAPTER XIII

Just before Christmas, after three weeks in London, Silvia was driving down alone to Howes, in preparation for the party which was to arrive next day. Peter would come then: he had got a devastating cold, and it was far wiser, in this grim inclemency of weather, that he should not come down with her to-day, only to come up again for his work next morning. It was much more sensible—Silvia had suggested it—that he should nurse his cold that evening, and, well wrapped up, make a single instead of a double journey to-morrow. But that piece of good sense was subsidiary to the fact that she did not want, just for this evening, to be alone with him; even if his cold had not supplied an excellent argument in favour of this plan, she would have suggested her own solitary departure.

Wilton, the correct virginal Wilton, sat opposite her on the front seat. Wilton had, at the start, deposited herself next the chauffeur, but Silvia had made her come inside. But there was little use, so thought Wilton, in coming inside, if her mistress still kept both windows open.

The sleet had turned to uncompromising snow, and Silvia seemed to notice it no more than if she were a Polar bear. Eventually, as the car flowed up the long hill through Putney, Wilton had been able to stand the draught no longer.

"You'll be catching a worse cold than Mr. Mainwaring's, ma'am," she said, "if you sit in that draught."... That made it more comfortable. Silvia roused herself for a moment.

"His man doesn't take such care of him as you do of me, Wilton," she said.

"And so much pneumonia about, ma'am," observed Wilton encouragingly.

Silvia began to think consecutively, starting not from far back, but from the immediate past. Nellie had lunched with her alone, just before she started, for Mrs. Wardour had been out, and Nellie had hailed this tête-à-tête as the most delightful thing that could have happened. Nellie had been at Wardour House, too, the night before for a concert; during this month of December, hardly yet three weeks old, she had been there half a dozen times, for Mrs. Wardour, resuming her social activities with extraordinary vigour after four months in the country, had, without the aid of any godmother, turned December into June.

"You know the real name of this delicious house, darling," Nellie had said. "Everyone calls it the New Jerusalem, because its gates are never shut day or night. Your mother brings light into the darkest homes of the upper classes. There's such dreadful discontent among them: if it wasn't for people—angels—like your mother, they would all go and live in converted garages or in country cottages, and pretend to be the proletariat. It's being amused and entertained that keeps the upper class together; otherwise they would be the leaders of Bolshevism. The Order of the British Empire now! Why isn't she the only Dame in it? The stability of the upper class depends on her, and the King depends on the upper class, and the Empire, in fact, if you see what I mean. I'm not quite sure that I do, but I do mean something. We should all have groaned and grumbled if your mother hadn't set such a brilliant example."

With Nellie's brilliant presence and charm to help out this engaging nonsense, it was a cheerful scintillation. Last June, so Silvia told herself, she would vastly have enjoyed such a month as she had just spent, and Nellie's *résumé* of it made her wonder whether she—only she—had been dull and unappreciative....

The snow was driven against the glass which Wilton had put up: she could hear it softly tap at the window....

"And Peter!" Nellie had said. "What have you done to him, darling, or rather what haven't you done to him? Everybody—I think I told you so once—used to be devoted to Peter: we used all to be in love with him, for he was so priceless, so marvellous, in not caring one atom for anybody. How long did it take you, do tell me, to discover his heart? Did you mine for it, and dredge for it, and blow up all the rocks round it? Or did you get an aeroplane and fly up to it. Perhaps, after all, it was in the sky—so tremendously remote that nobody ever thought of looking for it there. You and Peter, up in the blue like the queen bee and her lover! How wildly romantic! Or were you there, and did he fly up to you? You met in the blue, anyhow, and left us all staring up after you till our eyes watered with the glare."

Silvia, as the car hooted its way through Kingston, did not concern herself to recall with what small accompaniment she had sustained those arpeggios. She must have said something, for Nellie had gone on talking, talking.... Silvia had blinked before that brilliant vitality, which so decorated all that lay under its beams; but for the first time, when she spoke like that about herself and Peter, the light hurt her. It dazzled rather than illuminated, and when it fell on certain dark places it did not illuminate them, it only showed up their blackness. She, with Nellie's light, Nellie's impressions, to help her, peered into them. Such glimpses as she caught between the dazzle and the darkness made her turn away with protest against this bull's-eye that now seemed to intrude on privacy. What, after all, had her relations with Peter to do with Nellie?

The streets were slippery with the newly-fallen snow, and at some corner, while they were still passing through houses, there was a furious hooting of the horn outside, which to Silvia at that moment was not so much a warning of danger ahead on the road, as of danger lying somewhere deep within herself. They came to a dead stop, which made Wilton scream faintly and clutch the jewel-case, and for a yard or two they slid backwards. All that, too, seemed instantly translated in her mind into interior action, and, keeping pace with it, she slid a little farther back in her journey of thought.

She brought out from the locked cupboard of her very soul, where she had turned the key on it, one particular moment. It was yesterday that she had put it there. She was in a room of a house in Welbeck Street, and at the end of the consultation the great man, jovial and kindly, had got up from his chair, and smoothed the pillow of a sofa on which she had lain just before.

"Be quite active," Dr. Symes summed up, "without overtiring yourself. Appetite good? That's all right. Just go on with your ordinary life. What? No: no doubt of any kind. Your husband well? A cold? Everyone's got a cold."

Silvia paused over that while a wheel of her car slipped and skidded. Soon it hit the ground again. But in that pause she faced the fact that she had not told Peter. She meant to last night, but—but.... He had bewailed his cold; he had accepted her proposal that he should stop in London to-night. He had waved his hand at her and left her, not kissing her for fear of giving her his cold. But that was not the reason—it was only the excuse—for not telling him. She had welcomed it, at the time, as an adequate excuse; but if she had not found any such, she would have done without it.

For a second or two her thought paused, merely contemplating this fact as if looking at some picture. It seemed quite incredible that she had not gone straight to him with her news, blurted it, whispered it, kissed him with it. Yet if he had been sitting here now instead of Wilton, in this privacy of snow and twilight-travel, she knew that she would again be struggling, and in vain, to tell him.

From that point she swept back to one morning in October. It was then that some seed of knowledge which had previously lain dormant in her soul began to sprout. For two months now she had been conscious of its growth, and for two months she had steadily refused to acknowledge it. Her relations with him had been of the most normal and friendly, but the fact, as she saw now, of his content and tranquillity was sunshine and rain to the growth of it. Then, at the news Dr. Symes had given her, it burst into bitter blossom, and she could ignore it no longer.

Peter had never loved her: he had never, in finding her, lost himself. Mentally and sympathetically she knew that he liked her—liked her, she was prepared to say, immensely; physically she attracted and satisfied him. To think that he had married her "for" her money would be an exaggerated and hysterical estimate; her wealth had not been a counterweight that overcame some opposing disadvantage, but it was, so she now believed, a determining factor. Without it he would not have sought her.

It seemed odd to herself how little that mattered. Her wealth was an advantage—so, too, was her beauty; and even if he had married her "for" her wealth, that would have seemed to her no worse than if he had married her "for" her beauty, or "for" (had she been witty) her wit, or "for" any quality whatsoever of mind or body. All these were advantages, pleasant circumstances; but all of them, singly or together, compared with love, were no more than the bright shells on the seashore compared with the sea.

It was just here that she blamed him with a bitterness that appalled her; it was this that had made it possible for her to accept any excuse (or if necessary to have done without one) for not telling him what she had learned yesterday. He had bidden her shut her eyes, and picking up a shell had held it to her ear, and had told her that what she heard there was the sea.... He had looked, he had spoken, he had acted as if he brought close to her that splendid shining vastness. She had trusted him, and had listened with all the rapture of love to that murmuring. Therein he had cheated her, passed off on her a "fake" which, had she not been blinded by his hand over her eyes, he knew she must have recognized as such.

There was just one excuse for him; she hesitated to adopt it, because while it excused him, it far more terribly accused him. It was that he did not know what love meant. From the very first, from the day when he had asked her to marry him, he had not known. She had told him that all she wanted in the world was to be allowed to love him, and he had never seen that her surrender presupposed his own. He could not burn in her love without being alight himself. There was the root of it all, his ignorance.

At that, compassion deep as love itself inundated her bitterness, not diluting it, but from its very nature neutralizing it. Sorrow was there, but "without sorrow" (who had said that?) "none liveth in love." Not as by one drop out of the whole ocean was her love for him diminished; but, while he did not understand, he ploughed his way in drought and desert: he could not reach her.

It was through his constant affection for her and his gentleness, rather than through any failure in these, that the realization of this had come to her. She did not believe that she wearied him; she knew that she attracted him physically, that he was faithful to her not on principle, but by inclination, and yet all this was nothing. He had not begun (say for a minute or two) by loving her, and then dropped into mere affection, mere desire: simply he had never loved her at all as she understood loving. He did not love anybody else, and Silvia, so far from being consoled by that thought, found herself passionately wishing that he did. He might love Nellie, or that fool of a woman who screamed; for then, at any rate, he would know what love meant, and they would have common ground to meet on, though that very ground parted them. That might ruin her own life, which already she had given into his cool, careful hands; and if only, by smashing it to atoms, he could find his soul's salvation!

There were problems ahead, and how they should be solved she did not know: she only knew what the upshot must be. Inconceivably dear as the mere touch of his hand was to her, she knew that never again, unless he learned what love was, or she forgot it, could hand clasp hand and mouth meet mouth. Not again could she give him those symbols of the infinite as the playthings for enjoyment. All that she had or was, was his, except just that; unless he loved her, the banners of her love must stay unfurled. Somehow she must let him know that, just as, somehow and soon, she must let him know about what she learned yesterday.

As the car turned in through the park gates the snow beat in from the other window. It fell unheeded on her face and hands, till Wilton, encouraged to take care of her, drew up the sash.

Peter's head on her shoulder, his breath coming soft and slow through his mouth.... Peter's eyes close to hers, so that if he winked his eyelashes brushed her cheek.... Peter's arm lying languid and relaxed across her bosom.... She would give her body to be burned for him, but not with such burning as this. Anyone, not she alone, could supply such need as his; none could supply hers but he, and he only if he loved her. Loving him as she did, she could not (so the leaping firelight in her bedroom that night illuminated it for her), she could not shut out her ideal in some burning chamber of its own, and take the rest of her, in ordinary human manner, to him, nor could she take from him, even though it was the highest he could give, anything that made its approach on some other plane. He must want her as she wanted him, surrendered and lost, and found again in a new completeness, before they could come together as lovers. She conjectured that she was singular, exceptional in this: most men, most women gave what they could and got what they could. But there was no compromise possible for her that could produce this easily negotiable felicity. She could not, and if she could she would not, have accepted that in exchange for this drawn sword that lay between Peter and her. She had to tell him that.... She had to tell him also that the fruit of love on the one side, of affection on the other, was ripening. She must wait her occasion for that; some moment must be seized upon when he was most himself, most nearly, that is to say, what she had once thought him.

She had nothing of her own; all was his. That was her one inestimable possession, that she had given him all. Whatever happened, her utter penury was the one thing she must cling to.

Peter had rung up Dr. Symes before he left the Foreign Office that evening, asking for five minutes of his time at any hour of morning or afternoon next day. Perhaps it was rather fussy to consult a physician over a cold, but really there never had been such a cold. Dr. Symes gave you a cabalistic slip of paper which, being duly interpreted, proved to be some marvellous tonic stuff, or, when he had felt a pulse, and looked at a tongue, and tapped you on a stomach or made your knee jump in a curious manner, he even more probably told you that you had the constitution of an armadillo, and roared you out of his room for wasting his time. With a week of uncles and aunts ahead, even though Nellie was to partake in the secret joys of them, Peter felt he would like some robust reassurance of that sort. Or, on the other hand, since there never was such a cold — —

These speculations, as he drove to Welbeck Street next morning, were cut short by his arrival and his internment in a waiting-room. There were several persons there, reading illustrated papers with sad faces, who looked up when he entered, and thereafter regarded him with evident suspicion, fearing, so Peter figured it, that he might, though the latest arrival, be summoned before those who had waited longer. This, in fact, happened, and to the accompaniment of sour looks he was conducted down a long passage into the consulting room. As he went he considered whether he slept well, and whether he had a feeling of oppression on his chest, or a pain in his right side.

"How-de-do?" said Dr. Symes. "I've managed to squeeze you in between two of my patients, and I can give you just a couple of minutes, which will be quite enough. Naturally you wanted to see me. Well, there's nothing that should give you a moment's anxiety at present. Don't think about it at all, and don't let your wife think you're thinking about it."

He turned backwards over the leaves of his engagement book.

"Yes, as you know, I saw her the day before yesterday," he said. "All healthy and normal. But don't be fussed yourself, and certainly spare her all fuss. Of course, as I told her, there's no doubt at all. Let her—if she doesn't want to, *make* her—lead an ordinary active, normal life."

Peter had arrived by this time.

"My wife?" he asked.

Dr. Symes gave his great rollicking laugh.

"Yes, and your grandmother, too, for that matter," he said. "Don't let her confuse child-bearing with invalidism. They're radically opposed. Mind you, the way she spends these months is important. Make her go out, make her busy and employed. Don't let her get fancies into her head that she must coddle herself; there's no greater mistake."

"I see," said Peter.

"Just use your common sense," said the doctor. "She's got to bear a healthy child, and so she's got to be just as fit as we can make her. But take care of her too. What's her age now? Twenty-two, I suppose. Well, regard her as a woman of forty in robust health. Make her behave like an older woman than she is."

He rang a bell that stood on his table.

"I've told you everything," he said. "You look fit enough, anyway, though you've got a bit of a cold, haven't you? Getting down into the country for Christmas, eh? Change of air. I wish I was going to get some."

He looked at his table of appointments.

"Ask Mrs. Lucas to step this way," he said to the maid. "Good-bye. Good luck."

As Peter drove down to Whitehall he kept detached, as by some dexterous jerk, such part of his mind as dealt in emotion, and contemplated with the same isolation, as through his closed car-window he looked out on the snow-slushy street, what he had just learned. He wanted to assimilate it before in any sense he studied it, and to do that he had first to wipe off his sheer surprise, which stood like condensed vapour on the glass of this astounding picture which had just been presented to him. Again and again he had to wipe that away before he could get any clear vision of the fact itself, that Silvia knew that she was with child and had not told him. When he had assimilated that he could perhaps arrive at what it meant.

The glass was clear now; he had got it, and the enigma of it all stared him in the face; and the more he contemplated it the greater grew his bewilderment as to the meaning of it. How often, with the hesitation of an intensity that choked utterance, had she said a word or two, given him a glance, a smile that conveyed better than any stamped symbol of speech, what the incarnation of their union, his and hers, would be to her. She had wondered how, just how, she would tell him; no one knew into what shapes such joy would crystallize. And now it had come and she had not told him at all. Except for a trivial visit of his own, a superficial, unnecessary visit, he would still be ignorant. She had chosen to leave him in ignorance of what he had learned by accident.

Nellie had often told him that he went walking in the wet woods and telling nobody, and Silvia, in some frank chaffing discussion, had affirmed that she knew precisely what Nellie meant. Certainly, thought Peter now, it was likely enough she did know. Had anyone ever gone solitary so far into the wet woods as Silvia? Had anyone ever so immeasurably told nobody?

He searched back through his impressions and memories of these last two months to see if he could discover any clue that should lead him to an interpretation. As far as he knew, their relations had been uniformly harmonious, without hitch or check; there had been no sign, no warning of any sort on her part of an emotional change. As for himself— —

Yes, there had been a change. A change was here, and as it was not in her it must be in him. Some psychical pigment, grain after grain, had been dropping, continually dropping, into his clean cup of life, each sinking down into it quietly, lying there at the bottom. Now it seemed that the astonishment of this morning's discovery had violently stirred up the whole, and the whole, so he saw, was tinged with the colour of that which had been dissolving in the cool depths. For often and often, increasingly and ever more vividly—here was the dropping of those grains of colour— he had had the image of Silvia moving splendidly on sunny heights, the rays from which shone down on him through rent clouds and patches of blue. There those grains had settled, dissolving perhaps, but only locally tinging minute remote areas of his consciousness: they had not affected the full contents of the cup, that clear, cool, untroubled self of his. Now with this rough shaking and stirring, he was suffused with the colour of them. There, high above, was Silvia and her splendour, felt now, not only recognized. He had scrambled to his feet (was that it?), stung into standing, finger on mouth, instead of remotely contemplating. The ray that had merely shone on him now shone in him, and its light pierced the fogs of his egoism. It was the news itself, beyond doubt, not Silvia's withholding of it, which gave him that enlightenment, for to his feminine nature the fact of his impending fatherhood struck more intimately than it would have done on one more virile. It evoked, too, a dormant virility; his fatherhood was the sequel of another relationship. Clearer shone the ray; he must climb, he must go to her, he must give....

Close on the heels of that, and swiftly as reflection answers light, came the remembrance, lost for that moment, that Silvia had withheld the knowledge from him. He could guess now with a conjecture that verged on certainty what the reason for that was, and his egoism, his deep-rooted vanity, returned and reinforced, cried out against the outrage of it. She from those heights, shining no longer, but merely superior, looked down on him, and judged him unworthy to share that white joy which crowned and enveloped her love. All his pride stiffened at the thought. He knew how to walk in the wet woods, sufficient unto himself.

Of intention Peter had started from London rather late, so that he should find the little party already assembled. His father, he rested assured, would have taken on himself the mantle of host, and would be wearing it far more superbly than he. That he found to be the case: John Mainwaring had complete possession of the place and all the members of what was, with the exception of Nellie and her husband, the same unique little family gathering which had preceded Peter's marriage. There was Aunt Eleanor, stout and seal-like, there was a column of locomotive floral decoration around Aunt Joanna, there was Uncle Abe, now possessor of three monstrous cartoons, and Uncle Henry, the possessor of a nice stiff brandy and soda, for tea still continued to burn his heart. The cartoons, in fact, and the original sketches were the subject, as Peter entered, of debate between the aunts, to the glory and honour of their creator, who sat in clouds of incense. Mrs. Wardour had already got reconciled to the fact that her sister had been the purchaser, and bore it well.

"Lovely they look," said Aunt Joanna; "all three in a row, with the rest to come opposite. Many a half-hour do I spend at my buhl writing-table there, not getting along at all with my correspondence by reason of looking at them. I'm sure I don't know which I like best."

"Tea, Peter?" asked Silvia. She had looked up at his entry; now she kept her eyes on her tray.

"Yes, indeed," said Aunt Eleanor, "I'm sure they look very fine, Joanna. Three already finished! That's wonderful. I suppose, Mr. Mainwaring, you'll be soon wanting to borrow the fourth of my sketches?"

"Dear lady, I hesitate. I positively hesitate to ask you," said he, "for I know how you will hate parting with it even for a week or two. But without it I can never paint the larger version. The inspiration, the first rapture, is there; I must study it again."

Aunt Eleanor turned triumphantly to Nellie.

"You must positively come to see those sketches, Mrs. Beaumont," she said. "I have all the original sketches of Mr. Mainwaring's great cartoons. Such a treat!"

"I'm sure they're charming," said Nellie.

"Charming indeed! Masterpieces! Such fire! Such inspiration as never could be realized again."

"The three great cartoons," said Aunt Joanna firmly, while the floral decorations trembled, "fill up the whole side of Sir Abe's last addition to our house. A new wing, I may call it, with bedrooms above."

"My sweet little sitting-room," said Aunt Eleanor absently. "All the sketches: the fire...."

"Yes, dear, and as I was telling you, the great cartoons," said Aunt Joanna. "That was what I was telling you."

Uncle Henry made a diversion. He liked peace and plenty. "Capital good brandy this," he said. "You should try my plan, Abe. Have a drop of brandy and leave the tea alone. A'most a pity to put soda into it."

(He had not put much.)

"Well, I don't say you're not right, Henry," said Uncle Abe. "But to my mind what's given me at my dinner, if it's a drop of something good, tastes all the better if I haven't had — — There's some old dry Pétiot now. There's a wine! You must get on the right side of Peter for that."

Silvia handed Peter his cup.

"And your cold's better?" she asked.

"'Bout the same, thanks."

Nellie more than once had tried to catch Peter's eye in order to telegraph to him her rapt appreciation of the family. But though Peter had met her glance, he had nothing to send in reply.

"I see the whole history of the war in my sketches," proclaimed Aunt Eleanor. "News from headquarters, I call them. Such insight! And the fourth, dear Joanna, the submarine, you know. Ah, no, you haven't seen that yet, but if Mr. Mainwaring's cartoon from it comes up to the sketch, there'll be something for you to look at."

"Capital good brandy," said Uncle Henry. Something had to be said.

Peter drifted away from the tea-table and established himself next Nellie.

"So you got down all right," he said.

She let a circular sweeping glance pause infinitesimally four times, once for each of the aunts and uncles.

"Yes, and what a delicious room," she said. "You hadn't told me half."

Peter was surely rather distrait, she thought. Even now he didn't catch the point of her appreciation.

"It's good panelling," he said. "There's more of it in my sitting-room next door. We'll go there after tea."

She held out her cup. "Silvia, darling, one inch more tea, please," she said. "An inch. Pure greed."

Silvia had an absent smile for her but no speech, and took the cup from Peter's hand without looking at him till he had turned again towards Nellie with the desired inch. She then followed him, quick as a lizard, with one glance of mute raised eyebrows. Nellie got that, too; plucked it off, put it in her book. She felt that she was surrounded by interests: there were the priceless uncles and aunts; there was also something else going on, not so farcical, not farcical at all, perhaps, but quite as interesting.

"My dear, you have got a cold," she said to Peter.

"I thought I had," said he wheezily.

"I rather like having a cold," she went on. "It's an excuse for going to a doctor and being told that one has a brilliant constitution. That's Dr. Symes's cure. You're a Symite, aren't you?"

Peter looked right and left, then for a single second straight in front of him, where Silvia sat.

"Rather," he said. "We're all Symites."

He paused a moment.

"What a pity I didn't go to see him this morning," he said very deliberately, "before I left London. I might have been well by this time."

Silvia did not look up: she turned away to Mr. Mainwaring, who was on her right. Some jerked movement of her hand caused a teaspoon to clatter from its saucer and fall on the floor.

His father gave a little yodel, adapted to the drawing-room.

"Let me have a word with you sometime, my Peter," he said.

"Yes. I'll come to see you before I dress. Just now Nellie and I are going to have a talk. Will that do? Come, Nellie."

Peter drew two chairs up to the fire.

"That's nice," he said. "Priceless, aren't they? Aunt Eleanor is really the most wonderful. Can you bear it for three days, do you think? They go day after Christmas."

He lit a cigarette and threw it away again.

"Muck!" he said. "By the way, Nellie, do stop till we go up to town."

"Oh, my dear, I wish I could," said she. "But I know Philip's got some county business on the twenty-eighth that obliges him to go home. Something ridiculous about forbidding people to shoot golden orioles, of which there aren't any."

"Can't you let him go alone?" asked Peter.

"Well; yes, I think I might. I'll get my mother to go down. Mother will always go anywhere for board and lodging."

"Don't I remember that feeling!" said Peter. "So do stop. I heard Silvia ask my father."

Nellie produced an admirable mimicry of Aunt Eleanor's views on art, which, however, elicited from Peter only:

"Very funny: yes, very like her," and he subsided into silence and fire-gazing again.

"Silvia seemed rather silent," said Nellie at length.

Peter roused himself.

"Did she?" he said. "The aunts were talking so much that I didn't notice it. This is the panelling I spoke to you of, by the way."

"Charming. Just the same as in the drawing-room, isn't it?"

"The green drawing-room, please," said Peter.

"I beg its pardon," she said.

"Granted, I'm sure," said he without a smile.

Nellie tried a handful of other topics, and her curiosity to know what was the matter vastly increased. She had narrowed down the field of her conjectures to a certainty that, whatever it was, it concerned her host and hostess. Yesterday at lunch, when she had been alone with Silvia, she had the first impression of it, yet she had seen Peter that same evening in town (by way of nursing his cold he had come to the theatre with her), and he, in spite of that affliction, had been immensely cheerful, chuckling with prophetic delight at the feast that the uncles and aunts would spread for them. And he had not seen Silvia since (for she had already left London) until his entry into the green drawing-room half an hour ago.

She would much have preferred, as on that evening a month ago, when they dined alone together in London and he had been so pointedly reticent on the subject of Silvia, that he should volunteer a statement, but his reticence then seemed of totally different quality from what it was now.... She tried one more topic.

"Peter, dear, isn't it lovely?" she said. "I'm going to have a baby."

Peter jerked himself upright in his chair. "Really?" he said. "And here are you telling me that!"

He broke off.

"What's the matter, my dear?" she said. "There's something wrong."

He got up and drove with his foot into the log fire.

"It's really screamingly funny that you should tell me that," he said.

Nellie felt that they were getting near it now.

"Funny?" she asked.

"Oh, Lord, I said funny, didn't I?" said he.

She got up too, laying a hand on his shoulder.

"My dear, we're very old friends," she said.

He turned round to her with some unspoken bitterness souring in his eyes.

"Then I'll let you have the joke," he said. "You tell me that, and yet my wife, who knows the same thing about herself, has not told me."

He paused a moment.

"I found it out by accident this morning," he said. "I went to see Dr. Symes about my cold—odd that you should have spoken of him—and before I told him anything he began telling me, and that was what he told me. Of course, he assumed I knew; thought that I had come to him for some general directions, which he gave me. Silvia had been to him two days before. She hasn't said a word to me. Not a word."

Nellie heard herself give some ejaculation.

"Now you're fond of psychological problems," he said. "Also you're a woman, and know how women feel. Under what circumstances, feeling *how*, in fact, would a woman do that? Interesting point, isn't it? It's beyond me."

"No quarrel? No misunderstanding? Nothing of that sort?"

"None. I've felt she was watching me sometimes. I've——"

"Well? Can you describe that? " she asked.

"I've only thought of that this minute," he said, "and now I don't really see any connexion. But when my father knew my mother had gone, and was posing and posturing as a lost and stricken man, Silvia was watching me to see, I think, if I had real sympathy, real pity for him. I did feel then as if I was being tested. But I made that all right. I did it cleverly. I gave the most cordial welcome to his stopping on here—Lord, what evenings they were!—for endless weeks, and left him to tell her about it."

"Are you quite sure you made it all right?" she asked.

"She told me she had been wrong; she told me she had misjudged me, when she thought me feelingless," he said. "But even if she made a reservation, or reconsidered it, what then?"

Nellie's hand still rested, now with pressure, on his shoulder.

"And what if Silvia put herself, so to speak, in your father's place?" she said. "What if it occurred to her that you had been charming with *her*, and clever with *her*? Mind, that's only a guess."

Again Peter thrust the logs together.

"She trusts me too much," he said at length, "She loves me too much."

This time Nellie was silent.

"Well?" said he at length.

"She thinks you've been clever with her and charming with her," she said. "That's it. I think that she was quite wrong in keeping this news from you, but that's why. Silvia isn't like us, you must remember. We may be complicated and clever in our way, but she's not like that. There's something tremendous about Silvia. A simplicity, a splendour."

"And just when I was beginning to realize that, to adore it, she does this. I can't forgive it," said he.

She felt then, as perhaps never before, the charm of his egoism: it really was such a charming fellow he was egoistic about.

"My dear, it's just because you, as you say, are beginning to realize that and to adore it, that you feel you can't forgive it. You would forgive it easily enough if you didn't care. But put yourself in her place. Assume, as I feel sure we're right in assuming, that we have got at the reason for her not telling you; it is exactly what a woman of that simplicity and splendour would do. With all there is of her, she loves you."

"A charming way of showing it," said Peter.

"You're hurt; you're smarting," she said. "Otherwise you wouldn't say that."

"She has spoiled everything," exclaimed Peter. "Just when——"

All through their talk Nellie had been conscious of a dual stirring, not only in him—that was clear enough—but in herself. Not many weeks ago she would certainly have had her whole sympathies enlisted on his side. She would have fanned, secretly and stealthily no doubt, the flame of his resentment against Silvia, and with the same hidden action have insinuated into his mind that there was somebody who was eager to console, to help him to forget—one who gave him a welcome.... Even now some breath of woodland irresponsibility, the morality of Dryads and Satyrs, swept over her, with the whispering of wild things and the stirrings in the bushes. Like sought like there, deriding the consequences to others. Should she twang that string, let the wind blow on that harp in the trees, she knew well that something would answer it. He was hurt and sore; there were woodland balms....

Something within her again jerked back the finger that hovered over the string, ready to pluck it, and turned her hand into a shield instead, that prevented the wind from making the harp vibrate. Silvia had her harp, too, and he had begun, ever so faintly, to vibrate in answer to Silvia's harp, and not to hers.... In this second impulse there was compassion for Silvia, there was motherhood. She made her choice.

"You can't say that she spoiled it, my dear," she said. "You know how she loved you when you asked her to marry you."

Peter had a frown for this.

"I thought——" he began.

"I know what you thought. Silvia very likely told you that she wanted just to be allowed——"

"I never told you that," said he quickly.

"Of course you didn't. But wasn't it clear that before you married, she loved you as a boy loves, with some tempestuous desire of possession?"

"But she's got me," said he. "It isn't as if there were anyone else."

"I know that, and she knows that for certain. It's nothing, of that kind that revolts her."

"Revolts?" asked he.

"Oh, my dear, short of that, wouldn't she have told you what she has known for two days, and suspected long before? But you would be quite wrong to think that she loves you any less. What you don't see, especially, beyond that, is that Silvia has become a perfectly changed person. She keeps her splendour. Keeps it? Good heavens! I should think she did. But what she learned the other day quite changes her. She has become a woman, and she must have not just a man to love, but a man to love her. You've hinted that she's on the way to get one. That's the sum of the consolation I've got for you."

Nellie, having determined, having chosen, was being magnificent just then, and all the time the Dryad within her scolded and derided her.

"You fool, you conventionalist," the Dryad shrieked. "He might be yours; he's as weak as water, and vain, vain! You want him: wait a few months and see how you want him! Idiot!"

Nellie heard all that as plainly as she heard the whistle of the wind in the chimney.

"It won't be easy," she said. "You've got to get out of yourself, Peter, a thing, by the way, that I've never succeeded in doing. And when you've got out of yourself you've got to convince her that you've got into herself. I wouldn't bet on your chance."

"Have I been a brute?" asked he.

Nellie hesitated: she had never yet realized how close to love had been her intimacy with Peter, or how far from love her own marriage-bond. And now, when, bitterly resenting what Silvia had done, he turned to her....

Peter, in her silence, repeated his question.

"A brute?" he asked, and now his voice shook.

She took her hand briskly off his shoulder. They had stood there like that, comrades and friends, for ten minutes now, and her fingers had dwelt on his shoulder, the bone and the muscle of it.

"Not a brute at all," she said. "You couldn't be a brute, you darling. But a liar and a cheat."

"Ha!" said Peter.

He walked round the room after this, with a whistle for her and him, and a kick for a footstool that got in his way.

"You don't help me," he said. "What's to be done?"

Somehow, at his absence of resentment at what she had said, and at his appeal to her for help, the old delightful level of comradeship smoothed itself out.

"Tell her that you know," suggested Nellie. "Do it nicely."

"I couldn't possibly do it nicely. Confound it all— —"

She considered this.

"If you can't do it nicely, it will only make it worse," she conceded.

"What then?"

"Wait."

"For her to tell me?" demanded Peter.

"Yes, or for you just to know. It won't come to that. Oh, you absurd people! Shall I tell her that you know?"

Peter thought over this.

"It's becoming comic," he said presently. "That's the silliest thing you've said yet."

"Perhaps. But it isn't comic, my dear."

"I know it isn't. That's my ferocious flippancy. Gravediggers."

"And it isn't comic for Silvia," she added.

The spasm of the woodland died away again.

"She hasn't told me," said Peter hopelessly. "I can't get over that."

"You've got to get over that. Otherwise there's nothing ahead. She's got to get over more than that."

All the worst of him returned.

"You speak as if I hadn't given her all I had got," he said.

"You're getting more, my dear. Keep on getting it, and keep on giving it."

Peter looked at the clock.

"Here endeth the first lesson," he said. "Not even out of the prophets. I must go and see my father. More acting. Necessary, you know."

He flung his arms out.

"I daren't be real," he said. "No one knows what an abomination I am."

Quite unexpectedly Nellie felt weary and done for. She pulled herself together for a final encouragement.

"Ah, what a hopeful sign!" she said.

He lingered a moment.

"Quarter to eight," he said. "We dine at half-past. Think of the old quarter-to-eights! Ritz, opera, Mrs. Trentham! Charlie and Bobby and Tommy and me and you, and Sophy and Ella and any fool you like to mention. Lord Poole, now——"

"No, that won't do," said she. "He was real. I grant you the rest weren't. But he was real: he completely enjoyed himself—does still, bless him!"

"Wish I did," said Peter. "I used to. And I don't."

"You won't as long as you think about it."

There was the woodland touch to finish with.

"You're only ninety, are you?" she said. "Or is it ninety-one?"

"Ninety," said Peter, grinning.

CHAPTER XIV

The grin soon cleared off. His father rose from the sofa on which he had been so elegantly resting, as Peter entered, and clasped his hand, though he had seen him at tea a couple of hours before.

"Have you heard from your mother?" he asked. "My loved and lost one?" He smoothed his velveteen coat as he spoke.

My loved and lost one! The velveteen coat!... The little demons swarmed into Peter's soul—the demons of ridicule and cynicism and contempt and all the host of such. But rebel and ridicule as he might, he knew that he had been sham and charlatan on an immeasurably greater scale than his father.

"I had a report of her a couple of days ago," he said. "Just a message through her solicitors."

Mr. Mainwaring put the tips of his fingers in a neat row into his mouth, as if, in his suspense, to gnaw the nails of them. But he committed no such feat of violence. He merely sucked them, and took them out again.

"Tell me," he said.

Peter tried to evoke any sort of kindliness or sympathy from his mind, and failed.

"She is quite well apparently," he said, "and she——"

"She asked after me?" suggested his father.

"Yes, she asked after you. She hoped you were—comfortable, I think she said."

"Comfortable! My God! Comfortable!"

Peter waited till this paroxysm of irony was spent.

"I ought to have written to her to-day," he said, "but I didn't. I shall write to-morrow. What shall I tell her about you?"

"What your heart bids you," said he. "Tell her about me, as I am. Miserable, homeless, except for the charity of my children. I count Silvia as a child," he explained.

Peter felt absolutely relentless.

"So you long for her to come back to you," he said. "I will tell her."

He regarded Peter with his chin in the hollow of his hand.

"You don't understand, my dear, the depth——" he began.

"Explain it to me, then, father," said he.

"Take your own case, then. Supposing Silvia—I use your case for the absurdity of it—supposing Silvia left your house. What would you do? Would you not give her complete freedom to return or not to return? Would not your heart say, 'My love for her wants only what she wants'?"

"Then I won't say that you long for her to come back to you," said Peter. "I only want to know your wishes. I will transmit them. But—but why not do it yourself? You know her solicitors. Anything you send them will be forwarded to her."

"The scoundrels!" cried Mr. Mainwaring.

"Oh, I don't see that," said Peter. He stifled a yawn: it was all too stupid.

"Scoundrels!" cried Mr. Mainwaring. "Aren't they——" He appeared unable to say exactly what they were, and Peter got up.

"I'll convey any message you like, father," he said. "I only suggest that you might just as well send it yourself. There are two things you can do. You can summon my mother back, and, if you choose, divorce her if she doesn't come, on the grounds of desertion. The other is to acquiesce in her stopping away as long as she chooses. I don't see why you put a hypothetical case about Silvia and me. You want her to come back, or you don't."

This point of view necessitated some more stridings on the part of Mr. Mainwaring".

"My angel, your angel, your Silvia," he said, "has asked me if I would not like to spend the rest of the winter on the Riviera. A little sun for me, she said only to-night, a little change, a little chance of the healing of my wound. She offers me two months on the Riviera. Should not I be wrong if I did not accept her sweet charity?"

"Leave it over, you mean, about my mother," asked Peter, "till you get back? Get a little sun first, and that sort of thing. I think that would be a very sensible arrangement. That was a charming idea of Silvia's."

He laid his hand on Peter's shoulder, and his voice broke.

"Make Silvia happier than I have made my Maria," he said. "The love of a good woman! My God! What brutes we men are! No, not brutes: heaven forbid that I should call you, or indeed myself, a brute. But more tenderness, my Peter, more making of allowances. *Experto crede.*"

He paused a moment in a fine attitude.

"Abe Darley!" he said. "Henry Wardour! They and their wives! Their pleasant chaff: their gentle fun! Yes, when you begin to step down from the tableland of life you want to find such hands as those in yours. A brilliant woman, too, is Joanna Darley. How she appreciates the cartoons. And your Aunt Eleanor! Eleanor, as she suggested that I should call her. We are John and Eleanor. She has commissioned me to do her portrait before I attack the fourth, the tremendous cartoon. Submarines: you remember my sketch for it."

Peter went down the corridor to his room and Silvia's with the gravity that attaches to the conclusion of a comic interlude. The tragic burden, all the worse for its temporary suspension, must be taken up again, and the interlude had hardened rather than softened him. He despised his father for being a "fake," and that contempt stung him also, as with the back-stroke of his own lash. Smarting from that his mind went back to what Silvia had withheld from him, and there was the shrewdest hurt of all....

His bath was ready for him, and as he soaked and sprayed himself some tautness of physical vigour pictured the usual sequence to his bath, the dressing-gowned and drying séance in the chair close to Silvia's toilet table. He would sink his resentment; he would tap at her door and go in to her with a flood of normal nonsense. Then, if she told him now, as she must surely do, the news she had withheld, he would receive it as news hitherto unknown to him.

He arrived at this stage of resolution, finished his bath and came out. And at that moment, even as his knuckles were raised to inquire at her door, his resentment against her, seizing upon some new pretext of bitterness, poured over him again. His hand dropped as he turned and went into his own room. He was late also—that served for an excuse—for at the moment the sonorous bell in the turret above Silvia's room made its proclamation to the listening earth that dinner was served at Howes.

On the other side of the door Silvia, fully dressed and following the familiar sounds, was waiting for him to enter. How often had she waited like that, longing for him! She longed for him now, though dreading his coming, and so intertwined were these two that she could not disentangle the one from the other. She would tell him just what she had determined that he must know, she would ask his pardon for not having told him of the news before. She had used up, so it seemed to her, all the emotion of which she was mistress; what lay immediately in front of her covered like some hard integument the longing and dread with which she waited for him, though it left her superficial perceptions alert. The clink of the coals in the grate, the flapping of the flame there, were more vivid to her senses than anything else. There was the beating of rain on her windows, for the snow had ceased, and a wind from the south-west was beginning to bluster outside.... Then she heard Peter come out of his bathroom, and presently the door of his bedroom shut. Already the bell sounded sonorously above her: she must tell him then that night, when he came up to bed. There was relief in that. For an hour or two more the only barrier between him and her was in her own knowledge: it was not formally erected. She was conscious now that her heart had been beating fast in the anticipation of his coming, and she sat down for a few minutes (Peter would be late also) to recover her poise before she went downstairs. There was to be a jollification that night for tenants and servants: a dance for the elders, a Christmas tree for the children.

The wind which just now she had heard flinging the rain against her windows rose to a scream, and Peter, hurrying on with his dressing next door, saw a cloud of smoke driven out from his grate, followed by another and yet another, till in a few minutes the room was thick with its pungency. He remembered then that the Jackdaw had told him that something had gone wrong with the cowl of the chimney, and no doubt this change of wind caused this regurgitation ... these things always happened just before Christmas or bank holidays, when the British work-man became even more deliberate than usual. Opening the window seemed only to make things worse, and, heavy with his cold, he had no intention on this chill and bitter night of sleeping fireless. As with choking throat and streaming eyes he redoubled the speed of his dressing, he rang his bell and told his servant to transfer the necessaries for sleep and toilet to some other room. The uncles and aunts occupied the next suites, but farther along, beyond the head of the main stairs, was an unoccupied bedroom and dressing room, and he ordered that a fire should be lit there, and the change made during dinner, so that he would find the room ready for his tenancy that night. As he came out from that mephitic fog on to the corridor Silvia also emerged from her room.

"My chimney's smoking like the devil," he said. "I remember now that the Jackdaw told me there was something wrong with it. It's quite impossible to sleep there. I'm having my room changed."

He finished buttoning a shirt-link as he spoke, not looking at her. Somehow this set a key of coolness, of casualness.

"How tiresome for you," she said. "Where"—she stumbled over the question—"where have you gone?"

"Oh, somewhere down the passage," said Peter.

Just now, if he had come in to talk to her after his bath, she would have told him what he had to know. Now her resolution had a little cooled: it was not hot enough to enable her to ask him to come and talk to her when he came upstairs that night, nor yet to ask him more definitely where his room was. Besides, with the entertainment for the servants they would all be very late, and to-morrow would furnish a more convenient occasion. Or if not then, and not spontaneously on her part, he would come to her some night, seeking her, and then she would tell him.... In the interval there was the family farce of jollity to be kept up: it would only add to the difficulty of that if from her communication to him something unconjecturably critical arose. She had no idea how Peter would take it: there could be no mortal wound, for that implied that she was to him all that she missed being. But his pride, his vanity; how she longed to kill it, and how she hated to hurt it.

On his side, as they went down the broad stairs, resentment at what he knew she had withheld out-shouted all the counsel Nellie had given him, out-shouted, too, the authentic whisper of his own heart. He had but to listen to that, to act when action came, and always to think and to feel and to be without forethought, just blindly following its suggestions. But for that small voice to be heard he must unstopper his ears from that cotton-wool of vanity which shut out from his hearing all but the complaints and self-justifications which trickled through it. It had been and it was her business to tell him....

"My father says you have treated him to a month or two in the South," he said. "That is very good of you: he will enjoy it."

There was the ring as of a duty discharged in this that robbed it of spontaneousness, and it gave to her its own woodenness. Peter had not meant it like that: he wanted to thank her for her kindness, to let her know that he appreciated it. But all that passed now had to travel through the falsity of that situation between them, as through some mould which made it take a shape not truly its own, and come out at the end grimed and distorted.

"January and February are delightful on the Riviera," she said. "A change will do him good."

To him that seemed to double-lock the wards of the gate that should have stood open. They looked at each other through its bars: the very attempt on both sides to meet the conventional needs of the moment—the friendly word or two on the stairs—had but served to sever them. The femininity of his nature, already resentful at what had been withheld from him, construed her reply into a further withdrawal of herself, overlooking the fact that it was his own resentment that had led him into conventionalities of speech.

His pride choked him: was it nothing to her that she was ripening with his fatherhood? Had she no inkling that not his head only but his heart was, as in some belated dawn, beginning to glow with her splendour? The male element in him was awaking, like Adam from the sleep which the Lord God had laid on him, and was beginning to find, to realize that what he expunged and expelled from himself became the living glory and the complement of him. All such perception was still clouded with the blanketing vapours of his own resentment and egoism, but through the rifts, from high above Silvia shone....

His pride choked him. What choked her was her love, that could not breathe but in its own high air.

Uncle Henry, on the occasion of his first visit to Howes, just before Silvia's marriage, had found (and deplored) a certain "standoffishness," so he expressed it, in his new nephew. His wife had not agreed with him; she found Peter to be "very refined." But during the three days that now followed Uncle Henry quite scrapped his previous verdict. There could not have been a more seasonable host: Peter was full of fun, and indeed Aunt Eleanor was almost disposed to follow her husband's example and reconsider her favourable opinion of Peter's refinement. It was really naughty of him to put up that bit of mistletoe without warning her of it, and Mr. Mainwaring's chaste salute had come as a great surprise to her, before she realized the public temptation she was making of herself by standing so squarely and indubitably just below it. But there was no harm in a good old-fashioned Christmas, and if Peter would insist on having a bowl of wassail to usher in the midnight, after all, he was the host, and it would have been mere churlishness to refuse to drink that second (or was it third?) glass that he filled up for her when she was not looking. There were foolish games on these evenings, and when the ladies went to bed roars of laughter ascended from the billiard-room, where the men "kept it up" till any hour. There was no harm in being young, so she and Aunt Joanna agreed, melted into unwilling cordiality over this riotous hospitality.

Indeed, if there was any "standoffishness" to be detected, it was Silvia who must be impeached. Yet "standoffishness," even to Uncle Henry's limited power of analysis, did not quite express Silvia's quality. "Just a bit under the mark, not up to romps," was the definition that he and Uncle Abe arrived at, as, after waving their fat hands from the window of the motor that took them to the station at the conclusion of their visit, they lit the first cigars of Peter's Christmas present to them. Naturally they had not begun on them when they were staying with him, for there was always a box open in the smoking-room.

"Come on wonderful, has Peter," said Uncle Henry. "A jolly boy. Handsome, too. Not much wrong with that marriage."

Uncle Abe had a short attack of what he called his "morning cough." Joanna, who was in the other motor, called it "smoke and drink."

"Shouldn't wonder if you're right, Henry," he said when he recovered. "I had the same idea."

"Well, I must say it occurred to me," said Henry. "She seemed a bit thoughtful. And that would account for Peter's high spirits. Amazing!"

Uncle Abe put up his window.

"I've a bit of a cough this morning," he said. "And there's a pretty fortune for any child to come into."

Peter was sitting over the fire in his bedroom that night watching it, and trying to determine that when a certain coal ceased flaring with its spray of bubbling gas he would go to Silvia's room, and, one way or another, make an end of an intolerable situation. He had no idea (so much depended on her) what his "line" would be. Certainly he would tell her that he knew what she, all these days, had kept from him; but, beyond that, he could not, in the vaguest manner even, forecast the development of the situation. During these four days she had shown him nothing that he could construe into a signal; not once had he seen her privately, and, when in public, he had kept up his rôle of the rollicking host. He had no idea, for instance, whether she knew into what lodging his surly chimney, not yet coaxed into proper behaviour, had driven him. She had asked no further question since that general inquiry on the stairs, and he had volunteered no information. Equally had he avoided any private conference with Nellie; sometimes in a casual meeting of their eyes he had conjectured an unspoken communication; but he knew her views, as the situation concerned himself and Silvia, and there was no use in hammering at that any further. Nothing else, comparatively, concerned him.

There had been a general air of fatigued reaction abroad this evening. Mrs. Wardour, Silvia, and Nellie had gone to bed within a couple of hours of the termination of dinner, and he and his father had had but a short *séance* in the billiard-room before parting. Peter had an excuse for this early dispersal, for he must be at Whitehall by ten o'clock to-morrow morning, to deal with accumulations.

Yes; when that lump of coal collapsed he would go to Silvia. Sleepily he watched it, trying in some ill-defined manner to abstract himself from agitating thought, to give himself a rest before he plunged into some sort of breaking waves. He drowsed for a little, and, still looking at his fire between half-closed lids, he fell fast asleep.

The fire had gone out except for a glimmer of dying embers, and for the moment of bewildered awakening before he realized that he was still in his armchair in front of the grate he thought that he was back in his old room, and that the chimney was smoking. As he came to himself, he realized where he was, and even more keenly realized why his mind had caught hold of that idea of the smoking chimney. There was a strong smell of smoke in the room, and, jumping up, he turned on the switch of the electric light, which was close to his hand. He heard it click, but there was no illumination in answer. He had matches in his pocket, and, lighting one, kindled one of the candles that stood on the mantelpiece. Wide awake now, he was more than ever conscious of that smell of burning, and going to the door he opened it. A great swirl of smoke came in, bellying up from the main staircase on the left. Through it there came the noise of crackling wood, and a shoot of veiled flame.

Peter gripped his own mind. On his right, close at hand, were the rooms where his father and Nellie slept. Farther along to the right was a second staircase, communicating with the ground floor, and communicating also with the servants' wing. Half shutting his eyes against the sting of the smoke, he groped his way first to Nellie's door.

"Nellie," he cried, throwing it open, "get up at once: there's a fire in the house."

He never felt more completely himself; all his brain was tinglingly awake, and behind his brain something else....

"Don't wait a moment," he said. "Get along the passage and down the stairs. I'll send my father to you."

He saw her on her way and plunged into his father's room.

"House on fire, father," he said. "Go straight through to your right into the servants' wing, and bang on every door. Wake Mrs. Wardour, two doors away. Then join Nellie downstairs. Don't wait: I don't know how serious it is."

Away to the left, beyond that column of smoke now pouring up the main staircase, was the baize door behind which were the rooms that he and Silvia had occupied, and where now she was alone. He tried to dash along the corridor to reach them, but the heat drove him back. Already tongues of flame licked through the banisters of the main staircase, past which he had to go in order to get to her. He was cut off from that access.

Suddenly and serenely he remembered another access. Along the front of the house below the windows of the room he at present occupied and those rooms behind the baize door beyond the flaming staircase, there ran externally the coping which had reminded him of that which ran along the flat belonging to Nellie's mother in London. He remembered in the same flash the discussion that Nellie and he had held: how she had told him that, if he ever loved, he would be forced to make the passage of such a road at the bidding of that divine compulsion. It would not concern him, so she had said, that he incurred a mortal and a useless risk. He might not be able to rescue (here was the thesis) the beloved of his soul: any thought of rescue was outside the question. But, so she argued, he would not be able, if he loved, to resist the imperishable impulse.

Through the thick scorching air, with his candle guttering in the heat, he groped his way back to his room, and shutting the door against that burning blast, he went to the window. The gleam of the white stone coping was just visible, and taking off his coat and waistcoat, so as to be able to get closer to the wall, and kicking off his shoes, so as to secure a better grip, he let himself down on to it. There it was some ten or twelve inches in width; by standing very straight up, with his arms flat out against the wall of the house, he had his balance well below him.

He moved his left foot first and brought the right foot up to it. He rocked at this first movement, and recovered himself.... And then when once he had started on his perilous way, the dawn and morning of it all broke on him. Cautiously and clingingly he advanced, but the caution—there was the sunlight of it—was no longer for himself, but for her whom he sought. For himself it seemed to matter not at all whether an unnerved step terminated his expedition: the object of it, the necessity, sheer as the drop below him, of reaching Silvia was utterly dominant. He could hear a dim roaring inside the house, but it neither delayed nor hastened him.

He had come to the window of her room, and now he could lean an elbow on the sill of it, while he rattled at the sash and tapped at the glass. Through her blind he saw her room spring into light, and found himself recording the fact that this electric circuit was still working. Immediately he heard her voice:

"Who is it?" she cried. "What is it?"

"Peter," he said. "Open the window quickly."

The sash flew up, and she was there, close to him.

"Give me a hand, darling," he said. "Just pull me in. Don't ask any questions."

The window-sill was high above the coping, but with her hands, firm and strong as a boy's, on his arm, he scrambled into the room.

"The house is on fire," he said. "We're cut off. The main staircase is blazing. But it will be all right: don't be frightened. My father will have roused the servants by now."

He paused, panting from some retarded terror of his climb, unfelt while he made it.

"Silvia!" he said.

She stared at him a moment.

"But you were safe, Peter," she said. "What good was it that you came? Along that coping, did you come, all the way from your room?"

"I'm here anyhow; good, broad coping," he said. "Now, can we do anything more? Let's be practical: let's think."

For an immortal second she held him close.

"The big bell in the turret!" she said. "The rope goes through the corner of the little lobby outside my bathroom."

"Oh, good thought," said he. "Come and help me to pull it. We'll talk afterwards, when we've done all we can."

The sound of that reached the little town a mile away; the glare on the sky endorsed the signal. Outside on the terrace, facing the lake, and now vividly illuminated, were the other occupants from the house, busy with rescuings, and presently, shouted up to the two through the open window by which Peter had climbed in, came the news, conveyed here by telephone, that the fire-engines were on their way. A ladder was being fetched from the stable.... Had they no rope?... Then, as the conflagration spread, the electric light snapped itself out.

They had gone back, when the bell had done its work, to Silvia's room. The angry glare from outside shone in through the window, and smoke drifted in from below the baize door that shut them off from the burning corridor. Already the fog of it obscured the glare.

"That's all we can do," said Peter. "Come close, my dear. You mustn't be afraid. There's no need.... We— —"

She was clinging to him now.

"I have something to tell you," she said.

"You needn't," said he quickly. "I know it."

"You can't," said Silvia.

"But I do: your baby you mean, bless you."

Suddenly her mouth began to quiver.

"Oh, my God! why did you come here?" she said. "You were safe."

Outside beyond the baize door there was a crash of something falling, and she shrank into him.

"Why did you come?" she repeated.

"Because I couldn't help myself. It wasn't my fault. You don't understand— —"

"You had to, do you mean?" she asked.

He made no reply to this: his presence answered for him.

"Oh, go back," she cried. "You can go back still. If you love me— —"

He took her close into one great enfoldment.

The roaring of the burning house, the glare of its great beacon, grew momently more vivid. Then from outside came a yell of voices, and they went to the window.

"They've come," said Peter quietly.

A grinding of the gravel below, shouted orders, a raising of a ladder....